THE ARCHAEOLOGICAL EXCAVATION DICTIONARY

THE ARCHAEOLOGICAL EXCAVATION DICTIONARY

Anna Kieburg

PEN & SWORD
ARCHAEOLOGY

First published in Great Britain in 2016 by
PEN & SWORD ARCHAEOLOGY
an imprint of
Pen and Sword Books Ltd
47 Church Street
Barnsley
South Yorkshire S70 2AS

ISBN 978 1 78346 371 8

A CIP record for this book is available from the British Library

Printed and bound in England
by CPI Group (UK) Ltd, Croydon, CR0 4YY

Typeset in Times New Roman by
CHIC GRAPHICS

Pen & Sword Books Ltd incorporates the imprints of
Pen & Sword Archaeology, Atlas, Aviation, Battleground, Discovery,
Family History, History, Maritime, Military, Naval, Politics, Railways,
Select, Social History, Transport, True Crime, Claymore Press,
Frontline Books, Leo Cooper, Praetorian Press, Remember When,
Seaforth Publishing and Wharncliffe.

For a complete list of Pen and Sword titles please contact
Pen and Sword Books Limited
47 Church Street, Barnsley, South Yorkshire, S70 2AS, England
E-mail: enquiries@pen-and-sword.co.uk
Website: www.pen-and-sword.co.uk

Introduction

"Dov'è la cazzuola?" – "I beg your pardon?"

Who has not experienced the dilemma of not understanding colleagues and team members on an excavation? This excavation dictionary is for anyone who wants to avoid these sticky situations and allow conversations to flow so that digs can be more productive, enjoyable and memorable.

The terms chosen originate mainly from the technical and specialised terminology used on excavations and in the discussion groups which develop in this environment. These terms include materials and their forms; technology; methodology; topographic and geographic terms; architecture; indications of measurement and time; and neighbouring and related fields of research, including conservation and monument preservation.

It should be pointed out that this dictionary is not exhaustive of all of the terms associated with archaeological excavation. In particular, in the field of ceramic studies, many terms concerning specific vessel forms, decoration techniques and typological terms. For example, black-slipped ware, Linear Pottery, terra sigillata etc. could not be incorporated.

In addition to the phonetic spelling of the Arabic and Greek terms, we have also included the terms written out in the Arabic and Greek script in order to help both parties of the conversation as fully as possible.

Sincere thanks are given to all collaborators in this book, as well as Selma Abdelhamid (MA), Dr Raimon Graells I Fabregat, Dr Cecilia Moneta, Michaela Reinfeld (MA) and many colleagues at the RGZM Mainz, who have helped to realise this book. Special thanks go to Constanze Holler of the Philipp von Zabern publishing company who supervised the development of this book for the original publication in the German language.

The Collaborators

Jenny Abura, born 1981, studied Christian and Classical Archaeology and Byzantine History of Art in Göttingen and Oviedeo, Spain. During long visits and fieldwork seasons Jenny applies herself to her research focusing on early Christian church architecture, architectural sculpture in Late Antiquity and iconography of Hispania.

Gülten Adigüzel, born 1979, studied Classical Archaeology at the Adnan Menderes Üniversitesi in Aydın, Turkey and at the Humbodlt University Berlin. Gülten has taken part in excavations in Alabanda and Ephesos.

Giacomo Bardelli, born 1984, studied Classical Archaeology at the universities of Pavia and Innsbruck. Since 2011 he has held a fellowship at the society of the friends of the RGZM Mainz. Since 2008 he has regularly participated in excavation seasons with the University of Perugia near Campo della fiera (Orvieto).

Yves Gautier, born 1952, studied Prehistory, Classical Archaeology and Botany at the university of Bern, Switzerland. As field archaeologist Yves directed excavations for the country of Brandenburg. Since 1996 he has worked as a freelance translator in Brussels (www.archaeotrad.com).

Anna Kieburg, born 1977, studied Classical Archaeology, Ancient History and Biblical Archaeology at the University of Hamburg. Field research and excavations brought her to Xanten, Thessaloniki, Lake Garda, and to Rome, Pompeii, Herculaneum and Ostia. Since 2010 Anna has worked freelance for the RGZM Mainz.

Youssef Mohamed, born 1975, studied German and Egyptology at the universities of Cairo and Mainz. Youssef operates a successful travel company for study and individual tours of Egypt (www.meret-reisen.de).

Evan Proudfoot, born 1984, studied Classical Archaeology at the universities of Michigan, USA and Oxford. Excavations and field research brought Evan to Alaska,

USA, Romania and Italy. Since 2006 he has conducted research with emphasis on ceramics and door systems in Pompeii.

Efthymios Rizos, born 1981, studied Archaeology and Byzantine History of Art in Thessaloniki and obtained his Ph.D. from Oxford University. Efthymios undertook research as a scholarship holder at the Koç University in Istanbul and took part in excavations in Northern Greece and Albania.

8

English	German	French	Italian	Spanish
abacus	Abakus *m*	abaque *m*	abaco *m*	ábaco *m*
abbey	Abtei *f*	abbaye *f*	abbazia *f*, badia *f*	abadía *f*
ablate, wear out	abtragen	éroder	erodere, spianare	aplanar, derribar
abrasion, fading	Abnutzung *f*	détérioration *f*, usure *f*	logorio *f*, usura *f*	desgaste *m*, uso *m*
abrasion, scoring	Abrieb *m*	abrasion *f*, frottis *m*	abrasione *f*, consumo *m*	abrasión *f*
absence, lack (of)	fehlen	manquer	mancare	faltar
absolute	absolut	absolu/-e	assoluto/-a	absoluto/-a
absolute chronology	absolute Chronologie *f*	chronologie *f* absolue	cronologia *f* assoluta	cronología *f* absoluta
absolute dating	absolute Datierung *f*	datation *f* absolue	datazione *f* assoluta	datación *f* absoluta
absolute humidity	absolute Feuchtigkeit *f*	humidité *f* absolue	umidità *f* assoluta	humedad *f* absoluta
acanthus	Akanthus *m*	acanthe *f*	acanto *m*	acanto *m*
accession/ finds number	Fundnummer *f*	numéro *m* de trouvaille	numero *m* di reperto	número *m* de hallazgo
accordance, agreement	Übereinstimmung *f*	concordance *f*	concordanza *f*	coincidencia *f*
accumulation	Anhäufung *f*, Akkumulation *f*	accumulation *f*	accumulo *m*	acumulación *f*
accumulation	Ansammlung *f*	acculmulation *f*	accumulazione *f*	aglomeración *f*
accuracy	Sorgfalt *f*	diligence *f*, soin *m*	accuratezza *f*	cuidado *m*
accurate	sorgfältig	soigné/-e	accurato/-a	cuidadoso
aceramic neolithic	akeramisches Neolithikum *n*	Néolithique *m* précéramique	neolitico *m* aceramico	neolítico *m* aceramico
acerbic, sour	sauer	acide, aigre	acido/-a	agrio/-a, acido/-a
acid	Säure *f*	acide *m*	acido *m*	ácido *m*
acidity	Säuregehalt *m*	acidité *f*	acidità *f*	acidez *f*
acoustic radar, sonar	Sonargerät *n*	sonar *m*	sonar *m*	sonar *m*
acropolis	Akropolis *f* / Stadtburg *f*	acropole *f*	arcopoli *f*	acrópolis *f*
acroterion	Akroterion *n*	acrotère *m*	acroterio *m*	acrotera *f*
acrylic resin	Acrylharz *n*	résine *f* méthacrylique	resina acrilica *f*	resina acrílica
adaptation	Adaptierung *f*	adaptation *f*	adattamento *m*	adaptación *f*
adhesive, glue	Kleber *m*	colle *f*	adesivo *f*, collo *m*	adhesivo *f*
adhesive, sticky	klebrig	adhésif/-ve, collant	colloso/-a	pegajoso/-a
adhesive/ sticky tape	Klebeband *n*	ruban *m* adhésif	nastro *m* adesivo	cinta *f* adhesiva
adjustment, alignment	Ausrichtung *f*	alignement *m*, orientation *f*	aggiustaggio *m*, allineamento *m*	alineamiento *m*, disposición *f*
adjustment, alignment, assimilation	Angleichung *f*	adaptation *f*, ajustement *m*	livellazione *f*	adaptación *f*, ajuste *m*
administration of finds	Fundverwaltung *f*	gestion *f* des trouvailles	gestione *f* dei reperti	administración *f* de los hallazgos
adornment	Zierde *f*	décor *m*	ornamento *m*	adorno *m*
advance, ledge	Vorsprung (am Bau) *m*	éperon *m*, saillie *f*	aggetto *m*	resalto *m*

Greek		Turkish	Arabic	
άβαξ/άβακας *m*	avax/avakas	abaküs	حجر على رأس أعمدة	hagar ala raas aamedah
αββαείο *n*	avvaeio	manastır	دير	deer
αφαιρώ	afairo	cıkarmak, kaldırmak	يُزيل	yoziel
φθορά *f*	fthora	aşınma	إستهلاك	istehlak
τριβή *f*	trivi	yıpranma	كشط	kaschat
λείπω, μου λείπει	leipo, mou leipei	bulunmama, yokluk	يخطئ	yochtea
απόλυτος	apolitos	mutlak, kesin	مطلق	motlak
απόλυτη χρονολόγηση *f*	apoliti chronologisi	mutlak kronoloji	التسلسل الزمني المطلق	eltasalsul elzamani elmotlak
απόλυτη χρονολόγηση *f*	apoliti chronologisi	kesin tarihleme, kesin tarihlendirme	التأريخ المطلق	eltariech elmotlak
απόλυτη υγρασία *f*	apoliti igrasia	bağıl nemlilik	الرطوبة المطلقة	elrotuba elmotlakah
άκανθα *f* άκανθος *f*	akantha/ akanthos	akanthus	نوع من الشوك	nua men elschuk
αριθμός *n* ευρήματος	arithmos evrimatos	buluntu numarası	رقم الإكتشاف	rakam elektischaf
συμφωνία *f*	simfonia	anlaşma, fikir birliği, uyuşma	تطابق	tatbok
συσσώρρευση *f*	sissorrevsi	birikme, toplanma, topak	تراكم	tarakum
συγκέντρωση *f*	sigkentrosi	kalabalık, yığıntı	إجتماع	igtemaa
φροντίδα *f* επιμέλεια *f*	frontida, epimeleia	dikkat, özen	دقة	deka
προσεχτικά, επιμελώς	prosechtika, epimelos	dikkatli, özenli	بدقة	bedeka
Ακεραμική Νεολιθική *f*	Akeramiki Neolotchiki	Akeramik Neolitik Dönem	العصر الحجري الحديث الأكريمى	elasr elhagari elhadies elakrimie
ξυνός, όξινος	xinos, oxinos	asitli, ekşi	حامض	hamed
οξύ *n*	oxi	asit	حمض	hemd
οξύτητα *f*	oxitita	asit muhteviyatı	حموضة	homuda
συσκευή *f*	siskevi sonar	sonar cihazı	جهاز الموجات الصوتية	gehaz elmawgat elsawtija
ακρόπολη *f*	akropoli	akropolis/ yukarıda bulunan şehir	حصن	hesn
ακρωτήριο *n*	akrotirio	akroter	ركيزة	Acroterion
ακρυλική ρητίνη *f*	akriliki ritini	akrilik reçinesi	نوع من الصمغ الصناعى	nua men elsamg elsinaie
προσαρμογή *f*	prosarmogi	adaptasyon, uyarlama	تكيف	takayof
κόλλα *f*	kolla	yapışkan, yapıştırıcı	لاصق	lasik
κολλώδης	kolladis	yapışkan	لزج	lazek
κολλητική ταινία *f*	kollitiki tainia	yapışkan bant	شريط لاصق	scherit lasik
ευθυγράμμιση *f*	efthigrammisi	ayarlama, doğrultu, düzenleme, oryantasyon	توجيه	tawgieh
αφομοίωση *f*	afomoiosi	ayarlama	محاذاة	mohazah
διαχείριση *f* ευρημάτων	diacheirisi evrimaton	buluntu idaresi	إدارة الإكتشافات	idaret elektischafat
κόσμημα *n*	kosmima	süs, takı	زخرفة	zachrafa
πρόοδος *f*	proodos	çıkma, çıkıntı, öncelik	افريز	iefriez

English	German	French	Italian	Spanish
adyton	Adyton *n*	adyton *m*	adyton *m*	adito *m* , ádyton *m*
aedicula	Aedicula/ Ädikula *f*	édicule *m*	edicola *f*	edícula *f*
Aegean	ägäisch	égéen, -enne	egeo/-a	egeo/-a
Aegean	Ägäis *f*	mer *f* Egée	Egeo *m*	Mar *m* Egeo
Aeolian	äolisch	éolien/-ienne	eolio/-a	eólico/-a
aeolian silt deposit, loess	Löß *n*	loess *m*	loess *m*	loess *m*
aerial photographic survey	Luftbildsurvey *m*	surveille *m* aérien	ricognizione *f* aerea	survey *m* de fotografías aereas
aerial picture/ photo	Luftaufnahme *f*	photo aérienne *f*	aerofotografia *f*	fotografía *f* aérea
aerosol spray can	Sprühflasche *f*	atomiseur *m* , vaporisateur *m*	vaporizzatore *m*	vaporizador *m*
agate (stone)	Achat *m*	agate *f*	agata *f*	ágata *m*
age	altern	vieillir	invecchiare	envejecer
age	Alter *n*	âge m	età *f*	edad *f*
age determination, dating	Altersbestimmung *f*	détermination *f* de l'âge	determinazione *f* dell'età	estimación *f* de la edad
aggradation, silting	Verlandung *f*	atterrissement *m*	interramento *m*	sedimentación *f*
agriculture	Landwirtschaft *f*	agriculture *f*	agricoltura *f*	agricultura *f*
agriculture, farming	Ackerbau *m*	agriculture *f*	agricultura *f*	agricultura *f*
aid, tool	Hilfsmittel *n*	moyen *m*	sussidio *m*	remedio *m*
air bubble	Luftblase *f*	soufflure *f*	bolla d'aria *f*	burbuja *f*
air humidity	Luftfeuchtigkeit *f*	humidité *f* de l'air	umidità *f* atmosferica	humedad *f* atmosférica
airproof, airtight	luftdicht	étanche	ermetico/-a	hermético/-a
air/ water level	Wasserwaage *f*	niveau *m* à bulle	livella *f* a bolla d'aria	nivel del agua *m*
akkadian	akkadisch	akkadien/-ienne	accadico/-a	acadio/-a
alabaster	Alabaster *m*	albâtre *m*	alabastro *m*	alabastro *m*
alabastron	Alabastron *n*	alabastre *m*	alabastron *m*	alabastrón *m*
alcohol	Alkohol *m*	alcool *m*	alcol *m*	alcohol *m*
alcove	Alkoven *m*	alcôve *f*	alcova *f*	alcoba *f*
alcove, niche	Nische *f*	niche *f*	nicchia *f*	nicho *m*
alder	Erle *f*	aune *m*	ontano *m*	aliso *m*
alignment, line, row	Reihe *f*	rangée *f*	fila *f* , serie *f*	fila *f*
alkaline	alkalisch	alcalin/-e	alcalino/-a	alcalino/-a
alkaline rocks	Alkaligestein *n*	roches *f pl* alcalines	pietra *f* alcalina	rocas *f pl* alcalinas
alley, lane	Gang *m* , Gasse *f*	allée *f*, ruelle *f*	vicolo *m*	calleja *f*, corredor *m*
alloy	Legierung *f*	alliage *m*	lega *f*	aleación *f*
alluvial clay deposits	Auelehmablagerung *f*	dépôt *m* de limon alluvial	deposito *m* di argille alluvionali	arcilla *f* aluvial
alluvium	Alluvium *n*	alluvions *m pl*	terreno *m* alluvionale	aluvión *m*
alluvium (geol.), mud	Schlamm *m*	boue *f*	fango *m* , melma *f*	lodo *m*
alteration, weathering	Verwitterung *f*	érosion *m*	degrado *m*	descomposición *f*, desmoronamiento *m*
altitude, height	Höhe *f*	altitude *f*	altitudine *f*	altitud *f*, altura *f*
alumin(i)um foil	Aluminiumfolie *f*	feuille *f* d'aluminium	foglio *m* di alluminio	papel *m* de aluminio
amber	Bernstein *m*	ambre *m*	ambra *f*	ámbar *m*

Greek		Turkish	Arabic	
άδυτο(ν) *n*	adito (n)	adyton	قدس الأقداس	kods elakdas
ναΐσκος *m*	naiskos	aedicula	تجويف لحفظ تمثال	taguief lehefz temsal
αιγαιακός	aigaiakos	Ege ile ilgili	بحر ايجه	bahr igah
Αιγαίο *n*	Aigaio	Ege	بحر ايجه	bahr igah
αιολικός	aiolikos	Aiolyalı	عولسي	aulasi
αιολικές αποθέσεις *f pl*	aiolikes apotheseis	lös	الراسب الطفلي	elraseb eltaflie
εναέρια έρευνα *f*	enaeria erevna	hava fotoğrafi ile inceleme yapmak	مسح جوي	mash gawie
αεροφωτογραφία *f*	aerofotografia	hava fotoğrafi	صورة من الجو	sura men elgaw
σπρέι *n* , φιάλη υπό πίεση *f*	sprei, fiali ipo piesi	sprey	بخّاخة	bachacha
αχάτης *m*	achatis	akik	عقيق	akiek
γερνώ, παλιώνω	gerno, paliono	yaşlanmak	يتقدم فى السن	yatakadam fi elsen
ηλικία *f*	ilikia	yaş	عصر	asr
χρονολόγηση *f*	chronologisi	yaş tayini	تحديد سن	tahdid elsen
απόθεση *f*	apothesi	alüvyonla tıkanma	ترسب الطمي	tarasob eltamei
γεωργία *f*	georgia	ziraat	زراعة	ziraa
γεωργία *f*	georgia	tarım	زراعة	zeraah
βοήθημα *n*	voithima	yardımcı araç	وسيلة مساعدة	wasila mosaada
φούσκα *f*	fouska	hava kabarcığı	فقاعة هواء	fukaat hawaa
ατμοσφαιρική υγρασία *f*	atmosfairiki igrasia	hava rutubeti	رطوبة جوية	rutuba gaweia
αεροστεγής	aerostegis	hava kaçırmaz	محكم الغلق	muhkam elgalk
αλφάδι *n*	alfadi	su terazisi	ميزان الماء	mizan elmaa
ακκαδικός	akkadikos	Akadlı, Akad ile ilgili	أكادية	akkadijah
αλάβαστρος *m*	alavastros	albatr, kaymaktaşı	مرمر	marar
αλάβαστρο(ν) *n*	alavastro (n)	alabastron	زخرفة الأجزاء العليا للمعبد	zachraft elagazaa elulija lelmaabad
αλκοόλ *n* , οινόπνευμα *n*	alkool, oinopnevma	alkol	كحول	kuhol
εσοχή *f*	esochi	yatak nişi	قبه	kubah
κόγχη *f*	kogchi	niş, mihrap	تجويف فى الحائط	tagwief fi elhaet
κλήθρα *f*	klithra	akça ağaç	نبات مائى	nabat maie
σειρά *f*	seira	dizi, sıra	صفّ	saf
αλκαλικός	alkalikos	alkalik	قلوي	kalaui
αλκαλικό πέτρωμα *n*	alkaliko petroma	alkali taşlar, kayalar	صخورقلوية	suchur kalauija
πάροδος *f*, αγυιά *f*	parodos, agiia	dar yol, geçit	حارة	hara
κράμα *n*	krama	alaşım	خليط معدني	chaliet madenie
αλλουβιακή απόθεση *f* πηλού	allouviaki apothesi pilou	alüvyal toprak birikintisi	ترسيب الطمي	tarsieb eltamei
ποτάμια απόθεση *f*	potamia apothesi	alüvyon	ترسب الطيني	tarasub tini
λάσπη *f*, ιλύς *f*	laspi, ilis	balçık	طمي	tamei
φθορά *f*, αποσάθρωση *f*	fthora, apo sathrosi	aşınma, bozulma	الأحوال الجوية	elahwal elgaweija
ύψος *n*	ipsos	seviye, yükseklik	ارتفاع	irtefaa
αλουμινόχαρτο *n*	alouminocharto	alüminyum folyo	ورق حراري	warak hararie
κεχριμπάρι *n* , ήλεκτρο *n*	kechribari, ilektro	kehribar	كهرمان	kahraman

English	German	French	Italian	Spanish
amethyst	Amethyst *m*	améthyste *f*	ametista *f*	amatista *f*
amorphic, shapeless	amorph, formlos	amorphe	amorfo/-a	amorfo/-a
amount of knowledge	Erkenntnisgewinn *m*	gain *m* de connaissances	incremento *m* di conoscenza	beneficio *m* de los resultados
amphiprostyle	Amphiprostylos *m*	amphiprostyle *m*	anfiprostilo *m*	anfipróstilo *m*
amphitheatre	Amphitheater *n*	amphithéâtre *m*	anfiteatro *m*	anfiteatro *m*
amphora	Amphore *f*	amphore *f*	anfora *f*	ánfora *f*
amulet, charm	Amulett *n*	amulette *f*	amuleto *m* , portafortuna *m*	amuleto *m*
anaerobic	anaerob	anaérobique	anaerobico/-a	anaerobio/-a
analogue	analog	analogue	analogo/-a	analógo/-a
analogy	Analogie *f*	analogie *f*	analogia *f*	analogía *f*
analyse	Analyse *f*	analyse *f*	analisi *f*	análisis *m*
analysis of diatoms	Diatomeeanalyse, Kieselalgenanlyse *f*	analyse *f* des diatomées	analisi *f* delle diatomee	análisis *m* de diatomeas fósiles
analytic	analytisch	analytique	analitico/-a	analítico/-a
anastylosis	Anastylose *f*	anastylose *f*	anastilosi *f*	anastilosis *f*
anathyrosis	Anathyrose *f*	anathyrose *f*	anatirosi *f*	anatirosis *f*
anatomical	anatomisch	anatomique	anatomico/-a	anatómico/-a
anatomy	Anatomie *f*	anatomie *f*	anatomia *f*	anatomía *f*
ancient	altertümlich	ancien/-ìenne, antique	antico/-a	antiguo/-a
andesite	Andesit *m*	andésite *f*	andesite *f*	andesita *f*
angle	Winkel *m*	angle *m*	angolo *m*	ángulo *m*
angled, bent	angewinkelt	angulaire, coudé/-e	ripiegato/-a	en un ángulo recto
animal	Tier *n*	animal *m*	animale *m*	animal *m*
animal remains	Tierreste *pl*	restes *m pl* d'animaux	resti *m pl* animali	restos *m pl* de animales
annexe	Anbau *m* , Nebengebäude *n*	annexe *f*	annesso *m*	accesori anejo *m*
anno domini (AD)	nach Christus (n. Chr.)	après Jésus-Christ (ap. J.-C.)	dopo Cristo (d.C.)	después de Jesucristo (d.J.)
annual/ tree ring	Jahresring *m*	cerne/ couche *m* annuelle	anello *m* di crescita	anillo *m* annual
annular, circular	ringförmig	annulaire	anulare	anular, circular
anomaly	Anomalie *f*	anomalie *f*	anomalia *f*	anomalía *f*
anta capital	Antenkapitell *n*	chapiteau *m* d'ante	capitello *m* d'anta	capitel *m* de antas
ante	Ante *f*	ante *f*	anta *f*	anta *f*
antechamber	Vorkammer *f*	antichambre *m*, vestibule *m*	anticamera *f*, vestibolo *m*	antecámera *m*, vestíbulo *f*
antefix	Antefix *n*	antéfixe *f*	antefissa *f*	antefijo *m*
anthropogenic	anthropogen	anthropogène	antropogenico	antroprógeno/-a
anthropology	Anthropologie *f*	anthropologie *f*	antropologia *f*	antropología *f*

Greek		Turkish	Arabic	
αμέθυστος *m*	amethistos	ametist	حجر أميثست	hagar ameset
άμορφος	amorfos	amorf, biçimsiz	غير متجانس	geer motaganes
πληροφορίες *f pl*	plirofories	bilgi arttırma, bilgi kazanma	اكتساب معرفة	iktesab maarefah
αμφιπρόστυλος ναός *m*	amfiprostilos naos	amphiprostylos	تخطيط معبد يوناني	tachtit maabad yunani
αμφιθέατρο *n*	amfitheatro	amfitiyatro	مسرح مكشوف	masrah makschuf
αμφορέας *m*	amforeas	amphora	قارورة بمقبضين	karurah bemakbadein
φυλαχτό *n* φυλακτήριο *n*	filachto, filaktirio	amulet	تميمة	tamima
αναερόβιος	anaerovios	anaerobik	بدون أكسجين	bedon oksugien
αναλογικός	analogikos	analog, benzer	مطابق	mutabek
αναλογία *f*	analogia	analoji, benzer	تطابق	tatabok
ανάλυση *f*	analisi	analiz, tahlil	تحليل	tahlil
κοκκομετρική ανάλυση *f*	kokkometriki analisi	diatom analizi	تحليل الطحالب	tahliel eltahaleb
αναλυτικός	analitikos	analitik	تحليلي	tahlili
αναστύλωση *f*	anastilosi	anastylosis	إعادة بناء	iadet binaa
αναθύρωση *f*	anathirosi	anathyrosis	تأهيل الحجر للبناء	taahiel elhagar lelbinaa
ανατομικός	anatomikos	anatomik	تشريحي	teschrihie
ανατομία *f*	anatomia	anatomi, beden yapısı	علم التشريح	elm eltaschrih
αρχαίος	archaios	ilkel	أثرى	asari
ανδεσίτης *m*	andesitis	andezit	حجر أملس	hagar amlas
γωνία *f*	gonia	açı	زاوية	zawija
καμπύλος	kabilos	açılı	مثنى	masni
ζώο *n*	zoo	hayvan	حيوان	hajawan
ζωϊκά κατάλοιπα *n*	zoika kataloipa	hayvan artıkları	بقايا حيوانات	bakaja hajawanaat
πρόσκτισμα *n*	prosktisma	ek bina	مبنى ملحق	mabna molhak
μετά Χριστόν (μ. Χ.)	meta Christon	Milattan Sonra (M.S.J.), Sa'dan Sonra (I.S.)	ميلادية (م)	miladija *m*
(ετήσιος) αυξητικός δακτύλιος *m*	(etisios) afxitikos daktilios	yaş halkası	حلقة نمو سنوية للخشب	salaket numo sanawija lelchaschab
δακτυλιόσχημος	daktilioschimos	halka biçiminde	حلقي الشكل	halakei elschakl
ανωμαλία *f*	anomalia	anormallik, aykırılık	إنحراف	inheraf
επίκρανο *n* παραστάδας	epikrano parastadas	ante başlığı	تاج عمود مزخرف	tag amud muzachraf
παραστάδα *f*	parastada	ante	واجهة عامودية للسور	wageha amudijah lelsur
προθάλαμος *m*	prothalamos	ön oda	حجرة أمامية	hugra amamija
ακροκέραμο *n*	akrokeramo	antefiks	واجهة مزخرفة للطوب	wageha muzachrafa leltub
ανθρωπογενής	anthropogenis	antropojen	إبتكار بشرى	ebtekar baschari
ανθρωπολογία *f*	anthropologia	Antropoloji	علم الأجناس البشرية	elm el agnas elbascharija

English	German	French	Italian	Spanish
anthropomorphic	anthropomorph	anthropomorphe	antropomorfo/-a	antropomorfo/-a
antiquarian	antiquarisch	d'occasion	antiquario/-a	de ocasión, de lance
antique	antik	ancien/-ìenne, antique	antico/-a	antiguo/-a
antiquity	Altertum *n*	antiquité *f*	antichità *f*	antigüedad *f*
antiquity	Antike *f*	antiquité *f*	antichità *f*	antigüedad *f*
antithetical	antithetisch	antithétique	antitetico/-a	antitético/-a
antlers	Geweih *n*	bois *m* de cerf	corna *f*	cornamenta *f*
anvil	Amboss *m*	enclume *f*	incudine *f*	yunque *m*
anvil technique	Ambosstechnik *f*	technique *f* sur enclume	tecnica *f* dell'incudine	técnica *f* del yunque
apodyterium	Apodyterium *n*	apodyterium *m*	apoditerio *m*	apoditerio *m*
apotropaic	apotropäisch	apotropaïque	apotropaico/-a	apotropaico/-a
appendant	zugehörig	correspondant (-e)	appartenente	perteneciente a
appendix	Anhang *m*	appendice *m*	allegato *m* , appendice *m*	apéndice *m*
apperance	Erscheinung *f*	apparition *f*	apparizione *f*	aparición *f*, fenómeno *m*
application	Applikation *f*	application *f*	applicazione *f*	aplicación *f*
apse	Apsis *f*	apside *f*, chevet *m*	abside *f*	ábside *m*
aqueduct	Aquädukt *m*	aqueduc *m*	acquedotto *m*	aqueducto *m*
arcade	Arkade *f*	arcade *f*	arcata *f*	arcada *f*, arquería *f*
archaeobotany	Archäobotanik *f*	archéobotanique *f*	archeobotanica *f*	arqueobotánica *f*
archaeochemistry	Archäochemie *f*	archéochimie *f*	archeochimica *f*	arqueoquímica *f*
archaeology	Altertumswissenschaft *f*	archéologie *f*	scienza *f* dell'antichità	ciencia *f* de la antigüedad
archaeology	Archäologie *f*	archéologie *f*	archeologia *f*	arqueología *f*
archaeometallurgy	Archäometallurgie *f*	archéométallurgie *f*	archeometallurgia *f*	arqueometalurgía *f*
archaeoseismology	Archäoseismologie *f*	archéosismologie *f*	archeosismologia *f*	arqueosismología *f*
archaeozoology	Archäozoologie *f*	archéozoologie *f*	archeozoologia *f*	arqueometría *f*
archaic	archaisch	archaïque	arcaico	arcaico
Archaic period	Archaik *f*	archaïsme *m*	arcaismo *m*	época *f* Arcaica
archaic smile	archaisches Lächeln *n*	sourire archaïque *m*	sorriso *m* arcaico	sonrisa *f* arcaica
archeomagnetic dating	archäomagnetische Datierung *f*	datation *f* archéomagnetique	archeomagnetismo *m*	datación *f* arqueomagnética
archetype, prototype	Prototyp *m*, Urform *f*	forme primitive *f*, prototype *m*	prototipo *m*	forma primitiva *f*, prototipo *m*
arching, vault	Wölbung *f*	voûte *f*	volta *f*	bóveda *f*, convexidad *f*
architect	Architekt *m*	architecte *m*	architetto *m*	arqueozoología *f*
architectural history	Bauforschung *f*	étude *f* des bâtiments	ricerca *f* edilizia	estudio *m* Arquitectónico
architectural remains	Architekturreste *m pl*	restes *m pl* d'architecture	resti *m pl* architettonici	elementos *m pl* arquitectónicos

Greek		Turkish	Arabic	
ανθρωπόμορφος	anthropomorfos	anthropomorphos	مُجسم فى شكل إنسان	mugasam fi schakl ensan
παλαιός	palaios	antika, antikacı	أثري	asari
αρχαίος	archaios	antik	قديم	kadim
αρχαιότητα *f*	archaiotita	İlk Çağ	العصور القديمة	elusur elkadimah
αρχαιότητα *f*	archaiotita	Antik Çağ/ Eski Çağ	العصور القديمة	alosur elkadima
αντιθετικός	antithetikos	antithetik	متناقض	mutanakid
κέρας *n* , κέρατο *n*	keras, kerato	geyik boynuzu	قرون متشعبة	koron motaschaeba
αμόνι *n*	amoni	örs	سندان الحداد	sendan elhadad
τεχνική *f* διαμόρφωσης με αμόνι	techniki diamorfosis me amoni	örs tekniği	تقنية السندان	teknijat elsendan
αποδυτήριο *n*	apoditirio	apodyterium, soyunma odası	حجرة خلع الملابس	hugret chalaa elmalabis
αποτροπαϊκός	apotropaikos	apotropaik	مُحصن	muhasen
ανήκων, συνανήκων	anikon, sinanikon	ait olan, bağıl	منتمي إلى	montamie ila
παράρτημα *n*	parartima	ek, ilave	ملحق	molhak
εμφάνιση *f*	emfanisi	görüntü, görünüm	ظاهرة	zahera
εφαρμογή *f*	efarmogi	uygulama	تطبيق	tatbiek
αψίδα *f*	apsida	apsis	قبو	kabu
υδραγωγείο *n*	idragogeio	aquaduct, su kemeri	مجرى مائى مرتفع	magra maie mortafia
τοξοστοιχία *f*	toxostoichia	arkad, sıra kemerler	رواق	ruwak
αρχαιοβοτανική *f*	archaiovotaniki	Arkeobotani	علم الآثار والنبات	elm elasar wi
αρχαιοχημεία *f*	archaiochimeia	Arkeokimya	علم الآثار والكيمياء	elm elasar wi e
αρχαιολογία *f*	archaiologia	Eskiçağ Bilimleri	علم الآثار	elm elasar elmasrjeh
αρχαιολογία *f*	archaologia	Arkeoloji	علم الآثار	elm elasar
αρχαιομεταλλουργία *f*	archaiometallourgia	Arkeometalurji	علم المعادن الأثرية	elm elmaaden elasarija
αρχαιοσεισμολογία *f*	archaioseismologia	Arkeosismoloji	علم الزلازل الأثري	elm elzalazel elasarie
αρχαιοζωολογία *f*	archaiozoologia	Arkeozooloji	علم بقايا الحيوانات	elm bakaja elhaiwanat
αρχαϊκός	archaikos	arkaik	ما قبل التاريخ	ma kabl atariech
αρχαϊκή περίοδος *f*	archaki periodos	Arkaik Dönem	حضارة ما قبل التاريخ	hadaret ma kabl atariech
αρχαϊκό μειδίαμα *n*	archaiko meidiama	Arkaik Gülümseme	ابتسامة تماثيل يونانية	ebtisama tamasiel yonanieh
αρχαιομαγνητική χρονολόγηση *f*	archaiomagnitiki chronologisi	Arkeomanyetik Tarihleme	تأريخ بأسلوب خاص	tagrich beuslub chas
αρχέτυπο *n*	archetipo	asıl, ilk biçim	النموذج الأصلي	elnamuzag elaslie
θόλος *m*	tholos	kemer, kubbe	تقوس	takawos
αρχιτέκτονας *m*	architektonas	mimar	مهندس معماري	muhandes meamari
ιστορία *f* της αρχιτεκτονικής	istoria tis architektonikis	yapı araştırması	بحث المبانى	bahs elmabani
αρχιτεκτονικά λείψανα *n* *pl*	architektonika leipsana	mimari kalıntı	بقايا معمارية	bakaja meamarijs

English	German	French	Italian	Spanish
architecture	Architektur f	architecture f	architettura f	arquitectura m
architrave	Architrav m	architrave f	architrave f	arquitrabe m
archive	Archiv n	archives m pl	archivio m	archivo m
archiving/ archival storage	Archivierung f	archivage m	archiviazione f	archivo m
arch, vault	Gewölbe n	voûte f	volta f	bóveda f
archway	Torbogen m	arc m de portail	arco m del portone	arco m (de un portal)
area	Gebiet n	région f, zone f	regione f	área m
area excavation	Flächengrabung f	fouille f de surface	scavo m d'estensione	excavación f en extensión
area of exploitation	Abbaufläche f	champ m d'exploitation, surface f à décaper	campo m di estrazione	campo m de explotación
area, plain	Fläche f	étendue f, surface f	pianura f, superficie f	área f, plano m
area, region, sector	Bereich m	domaine m, ressort m	area f, campo m	área f, sector m
area-wide	flächendeckend	complet/-ète, généralisé/-e, global/-e	capillare	completo/-a
arena	Arena f	arène f	arena f	arena f
arid	arid	aride	arido	árido
arrangement	Anordnung f	arrangement m, disposition f	collocazione f	ordenación f, disposición f
arrow	Pfeil m	flèche f	freccia f	flecha f
art	Kunst f	art m	arte f	arte m
artefact	Artefakt n	artefact m	artefatto m	artefacto m
artefact scatter, spread of artefacts	Artefaktstreuung f	répartition f des artefacts	dispersione f dei manufatti	dispersión f de artefactos
artificial	künstlich	artificiel	artificiale	artificial
artificial/ synthetic resin	Kunstharz n	résine f artificielle/ synthétique	resina f sintetica	resina sintética f
aryballos	Aryballos m	aryballe m	aryballos m	aríbalo m
ash	Asche f	cendre f	ceneri f, polvere f	ceniza f
ash/ burnt layer	Brandschicht f	couche f d'incendie	strato m di cenere	estrato m de ceniza
ashlar	Quader m	pierre f de taille	parallelepipedo m	sillar m
ash pit	Aschengrube f	fosse f à cendres	ceneratoio m	depósito m de ceniza
ash tree	Esche f	frêne m	frassino m	fresno m
askos	Askos m	askos m	askos m	ascos m, ascó m
asphalt, bitumen	Asphalt m	asphalte m, bitume m	asfalto m	asfaltado m
assignment	Zuordnung f	classement m	associazione f	coordinación f
assortment	Sortiment n	assortiment m	assortimento m	surtido m
Assyric	assyrisch	assyrien, -enne	assiro/-a	asirio/-a
Assyrology	Assyriologie f	assyriologie f	assirologia f	asiriología f
asymmetrical	asymmetrisch	asymétrique	asimmetrico/-a	asimétrico/-a
at risk, endangered	gefährdet	en danger, menacé/-e	compromesso/-a	en peligro
atrium	Atrium n	atrium m	atrio m	atrium m / atrio m

Greek		Turkish	Arabic	
αρχιτεκτονική *f*	architektoniki	mimari	الهندسة المعمارية	elhandasa elmeamarija
επιστύλιο *n*	epistilio	architrav	عتب	atab
αρχείο *n*	archeio	arşiv	أرشيف	arschif
αρχειοθέτηση *f*	archeiothetisi	arşivleme	حفظ	hefz
θόλος *m*	tholos	kemer, kubbe, tonoz	قبو	kabw
τόξο *n* , τοξωτή πύλη *f*	toxo, xoti pili	kapı kemeri	قبة البوابة	kobet elbawaba
περιοχή *f*	peiochi	alan, bölge	منطقة	manteka
εκτεταμένη ανασκαφή *f*	ektetameni anaskafi	yüzey temizliği	حفر المنطقة	hafr elmanteka
επιφάνεια *f* εξόρυξης	epifaneia exorixis	yongalanmış yüzey	منطقة تنقيب	mantekat eltankieb
επιφάνεια *f*, έκταση *f*	epifaneia ektasi	yüzey	مساحة / منطقة	misaha/ manteka
περιοχή *f*	periochi	bölüm	مجال	magal
εκτεταμένος	ektetamenos	bölgeyi kapsayan, yüzeysel	مستوعب المنطقة	mustawab elmanteka
αρένα *f*, κον ίστρα *f*	arena konistra	arena	حلبة	halbah
άνυδρος	anidros	kurak	قاحلة	kahela
κατάταξη *f*	katataxi	düzen, düzenleme, talimat	ترتيب	tartib
βέλος *n*	velos	ok	سهم	sahm elschmal
τέχνη *f*	techni	sanat	فن	fan
κατασκεύασμα *n* , τέχνεργο *n*	kataskevasma technergo	artifakt, ilk insan eliyle yapılan eser	قطعة أثرية	ketaa aserija
διασπορά *f* τεχνέργων ☐	diaspora technergon	artifakt dağılımı	قطع أثرية مبعثرة	kutaa aserija mobasara
τεχνητός	technitos	suni	صناعي	sinaie
τεχνητή ρητίνη *f*	techiti ritini	suni reçine	صمغ صناعى	samg sinaie
αρύβαλλος *m*	apivallos	aryballos	إناء للدهان	inaa leldahan
στάχτη *f*, τέφρα *f*	stachti tefra	kül	رماد	ramad
στρώμα *n* καύσης	stroma kafsi	yangın tabakası	الطبقة المحروقة	eltabaka elmahroka
γωνιόλιθος *m*	goniolithos	yontma yapı taşı	حجر مربع	hagar murabaa
αποθέτης *m* τέφρας	apothetis tefras	kül çukuru	حفرة رماد	hufrat ramad
φράξος *m*	fraxos	dişbudak ağacı	الرماد البركاني	elramad elborkani
ασκός *m*	askos	askos	إناء منتفخ	inaa montafech
άσφαλτος *f*	asfaltos	asfalt	أسفلت	asfalt
κατάταξη *f*	katataxi	sınıflandırma	إلحاق	elhaak
σειρά *f*	seira	mal çeşidi	مجموعة سلع	magmuat selaa
ασσυριακός	assiriakos	Asurca	آشوري	aschuri
ασσυριολογία *f*	assiriologia	Asuroloji	علم الآشوريات	elm elaschurijat
ασύμμετρος	asimmetros	asimetrik	غير متماثل	geer mutmasel
απειλούμενος, σε κίνδυνο	apeiloumenos, se kindino	tehlikede	مُعرض للخطر	moarad lelchatar
αίθριο *n*	aithrio	atrium	ردهة	rudha

English	German	French	Italian	Spanish
attachment, binding	Bindung *f*	fixation *f*	attacchi *m pl*, legame *m*	enlace *m*, fijación *f*
attempt, test	Versuch *m*	essai *m*	tentativo *m*	ensayo *m*, preuba *f*
attitude, point of view	Standpunkt *m*	point de vue *m*	punto di vista *m*	punto *m* de vista
attribute	Attribut *n*	attribut *m*	attributo *m*	atributo *m*
atypical	atypisch	atypique	atipico	atípico
authentic, genuine	echt	véritable, vrai	autentico/-a, vero/-a	auténtico/-a
authenticity	Echtheit *f*	authenticité *f*	autenticità *f*	autenticidad *f*
auxiliary line	Hilfslinie *f*	ligne *f* auxiliaire	linea *f* ausiliaria	línea *f* auxiliar
auxilliary	Neben-	périphérique, auxilliaire	addizionale, accessorio/-a	adicional, a lado de
axe, hatchet	Beil *n*	cognée *f,* hache *f*	ascia *f*, scure *f*	hacha *m*
axis	Achse *f*	axe *m*	asse *m*	eje *m*
axis of symmetry	Symmetrieachse *f*	axe *m* de symétrie	asse *m* di simmetria	eje *m* de simmetría
axonometric projection	Axonometrie *f*	axonométrie *f*	assonometria *f*	axonometría *f*
back, rear	hinten	derrière, à l'arrière	dietro	atrás
bacteria	Bakterien *f pl*	bactérie *f*	batteri *m*	bacteria *f*
bag	Tüte *f*	sac *m*	busta *f*	bolsa *f*
balsamarium	Balsamarium *n*	balsamaire *m*	balsamario *m*	lacrimatorio *m*
balsam, oinment	Balsam *m*	baume *m*	balsamo *m*	bálsamo *m*
band-aid	Pflaster (med.)	pansement *m*	cerotto *m*	emplasto *m*
bank, shore, strand, waterside	Ufer *n*	berge *f*, rivage *m*, rive *f*	riva *f*, sponda *f*	costa *f*, orilla *f*, ribera *f*
bar, batten	Latte *f*	latte *f*	assicella *f*	lata *f*
bar, batten	Leiste *f*	baguette *f*	listello *m*	listón *m,* moldura *f*
bar clamp	Schraubzwinge *f*	serre-joint *m*	morsetto *m*	tornillo *m* de apriete
bark	Baumrinde *f*	écorce *f*	corteccia *f* d'albero	corteza *f*
barley	Gerste *f*	orge *m*	orzo *m*	cebada *f*
barrel vault	Tonnengewölbe *n*	voûte *f* en berceau	volta *f* a botte	bóveda *f* en cañón
barrow	Schubkarre *f*	brouette *f*	carriola *f*	carretilla *f*
basalt, trap rock	Basalt *m*	basalte *m*	basalto *m*	basalto *m*
base, pedestal	Postament *n*	piédestal *m*	piedistallo *m*	pedestal *m*
base ring	Standring *m*	anneau *m* de base	base anulare *f*	base *m* anular
base, socle	Sockel *m*	piédestal *m,* socle *m*	zoccolo *m*	base *m,* pedestal *m*
basic form	Grundform *f*	forme *f* principale	forma *f* primitiva	forma *f* elemental
basic/ raw material	Werkstoff *m*	matériau *m*	materiale *m*	material *m*
basilica	Basilika *f*	basilique *f*	basilica *f*	basílica *f*
basis	Grundlage *f*	base *f*, éléments *m pl*	base *f*	base *f*
basket	Korb *m*	corbeille *f*, panier *m*	cesto *m*	cesta *f*
bas-relief	Flachrelief *n*	bas-relief *m*	bassorelievo *m*	bajorrelieve *m*
bastion	Bastei *f*, Bastion *f*	bastion *m*	bastione *m*	bastión *m*

Greek		Turkish	Arabic	
σύνδεση *f*	sindesi	bağlama, bağlanma	وصل	wasl
απόπειρα *f*, δοκιμή *f*	apopeira, dokimi	deneme	محاولة	muhawala
οπτική γωνία *f*, προσέγγισ η *f*	optiki gonia prosengisi	bakış noktası, durulan yer	نقطة الوقوف	noktat elwokuuf
εμβληματικό αντικείμενο *n*	emvlimatiko antikeimeno	attribut, nitelik	صفة	sefa
ατυπικός, μη τυπικός	atipikos, mi tipikos	alışılmamış, tipik olmayan	غير نمطي	geer namati
αυθεντικός, γνήσιος	afthentikos, gnisios	asıl, gerçek	حقيقي	hakiki
αυθεντικότητα *f*, γνησιότητα	afthentikotita, gnisiotita	doğruluk, saflık	الأصالة	alasala
βοηθητική γραμμή *f*	voithitiki grammi	yardımcı çizgi	خط إرشاد	chat erschad
δευτερεύων, παρ(α)-	defterevon, par(a)-	başka, dışında, yanına	جانبي	ganebie
πέλεκυς *m*, τσεκο ύρι *n*	pelekis, tsekouri	el baltası, keser, nacak	بلطة	balta
άξονας *m*	axonas	aks, dingil, eksen	محور	mehuar
άξονας συμμετρίας *m*	axonas simmetrias	simetri/ bakışım ekseni	محور التناسق	mehwar eltanasok
αξονομετρικό σχέδιο *n*	axonometriko schedio	aksonometri	أسلوب عرض هندسى	uslub ard handasi
πίσω	piso	arka, arkada	فى الخلف	fi elchalf
βακτήρια *n pl*	vaktiria	bakteri	بكتيريا	bakterja
σακούλα *f*, τσάντα *f*	sakoula, tsanta	torba	كيس	kiees
βαλσαμάριο *n*	valsamario	balsamarium	قارورة للدهان	karurah leldahan
αλοιφή *f*, βάλσαμο *n*	aloifi, valsamo	balsam, ilaç, merhem	بلسم	balsam
επίδεσμος *m*	epidesmos	plaster	ضمادة	damada
όχθη *f*, ακτή *f*	ochthi, akti	kıyı	ضفة	dafa
πήχυς *m*, σανίδα *f*	pichis, sanida	çıta	عارضة خشبية	arida chaschabeia
γοφός *m*, σαν ίδα *f*	gofos, sanida	pervaz	شريط	schariet
σφιγκτήρας *m*	sfigktiras	el mengenesi, kelepçe	قمّاطة	kamata
φλοιός *m*	floios	ağaç kabuğu	لحاء الشجر	lihaa elschagar
κριθάρι *n*	krithara	arpa	شعير	schaier
καμάρα *f*	kamara	beşik tonoz	قبو مُقوّس	kabo mukawas
καρότσι *n*	karotsi	el arabası	عربة يد	arabet yad
βασάλτης *m*	vasalitis	bazalt	بازلت	bazalt
βάθρο *n*	vathro	postament	قاعدة التمثال	kaedet eltemsal
δακτύλιος έδρασης *m*	daktilios edrasis	halka dip, kaide	حلقة الوقوف	halaket elwokuuf
βάση *f*	vasi	kaide, taban	قاعدة	kaeda
βασική μορφή *f*	basiki morfi	ana şekil	شكل أساسي	schakl asasie
πρώτη ύλη *f*, υλικό *m*	proti ili, iliko	ham madde, malzeme	مادة خام	mada cham
βασιλική *f*	basiliki	bazilika	كنيسة	kinisa
βάση *f*	basi	temel	قاعدة / أساس	kaida/ asas
καλάθι *n*	kalathi	sepet	سلة	salla
επιπεδόγλυφο *n*	epipedoglifo	alçak kabartma	نحت سطحى	naht sathie
προμαχώνας *m*	promachonas	bastiyon, burç	حصن	hesn

English	German	French	Italian	Spanish
bastion, bulwark, stronghold	Bollwerk *n*	bastion *m* , rempart *m*	baluardo *m*	baluarte *m* , bastión *m*
bead and reel	Perlstab *m*	rang *m* de perles	filo *m* di perle	astrágalo *m*
beaded rim, boltel	Wulst *m/f*	boudin *m*	cuscinetto *m*	bocel *m* , toro *m*
beaker	Becher *m*	gobelet *m* , timbale *f*	calice *m* , coppa *f*	cangilón *m*, vaso *m*
beak-spouted ewer	Schnabelkanne *f*	cruche *f* à bec	brocca *f* con beccuccio	jarra *f* de pico
beams, woodwork	Gebälk *n*	charpente *f*, entablement *m*	intravatura *f*	armadura *f*, envigado *m*
beam, timber	Balken *m*	poutre *f* , solive *f*	corrente *m* , trave *m*	viga *f*
bed load, rubble	Geröll *n*	cailloutis *m*, galet *m*	detriti *m pl*	rocalla *f*
bedrock	anstehendes Gestein *n*	roche *f* en place	roccia *f* in posto	roca *f* nativa / viva
bedrock	Felsboden *m*	sol *m* rocheux	superficie *f* rocciosa	suelo *m* rocoso
Beech tree	Buche *f*	hêtre *m*	faggio *m*	haya *f*
beer	Bier *n*	bière *f*	birra *m*	cerveza *f*
beeswax	Bienenwachs *n*	cire *f*	cera d'api *f*	cera de abeja *f*
before Christ (B.C.)	vor Christus (v. Chr.)	avant Jésus-Christ (av. J.-C.)	avanti Cristo (a.C.)	antes de Jesucristo (a. C.)
behind	hinter	derrière	indietro	detrás de
bell beaker	Glockenbecher *m*	gobelet *m* campaniforme	bicchiere campaniforme *m*	vaso campaniforme *m*
bell shaped	glockenförmig	campaniforme	campaniforme	campaniforme
bell-shaped crater	Glockenkrater *m*	cratère en cloche *m*	cratere *m* a campana	crátera *f* de campana
bench	Bank *f*	banc *m*	banco *m*	banco *m*
bend, curvature	Krümmung *f*	courbure *f*	curvatura *f*	curvatura *f*
biconical	bikonisch	biconique	biconico/-a	biconico/-a
biface, hand-axe	Faustkeil *m*	biface *m*	amigdala *f*, bifacciale *m*	pico *m* de puño
bilingual vase	Bilingue *f*	vase *m* bilingue	bilingue *m/f*	bilingüe *m*
billowy, waved	wellig	ondulé/-e	ondulato/-a	ondulado/-a
binder, binding material	Bindemittel *n*	liant *m*	collante *f*, legante *f*	aglomerante *m* , aglutinante *m*
biodegradable	biologisch abbaubar	biodégradable	biodegradabile	biodegradable
birch tree	Birke *f*	bouleau *m*	betulla *f*	abedul *m*
Bird's-eye view	Vogelperspektive *f*	vue *f* à vol d'oiseau	prospettiva *f* a volo d'uccello	a vista *f* de pájaro
bitumen	Bitumen *n*	bitume *m*	bitume *m*	bitumen *m*
black coal	Steinkohle *f*	houille *f*	carbone *m* fossile	carbón *m*
blade, knife	Klinge *f*	lame *f*	lama *f*	cuchilla *f*
blade, sword	Schwert *n*	épée *f*	spada *f*	espada *f*
blanket, ceiling, cover	Decke *f*	couverture *f*, plafond *m*	coperta *f*, soffito *m*	techo *m*
bleach	bleichen	blanchir	imbiancare	blanquear
bleach, whitener	Bleichmittel *n*	produit *m* de blanchiment	candeggina *f*	decolorante *m*
block recovery	Blockbergung *f*	sauvetage *m* en bloc	asportazione *m* di un blocco di terreno	extracción *f* en bloque

Greek		Turkish	Arabic	
προπύργιο *n*	propirgio	bastiyon, tam donanımlı toprak tesis	حصن	hesn
αστράγαλος *m*	astragalos	inci dizisi	إطار مُزخرف	itar muzachraf
χάντρα *f*	chantra	kabarıklık, şişkinlik	حافة مطرزة	boruuz
κύπελο *n*	kipelo	bardak	كوب	kub
ραμφόστομη οινοχόη *f*	ramfostomi oinochoi	gagalı ağızlı testi	إبريق بفوهة على شكل مُنقار	ibriek befowaha ala schakl monkar
δοκάρια *n pl* , δοκοί *f pl*	dokaria, dakoi	çatı kirişi, taban kirişi	دعامات خشبية	duamat chaschabija
δοκάρι *n* δοκός *f*	dokari/dokos	ağaç kiriş, kalas	دعامة	duama
φορτίο *n* πυθμένα	fortio pithmena	döküntü, moloz	أحجار مُكسرة	ahgar mokasarah
φυσικός βράχος *m*	fisikos vrachos	temel kaya	صخرة متبقية	sachrah motabakija
φυσικός βράχος *m*	fisikos vrachos	kayalık zemin	أرض صخرية	ard sachrija
οξιά *f* , φηγός *f*	oxia, figos	gürgen ağacı	خشب الزان	chaschab elzan
μπύρα *f*	bira	bira	بيرة	bira
μελισσοκέρι *n*	melissokeri	balmumu	شمع العسل	schama elasal
προ Χριστού (π. Χ.)	pro Christou	Milattan Önce/ İsa'dan Önce	قبل الميلاد (ق. م.)	kabl elmilad
πίσω από	piso apo	ardında, arkasına	خلف / وراء	chalf/ waraa
κωδωνόσχημο κύπελλο *n*	kodonoschimo kipello	çan biçimli akıtacak	كوب ناقوسى الشكل	kub nakusi elschakl
κωδωνόσχημος	kodonoschimos	çan biçimli	ناقوسى الشكل	nakusi elschakl
κωδωνόσχημος κρατήρας *m*	kodonoschimos kratiras	çan krater	إيناء ناقوسى الشكل	inaa nakusi elschakl
πάγκος *m* , θρανίο *n*	pagkos, thranio	bank, peyke, seki	دكّة	dekah
καμπύλη *f*	kabili	büklüm, büküntü	انحناء	enhinaa
αμφικωνικός	amfikonikos	bikonik, çift konik	محدب الوجهين	muhadab elwaghein
χειροπέλεκυς *m*	cheiropelekis	el baltası	فأس حجرى كالخابور	faas hagari kalchabur
δίγλωσσο αγγείο *n*	diglosso angeio	çift dilli	ثنائي اللغة	sunaie elluga
κυματιστός	kimatistos	dalgalı	متموج	motamaweg
συνδετική ύλη *f*	sindetiki ili	bağlayıcı, harç	وسيلة ربط	wasilat rabt
βιοδιασπώμενος	viodiaspomenos	biyolojik olarak tasfiyesi mümkün	قابل للتحلل الحيوى	kabil leltahlil elheiawi
σημύδα *f*	simida	kayın ağacı	شجر البتولا	schagar elbotola
προοπτική πουλιού *f*	prooptiki pouliou	kuşbakışı	منظور أعين الطيور	manzur aajon eltojur
πίσσα *f*	pissa	bitum, zift	زفت	zeft
λιθάνθρακας *m*	lithanthrakas	taş kömürü	فحم	fahm
λεπίδα *f*	lepida	bıçak ağzı	شفرة	schafra
σπαθί *n* , ξίφος *n*	spathi, xifos	kılıç	سيف	seif
οροφή *f*	orofi	tavan	سقف	sakf
λευκαίνω	lefkaino	ağartma, beyazlatma	يبيض	yobeid
λευκαντικό *n*	lefkantiko	ağartma maddesi, beyazlatıcı	مادة التبييض	madet eltabjed
ανάκτηση *f* ογκολίθου	anaktisi ogkolithou	blok kaldırma	إنقاذ كتلة	inkaz kutla

English	German	French	Italian	Spanish
blossom	Blüte *f*	fleur *f*	fiore *m*	flor *f*
blown	geblasen	soufflé/-ée	soffiato/-a	soplado/-a
blunt	stumpf	émoussé/-ee, obtus/-e	spuntato/-a	truncado/-a
board, plank	Brett *n*	planche *f*	asse *f*	sofito *m*
body	Leiche *f*	cadavre *m*, corps *m*	cadavere *m*	cadáver *m*
bog body	Moorleiche *f*	homme *m* des tourbières	resti *m pl* umani ritrovati in una palude	cadáver *m* conservado en un pantano
bone	Knochen *m* (Bein *n*)	os *m*	osso *m*	hueso *m*
book	Buch *n*	livre *m*	libro *m*	libro *m*
border	Grenze *f*	frontière *f*	frontiera *f*	frontera *f*, límite *m*
bore hole, drillhole	Bohrung *f*	forage *m*	trapanazione *f*	perforación *f*
botanic	botanisch	botanique	botanico/-a	botánico/-a
botany	Botanik *f*	botanique *f*	botanica *f*	botánica *f*
bothros	Bothros *m*	bothros *m*	bothros *m*	bothros *m*, botro *m*
bottle	Flasche *f*	bouteille *f*	bottiglia *f*	botella *f*
bottom load	Flussgeröll *n*	galet *m*, caillou roulé *m*	detriti *m pl* fluviali	cantos *m* rodados
boulder, cobblestone	Feldstein *m*	pierre *f*	sasso *m*	canto *m*
bouleuterion	Buleuterion *n*	bouleutêrion *m*	buleuterion *m*	bouleuterion, buleuterio *m*
boundary fence, enclosure	Einfriedung *f*	clôture *f*, enclos *m*	recinto *m*, recinzione *f*	cercado *m*, vallado *m*
boundary, limit	Begrenzung *f*	bornage *m*, limitation *f*	limitazione *f*	barrera *f*, limitación *f*
bound, linked	gebunden	lié/-e à	legato/-a	combinado/-a
bowl	Schale *f*	bol *m*, jatte *f*	scodella *f*	bandeja *f*
bowl	Schüssel *f*	grande jatte *f*, vasque *f*	ciotola *f*	fuente *f*, plato *m*
bowl, cup	Napf *m*	écuelle *f*, godet *m*	ciotola *f*	escudilla *f*
box	Kasten *m*	caisse *f*	cassa *f*	caja *f*
box, case	Schachtel *f*	boîte *f*, carton *m*	scatola *f*	caja *f*
bracelette	Armreifen *m*	bracelet *m*	bracciale *m*	brazalete *m*
bracket, console	Konsole *f*	console *f*	mensola *f*	consola *f*, repisa *f*
brass	Messing *n*	laiton *m*	ottone *m*	latón *m*
break	abbrechen	briser, rompre	abbattere, demolire	romper algo
break	Bruch *m*	rupture *f*, fracture *f*	frattura *f*, rottura *f*	rotura *f*, fractura *f*
breakable, fragile	zerbrechlich (fragil)	fragile	fragile	frágil, rompible
break, cleft, crack	Riss *m*	fissure *f*	crepatura *f*, fenditura *f*	fisura *f*, rotura *f*
breaking edge	Bruchkante *f*	cassure *f*	bordo *m* della rottura, frattura *f*	fractura *f*
breathing protection	Atemschutz *m*	protection *f* respiratoire	protezione *f* respiratoria	protección *f* respiratoria
brick	Ziegelstein *m*	brique *f*	laterizio *m*	ladrillo *m*
brick fragments	Ziegelbruch *m*	tuileau *m*	frantumazione *f* dei laterizi	material *m* latericio triturado
brick stamp	Ziegelstempel *m*	estampille *f* de tuile	bollo *m* laterizio	sello *m* (de ladrillos)

Greek		Turkish	Arabic	
άνθιση *f*	anthisi	çiçek, çiçek açma	ازدهار	izdehaar
φουσκωμένος	fouskomenos	şişirilmiş, üflenmiş	منفوخ	manfuch
αμβλύς	ablis	donuk, mat	تالم	talem
σανίδα *f*	sanida	tahta	لوح	luh
πτώμα *n*	ptoma	ceset	جثة	gusa
μούμια *f*, σαπωνοποιημένο πτώμα *n*	moumia, sapono poimeno ptoma	bataklıkta bulunan insan ölüsü artığı	جثة مستنقع	goset mostanka
κόκαλο *n* , οστό *n*	kokalo, osto	kemik	عظم	azm
βιβλίο *n*	vivlio	kitap	كتاب	kitab
όριο *n* , σύνορο *n*	orio, sinoro	sınır	حد	had
διάτρηση *f*	diatrisi	delme	حفر / تنقيب	hafr, tankieb
βοτανικός	votanikos	bitkibilimsel, botanik	نباتى	nabati
βοτανική *f*	votaniki	Bitki Bilimi, Botanik	علم النبات	elm elnabat
βόθρος *m*	vothros	bothros	حفرة للقرابين	hufra lelkarabien
μπουκάλι *n* , φιάλη *f*	boukali, fiali	şişe	زجاجة / قارورة	zugaga/ karurah
φορτίο πυθμένα *n*	fortio pithmena	nehir/ ırmak molozu	حصى النهر	hasa elnahr
κροκάλα *f* , λίθος *m*	krokala, lithos	sınır taşı	حجر ميدانى	hagar meidani
βουλευτήριο *n*	vouleftirio	buleuterionm, bouleuterion	قاعة إجتماعات شورى المدينة	kaat egtimaat schura elmadina
περίβολος *m*	perivolos	duvar, savunma duvarı	سياج	siyag
περιορισμός *m*	periorismos	sınırlama	تحديد	tahdid
δεμένος	demenos	bağlanmış, bağlı	مربوط	marbut
κούπα *f* , λεκάνη *f* , σκύφος *m*, φιάλη *f*	koupa, lekani, skifos, fiali	çanak, kase	قشرة / سلطانية	keschra/ soltanija
λεκάνη *f* , φιάλη *f*	lekani, fiali	çanak	سلطانية	soltanija
σκύφος *m* , λεκάνη *f*	skifos, lekani	çanak, kase	سلطانية	soltanija
κιβώτιο *n* , κουτί *n*	kivotio, kouti	kasa, kutu, sandık	صندوق	sanduk
κουτί *n* , θήκη *f*	kouti, thiki	kutu, paket	علبة	elba
βαχιόλι *n* , ψέλλιο *n*	vachioli, psellio	bilezik	أساور	asawer
κιλλίβαντας *m* , κονσόλα *f*	killivantas, konsola	denetim panosu, konsol	كونصول / حامل	konsul / hamel
ορείχαλκος *m*	oreichalkos	pirinç, sarı bakır	نحاس أصفر	nuhas asfar
διακόπτω	diakopto	kırmak	يقطع	yaktaa
θραύση *f* , ρήγμα *n*	thravsi, rigma	kırık	كسر	kasr
εύθραυστος	efthrafstos	kırılgan	قابل للكسر	kabel lelkasr
ρωγμή *f* , ράγισμα *n*	rogmi, ragisma	çatlak, yarık	صدع / شق	sadaa / schak
μέτωπο *n* ρήγματος	metopo rigmatos	kırık kenar	حافة الانهيار	hafat elenhiear
αναπνευστική προστασία *f*	anapnefstiki prostasia	maske, solunum *f* iltresi	حماية التنفسي	himajet eltanafos
πλίνθος *f* , τούβλο *n*	plinthos, touvlo	tuğla	قالب طوب	kaleb tub
θραύσματα πλίνθων *n pl*	thrafsmata plinthon	tuğla kırığı	كسورة طوب	kasret tub
πλινθοσφραγίδα *f*	plinthosfragida	atölye tuğla mührü	ختم الطوب	chetm eltub

English	German	French	Italian	Spanish
bright	hell	clair/-e	chiaro/-a	claro/-a
bright, lucent, shiny	leuchtend	lumineux/-euse	luminoso/-a, vivo/-a	luminoso/-a
bristles	Borsten	soie *f*	setole *f*	cerda *f*
brittle	spröde	cassant/-e	fragile/ screpolato/-a	quebradizo/-a
broken	gebrochen	brisé/-e, rompu/-e	fratturato/-a	rompado/-a, roto/-a
broken	kaputt	cassé/-ée	rotto/-a, rovinato/-a	estropeado/-a, roto/-a
bronze	Bronze *f*	bronze *m*	bronzo *m*	bronce *m*
Bronze Age	Bronzezeit *f*	âge *m* au Bronze	età *f* del bronzo	Edad *f* de Bronce
brooch, fibula	Fibel *f*	broche *f*, fibule *f*	fibula *f*	fíbula *f*
broom	Besen *m*	balai *m*	scopa *f*	escoba *f*
brush	Bürste *f*	brosse *f*	spazzola *f*	escobilla *f*
brush	Handbesen *m*	balayette *f*	scopetta *f*	escobilla *f*
bucket	Eimer *m*	seau *m*	secchio *m*	cubo *m*
buckle	Schnalle *f*	boucle *f*	fibbia *f*	hebilla *f*
bucrane/ bukranium	Bukranium *n*	bucrane *m*	brucranio *m*	bucráneo *m*
builder, constructor	Erbauer *m*	constructeur *m*, fondateur *m*	costruttore *m*	constructor *m*
building/ construction material	Baumaterial *n*	matériaux *m* pl de construction	materiale *m* da costruzione	material *m* de construcción
building, edifice	Gebäude *n*	bâtiment *m*	edificio *m*	edificio *m*
building, edifice, structure	Bauwerk *n*	édifice *m*, bâtiment *m*	edificio *m*	edificio *m*, obra *f*
building level	Bauschicht *f*	couche *f* de construction	strato *m* di costruzione	estrato *m* de construcción
building phase	Bauphase *f*	phase *f* de construction	fase *m* di costruzione	fase *f* de construcción
building system	Bausystem *n*	système *m* de construction	sistema *f* di costruzione	sistema *f* de construcción
bulbar surface	Abschlagfläche *f*	plan *m* d'éclatement, surface *f* de bulbe	superficie *f* di abbattimento	punto *m* área *f* de impacto
bulge	Ausbuchtung *f*	convexité *f*	curvatura *f*	convexidad *f*
bulky, thick	dick	épais, -aisse	grosso/-a	gordo/a, grueso/a
bulla	Bulla (Schmuck) *f*	bulle *m*	bulla *f*	bulla *f*
burial mound, tumulus	Grabhügel *m*, Tumulus *m*	tumulus *m*	tumulo *m*	túmulo *m*
burn	brennen	brûler	ardere, bruciare	arder, cocer
burnable	brennbar	inflammable	combustibile, infiammabile	combustible, inflamable
burning process	Brennvorgang *m*	processus *m* de cuisson	processo *m* di combustione	proceso *m* de cocción
burnt	gebrannt	brûlé/-e	bruciato/-a	cocido/-a
burnt clay	Brandlehm *m*	argile *f* cuite	argilla *f* bruciata	barro *m* cocido
bust	Büste *f*	buste *m*	busto *m*	busto *m*
Byzantine	byzantinisch	byzantin	bizantino/-a	bizantino/-a
C-14 method	C14-Methode *f*	méthode *f* de datation par le carbone 14	metodo *m* del carbonio 14	datación *f* por radiocarbono

Greek		Turkish	Arabic	
λαμπερός	laberos	açık, aydınlık	مضئ / فاتح	mudia/ fateh
φωτεινός	foteinos	aydınlatan, parlak	مشرق	muschrek
τρίχα *f*	tricha	kalın kıllar	شعر خشن	schaar cheschen
εύθραυστος, ευαίσθητος, εύθριπτος	efthrafstos, efaisthitos, efthriptos	kırılgan, kolay kırılır	هش	hasch
σπασμένος	spasmenos	kırılmış, kırık	مكسور	maksur
χαλασμένος	chalasmenos	bozuk, kırık	تالف	talef
μπρούντζος *m*	brountzos	bronz	برونز	bronz
Εποχή *f* του Χαλκού	Epochi tou Chalkou	Bronz Çğı	العصر البرونزي	elasr elbronzi
πόρπη *f*	porpi	çengelli iğne	مشبك	meschbak
σκούπα *f*	skoupa	süpürge	مكنسة	miknasa
βούρτσα *f*	vourtsa	fırça	فرشاة	furscha
βούρτσα *f*	vourtsa	el süpürgesi	مقشة يد	mekaschat jad
κάδος *m*	kados	kova	جردل	gardal
πόρπη *f*	porpi	kenet, toka	مقبض	mekbad
βουκράνιο *n*	voukranio	bukranion	جمجمة الثور	gomgomat elsor
χτίστης *m* , κατασκευαστής *m*	chtistis, kataskefastis	inşa eden, kurucu, yapan	بانى	bany
οικοδομικό υλικό *n*	oikodomiko iliko	yapı malzemesi	مواد البناء	mawad elbinaa
κτίριο *n* , κτίσμα *n*	ktirio, ktisma	bina, yapı	مبنى	mabna
δομική κατασκευή *f*	doumiki kataskevi	yapı	مبنى	mabna molhak
επίπεδο *n* δόμησης	epipedo domisis	yapı tabakası	مستوى بناء	mustawa binaa
οικοδομική φάση *f*	oikodomiki fasi	inşa safhası	مرحلة بناء	marhlat binaa
σύστημα *n* δόμησης	sistima domisis	yapı sistemi	نظام بناء	nisam binaa
επιφάνεια *f* απόκρουσης	epifaneia apokrousis	yongalanmış yüzey	منطقة مُنقبة	manteka monakabah
διόγκωση *f*, εξόγκωμα *n*	diogkosi, exogkoma	kabartı, çıkıntı	نتوء	notua
αδρός, ογκώδης	adros, ogkodis	kalın, iri	سميك	samik
βούλλα *f*	voulla	bulla	الثور الذهبي	alsor elzahabi
τύμβος *m*	timvos	tümülüs	تل المقبرة	tall elmakbara
καίω	kaio	yanmak	يشعل	yoscheal
εύφλεκτος, καύσιμος	efflektos kafsimos	yanıcı	قابلة للاشتعال	kabila leleschtiaal
διαδικασία *f* όπτησης	diadikasia optisis	yakma süreci	احتراق	ehtirak
καμένος	kamenos	pişmiş, yanmış	محروق	mahruk
ψημένος πηλός *m*	psimenos pilos	pişmiş balçık	طين محروق	tien mahruk
προτομή *f*	protomi	büst	تمثال نصفي	temsal nesfi
βυζαντινός	vizantinos	Bizans ile ilgili	بيزنطي	bizanti
Χρονολόγηση *f* με άνθρακα δεκατέσσερα	Xronologisi me anthraka dekatessera	C14 Metodu	الطريقة C14	eltarika C14

English	German	French	Italian	Spanish
calcite	Kalzit *n*	calcite *f*	calcite *f*	calcita *f*
calcium	Kalzium *n*	calcium *m*	calcio *m*	calcio *m*
calculator	Taschenrechner *m*	calculette *f*	calcolatrice *f*	calculadora *f* de bolsillo
caldarium	Caldarium *n*	caldarium *m*	caldario *m*	caldario *m*
calibration	Kalibrierung *f*	calibration *f*	calibratura *f*	calibración *f*
calibration technique	Vermessungstechnik *f*	technique *f* d'arpentage	tecnica *f* di misurazione	técnica *f* g eodésica
calliper	Schieblehre *f*	pied *m* à coulisse	calibro *m* a corsoio	pie *m* de rey
cameo	Kamee *f*	camée *m*	cammeo *m*	camafeo *m*
camera	Fotoaparat *m* , Kamera *f*	appareil *m* photo, caméra *f*	apparecchio *m* fotografico, camera *f*	aparato *m* fotográfico, cámara *f* (fotográfica)
campaign	Kampagne *f*	campagne *f*	campgna *f* di scavo	campaña *f*
campsite	Lagerplatz *m*	campement *m*	campo *m*	campamento *m*
canal, ditch	Kanal *m*	canal *m*	canale *m*	canal *m*
canalisation, drainage system	Kanalisation *f*	canalisation *f*, égouts *m* *pl*	canalizzazione *f*	canalización *f*
can (American), tin	Dose *f*	boîte *f*	Lattina *f*	lata *f*
canteen, water bottle	Feldflasche *f*	gourde *f*	borraccia *f*	cantimplora *f*
canyon	Schlucht *f*	gorge *f*, ravin *m*	burrone *m*	barranco *m*
capital	Hauptstadt *f*	capitale *f*	capitale *f*	capital *f*
capital	Kapitell *n*	chapiteau *m*	capitello *m*	capitel *m*
carbonate	Kohlenstoff *m*	carbone *m*	carbonio *m*	carbono *m*
carbon concentration	Carbongehalt *m*	teneur *f* en carbone	contenuto *m* di carbone	contenido *m* de carbono
carefully	vorsichtig	prudent/-e	prudente	cuidadoso
carination	Knickwand (Gefäß) *f*	carène *f*	a collo distinto	de pared doblado
carpentry	Zimmererhandwerk *n*	charpenterie *f*, métier *m* de charpentier	carpenteria *f*	carpintería *f*
carton	Karton *m*	carton *m*	scatola *f*	cartón *m*
carving	Schnitzerei *f*	sculpture (sur bois) *f*	intaglio *f*, scultura in legno	entalladura *f*, talla *f* (de madera)
casket, coffin	Sarg *m*	cercueil *m*	bara *f*	ataúd *m*
cast	Abguss *m*	copie *f*, moulage *m*	fusione *m* , calco *m*	vaciado *m*
cast	gegossen	coulé/-ée	fuso/-a	realizado a molde
cast	Guss *m*	fonte *f*	colata *f*	fundición *f*
casting mould	Gussform *f*	moule *m*	forma di fusione *f*	molde *m*
castle	Kastell *n*	fort *m* romain, castrum *m*	castello *m*	castillo *m*
castle, fortress	Burg *f*, Festung *f*	château-fort *m*, citadelle *f*, *f* orteresse *f*	castello *m*	castillo *m* , fortaleza *f*, fortín *m*

Greek		Turkish	Arabic	
ασβεστίτης *m*	asvestitis	karbonatlı kireç, saydam mermer	كالسيت	kalsiet
ασβέστιο *n*	asvestio	kalsiyum	كالسيوم	kalsium
αριθμομηχανή *f*	arithmomichani	hesap makinesi	آلة حاسبة	ala hasba
caldarium *m*	caldarium	sıcaklık odası	حمام بُخار ساخن	hamam buchar sachen
βαθμονόμηση *f*, διακρίβωση *f*	vathmovomisi, diakrivosi	ayarlama	معايرة	muajara
τεχνική μέτρησης *f*	techniki metrisis	ölçüm tekniği	تقنية القياس	teknijat elkijaas
παχύμετρο *n*	pachimetro	kompas, sürgülü hesap cetveli	آلة لقياس الأبعاد	ala lekijas elabaad
καμέος *m*	kameos	renkli kabartma	حجر كريم منقوش عليه صورة	hagar karim mankusch aleih sura
φωτογραφική μηχανή *f*	fotografiki michani	fotoğraf makinası, kamera	كاميرا	kamera
εκστρατεία *f*	ekstrateia	kampanya	موسم عمل الحفريات	musem amal elhafrijat
χώρος κατασκήνωσης *m*	choros kataskinosis	depolama/ kampa yeri	مكان للتخزين	makan leltachzin
οχετός *m* , κανάλι *n*	ochetos, kanali	kanal	قناة	kana
αποχέτευση *f*	apochetefsi	kanalizasyon	مجاري	magari
κουτί *n*	kouti, thiki	kutu, tabaka	علبة	elba
παγούρι *n*	pagouri	matara	زمزمية	zamzamija
φαράγγι *n*	farangi	dağ geçidi, patika	واد ضيق عميق	wadie deijek amiek
πρωτεύουσα *f*	protefousa	başkent	عاصمة	asema
κιονόκρανο *n*	kionokrano	kapitel / sütun başlığı	تاج عمود	tag amud
άνθρακας *m*	anthrakas	karbon	كربون	karbon
περιεκτικότητα *f* σε άνθρακα	periektikotita se anthraka	karbon miktarı	محتوى الكربون	mohtawa alkarbon
προσεχτικά	prosechtika	dikkatli, itinalı	بحذر	behazar
		keskin profil	حائط منحنى	haet monhanie
ξυλουργική *f*	xilourgiki	marangoz	نجارة	nigara
χαρτοκιβώτιο *n*	chartokivotio	karton	كارتون	karton
σκάλισμα *n*	skalisma	heykel, oymacılık	نحت	naht
φέρετρο *n*	feretro	tabut	تابوت	tabut
εκμαγείο *n*	ekmageio	döküm	شكل مصبوب	schakal mesbub
χυτός	chitos	dökme	مصبوب	masbub
εκμαγείο *n*	ekmageio	döküm	سبك	sabk
μήτρα *f*	mitra	dökme kalıbı	قالب السّباكة	kaleb elsibaka
φρούριο *n* , κάστρο *n*	frourio, kastro	hisar, kale	حصن	hesn
οχυρό *n* , φρούριο *n*	ochiro, frourio	kale	قلعة	kalaa

28

English	German	French	Italian	Spanish
castle, palace	Schloss *n*	château *m*	castello *m*	castillo *m*
casual, frail, loose	locker	branlant/-e, meuble	leggero/-a, lento/-a	flojo/-a, suelto/-a
category	Kategorie *f*	catégorie *f*	categoria *f*	categoría *f*
category, sort	Gattung *f*	genre *m*	genere *m*	género *m*
cattle	Rind *n*	boeuf *m*	bovino *m*	bovino *m*, buey *m*
cattle	Vieh *n*	bétail *m*	bestiame *m*	ganado *m*
cauldron, kettle	Kessel *m*	chaudron *m*	calderone *m*	caldera *f*
caution (!)	Vorsicht *f*	attention(!) *f*, précaution *f*, prudence *f*	Attenzione! *f*, precauzione *f*	Atención *f*, Cautela *f*, precaución *f*
cave	Höhle *f*	caverne *f*, grotte *f*	cava *f*	cueva *f*
cavea	Zuschauerraum *m*, Cavea *f*	cavea *f*	cavea *f*	cavea *f*
cave research, speleology	Höhlenforschung *f*	spéléologie *f*	speleologia *f*	espeleología *f*
cavern, den, dump	Grube *f*	fosse *f*	fossa *f*	fosa *f*
cavernous, hollow	hohl	creux/-euse	cavo/-a	cavernoso/-a, hueco/-a
cave/ rock painting	Höhlenmalerei *f*	peinture *f* rupestre	pittura *f* rupreste	pintura rupestre *f*
cave settlement	Höhlensiedlung *f*	habitat *m* rupestre	abitazioni *f* rupestri	colonia *f* de caverna
cavity, void space	Aushöhlung *f*	cavité *f*, creux *m*	cavità *f*	cavernosidad *f*, socavón *m*
cedar	Zeder *f*	cèdre *m*	cedro *m*	cedro *m*
cella	Cella *f*	cella *f*	cella *f*	cella *f*
cellulose	Zellulose *f*	cellulose *f*	cellulosa *f*	celulosa *f*
celtic	keltisch	celtique	celtico/-a	céltico/-a
cement	Zement *m*	ciment *m*	cemento *m*	cemento *m*
centimetre	Zentimeter *m*	centimètre *m*	centimetro *m*	centímetro *m*
centre	Zentrum *n*	centre *m*	centro *m*	centro *m*
century	Jahrhundert *n*	siècle *m*	secolo *m*	siglo *m*
ceramic	Keramik *f*	céramique *f*	ceramica *f*	cerámica *f*
cereal	Getreide *n*	céréales *m pl*	cereali *m pl*	cereales *m pl*, grano *m*
ceremonial	zeremoniell	de culte, rituel/-le	ceremoniale	ceremonioso/-a
ceremony	Zeremonie *f*	cérémonie *f*	cerimonia *f*	ceremonia *f*
cesspit, -pool	Senkgrube *f*	puisard *m*	pozzo *m* nero	sumidero *m*
Chalcolithic, Copper Age	Chalkolothikum *n*, Kupfersteinzeit *f*	âge *m* du Cuivre, Chalcolithique *m*	calcolitico *m*, età *f* del rame	Calcolítico *m*, Edad *m* del Cobre
chalice, goblet	Kelch *m*	calice *m*	calice *m*	copa *f*
chalice, goblet	Pokal *m*	calice *m*, coupe *f*	poculo *m*	copa *f*
chalk	Kreide *f*	craie *f*, crayon *m*	creta *f*, gresso *m*	clarión *m*, tiza *f*
chamber, room	Raum *m*, Zimmer *n*	chambre *f*	stanza *f*	cuarto *m*, habitación *f*
chamber tomb	Kammergrab *n*	tombe *f* à chambre	tomba *f* a camera	sepultura *f* de cámera
change, shift, transformation	Veränderung *f*	altération *f*, modification *f*, transformation *f*	cambiamento *m*	alteración *f*, modificación *f*

Greek		Turkish	Arabic	
ανάκτορο *n* , κάστρο *n*	anaktoro, kastro	şato, saray	قصر	kasr
χαλαρός	chalaros	bol, gevşek, oynak	مُرتخ	murtachie
κατηγορία *f*	katigoria	kategori	صنف	sanf
κατηγορία *f*	katigoria	tür	فصيلة / نوع	fasila/ nua
βοοειδές *n*	vooeides	sığır	بقر	bakar
βοοειδή *n pl*	vooeidi	besi hayvanı	ماشية	maschija
λέβητας *m*	levitas	kazan	قِدر / مرجل	kedr/ mirgal
προσοχή *f*	prosochi	dikkat, itina, sakınma	حذر	hazar
σπηλιά *f*, σπήλαιο *n*	spilia, spilaio	mağara, in	كهف / مغارة	kahf / magara
κοίλο *n*	koilo	cavea	قاعة المشاهدين	kaat elmoschahdin
σπηλαιολογία *f*	spilaiologia	inbilim	استكشاف الكهوف	estekschaf elkohuf
λάκκος *m* , σκάμμα *n*	lakkos, skamma	çukur	حُفرة	hofra
κούφιος	koufios	içi boş, oyuk	مجوف	mogawaf
σπηλαιογραφία *f*	spilaiografia	mağara resmi	نقش على حوائط الكهوف	naksch ala hawaet elkohuf
σπηλαία εγκατάσταση *f*	spilaia egkatastasi	mağara yerleşme/yerleşim	مستوطنة الكهوف	mostawtanat elkohuf
κοιλότητα *f*, υπόγεια διάβρωση *f*	koilotita, ipogeia diavrosi	çukur, oyuk	تجويف	tagwif
κέδρος *m*	kedros	katran ağacı	أرز	arz
σηκός *m*	sikos	cella	الغرفة الرئيسية فى المعبد	elorfa elraisia fi almaabad
κυτταρίνη *f*	kittarini	selüloz	سللوز	selolooz
κελτικός	keltikos	kelt	سِيلتىّ	sieltie
τσιμέντο *n*	tsimento	çimento	أسمنت	asmant
εκατοστόμετρο *n*	ekatostometro	santim, santimetre	سنتيمتر	sentimeter
κέντρο *n*	kentro	merkez	مركز	markaz
αιώνας *m*	aionas	asır, yüzyıl	قرن	karn
κεραμική *f*	keramiki	keramik, seramik	فخار	fuchar
δημητριακά *n pl*	dimitriaka	ekin, tahıl	حبوب	hubob
τελετουργικός	teletourgikos	törensel	طقسي	taksie
τελετουργικό *n*	teletourgiko	merasim, tören	طقس ديني	taks dienie
βόθρος *m*	vothros	lâğım çukuru	بالوعة	baluaa
Χαλκολιθική *f*	Chalkolithiki	Kalkolitik Çağ/ Bakır Çağı	العصر النحاسى	elaser elnahasi
κύπελλο *n* , ποτήρι *n* , κάλυκας *m*	kipello, potiri kalikas	büyük kadeh	كأس	kaes
κύπελλο *n*	kipello	kupa	كأس	kaas
κιμωλία *f*	kimolia	kretase, tebeşir	طباشير	tabaschir
δωμάτιο *n*, χώρος *m*	domatio, choros	oda	حجرة	horga
θαλαμοειδής τάφος *m*	thalamoeidis tafos	oda mezar	مقبرة ذات حجرات	makbara zat hograt
αλλαγή *f*	allagi	değişim	تغيير	tagjier

English	German	French	Italian	Spanish
channelling	Kannelur *f*	cannelure *f*	scanalatura *f*	acanaladura *f*
characterisation	Charakterisierung *f*	caractérisation *f*	caratterizzazione *f*	caracterización *f*
characteristic, feature	Merkmal *n*	caractéristique *f*	cratteristica *f*	marca *f*, señal *f*
characteristic, nature	Eigenschaft *f*	caractère *m*, qualité *f*	caratteristica *f*, proprietà *f*	propiedad *f*
charcoal	Holzkohle *f*	charbon *m* de bois	carbone *m* di legno	carbón *m* vegetal
chariot/ wagon burial	Wagengrab *n*	tombe *f* à char	tomba *f* con carro	tumba *f* de carro
charred	verkohlt	carbonisé/-ée	carbonizzato/-a	carbonizado/-a
chart, diagram, graph	Grafik *f*	graphique *m*	grafica *f*	gráfico *m*
cheap, low-grade	minderwertig	de mauvaise qualité, inférieur/-e	inferiore	inferior
chemical	chemisch	chimique	chimico/-a	químico/-a
chest	Kiste *f*	boîte *f*, caisse *f*	cassetta *f*	caja *f*
chieftain	Häuptling *m*	chef *m*	capo *m*	jefe *m* de tribu
chimney, smoke stack	Schornstein *m*	cheminée *f*	comignolo *m*	chimenea *f*
chinaware, porcelain	Porzellan *n*	porcelaine *f*	porcellana *f*	porcelana *f*
chisel	Meißel *m*	burin *m*	scalpello *m*	cincel *m*
chitin carapace	Chitinpanzer *m*	carapace *f* de chitine	cuticola *f*	carparazón *m* de quitina
chonological, seasonal	zeitlich	chronologique, temporel/-elle	cronologico/-a, temporale	temporal
chopper	Hackmesser *n*	hachoir *m*	scure *f*	hacha *f*
chronology	Chronologie *f*	chronologie *f*	cronologia *f*	cronología *f*
church	Kirche *f*	église *f*	chiesa *f*	iglesia *f*
chute	Trichter *m*	entonnoir *m*	imbuto *m*	embudo *m*
circle	Kreis *m*	cercle *m*	circolo *m*	círculo *m*
circle	Zirkel *m*	compas *m*	compasso *m*	círculo *m*
circular	kreisförmig	circulaire	circolare	circular
circular disc	Kreisscheibe *f*	disque *m*	disco circolare *m*	disco *m*
circus, hippodrome	Hippodrom *n*, Zirkus *m*	cirque *m*	circo *m*	circo *m*
cistern, reservoir	Zisterne *f*	cisterne *f*	cisterna *f*	aljibe *m*, cisterna *f*
civilisation	Zivilisation *f*	civilisation *f*	civiltà *f*	civilización *f*
clam, mussel, sea shell	Muschel *f*	moule *m*	conchiglia *f*	concha *f*
clan, tribe	Sippe *f*, Stamm *m*	clan *f*, parenté *f*, tribu	tribù *f*	tribu *f*
class	Klasse *f*	classe *f*	classe *f*	clase *f*
classic	klassisch	classique	classico/-a	clásico/-a
Classic Era	Klassik *f*	période *f* classique	età *f* classica	época *f* clásica
classification	Systematik *f*	systématique *f*	sistematica *f*	orden *m*, sistemática *f*
clay	Ton *m*	argile *f*	argilla *f*	arcilla *f*
clay brick	Lehmziegel *m*	adobe *m*, brique crue *f*	mattone crudo *m*	adobe *m*

Greek		Turkish	Arabic	
ράβδωση *f*	ravdosi	yiv	أخدود رأسى فى جذع العمود	uchdud raasi fi geza elamud
χαρακτηρισμός *m*	charaktirismos	karakterize etme	توصيف	tawsif
χαρακτηριστικό *n*	charaktiristiko	karakteristik, özellik	ميزة	miza
ιδιότητα *f*	idiotita	ayırıcı özellik, nitelik	صفة	sefah
ξυλάνθρακας *m*	xilanthrakas	odun kömürü	فحم نباتى	fahm nabati
ταφή με άμαξα *f*	tafi me amaxa	arabalı gömü defin	قبر للعربة	kabr lelaraba
απανθρακωμένος	apanthrakomenos	kömürleşmiş	متفحمة	motafahema
σχεδιάγραμμα *n*	schediagramma	grafik	رسم تصويرى	rasm taswirie
ευτελής	eftelis	düşük kaliteli, ikinci el, niteliksiz	قليل القيمة	kalil elkima
χημικός	chimikos	kimyasal	كيميائي	kimjaie
κιβώτιο *n* , κίστη *f* , κουτί *n*	kivotio, kisti, kouti	kasa, kutu, sandık	صندوق	sunduk
φύλαρχος *m*	filarchos	elebaşı, kabile reisi	رئيس قبيلة	raies kabila
καπνοδόχος *f/m* , καμινάδα *f*	kapnodochos, kaminada	baca	مدخنة مُرتفعة	medchana mortafia
πορσελάνη *f*	porselani	porselen	خزف	chazaf
ξύστρα *f*	xistra	keski	إزميل	azmiel
κέλυφος χιτίνης *f*	kelifos chitinis	kitin	درع كيتين	dera keitien
χρονικός	chronikos	zaman itibariyle, zamansal	زمني	zamanie
μπαλτάς *m*	baltas	satır	ساطور	satur
χρονολογία *f*, χρονολόγηση *f*	chronologia, chronologisi	kronoloji	التسلسل الزمني	eltasalsul elzamani
εκκλησία *f*	ekklisia	kilise	كنيسة	kanisa
χοάνη *f*	choani	huni	قمع	komaa
κύκλος *m*	kiklos	daire	دائرة	daera
κύκλος *m*	kiklos	çember, pergel	برجل	bargal
κυκλικός	kiklikos	daire şeklinde	دائري	daeri
κυκλικός δίσκος *m*	kiklikos diskos	dairesel disk	قرص دائري	kurs daeri
ιππόδρομος *m*	ippodromos	hipodrom	سيرك، ميدان سباق الخيل	midan sebak elcheel, serk
δεξαμενή *f*, κιστέρνα *f*	dexameni, kisterna	sarnıç	صهريج	sehrieg
πολιτισμός *m*	politismos	medeniyet, uygarlık	حضارة	hadara
όστρεο *n*	ostreo	midye	صدفة	sadafa
φυλή *f*	fili	kabile	قبيلة	kabila
τάξη *f*	taxi	sınıf	فصل	fasl
κλασσικός	klassikos	klasik	كلاسيكي	klasiki
Κλασσική Περίοδος *m*	Klassiki Periodos	Klasik Çağ, Klasisizm	العصر الكلاسيكى	elaser elklasiki
ταξινόμηση *f*	taxinomisi	sınıflama	نظام	nizam
πηλός *m*	pilos	balçık, kil	صلصال / طين	selsaal/ tien
οπτόπλινθος *f*, τούβλο *n*	optoplinthos, touvlo	balçık tuğla	طوب طيني	tub tienie

English	German	French	Italian	Spanish
clay brick wall	Lehmziegelwand *f*	mur *m* en adobe	muro *m* di mattoni crudi	muro *m* de adobe
clay, loam	Lehm *m*	glaise *f*	argilla *f*	barro *m*
clay seal	Tonsiegel *n*	sceau en terre cuite	sigillo *m* argilloso	sello *m* de barro
clay soil	Lehmboden *m*	sol *m* glaiseux	suolo *m* di argilla	suelo *m* arcilloso
clay-state, unburnt	ungebrannt	cru/-e	incombusto/-a	crudo/-a, sin cocer
clay ware	Tonware *f*	céramique, poterie *f*	terracotta *f*	alfarería *f*
cleaning	Reinigung *f*	nettoyage *m*	pulizia *f*	limpieza *f*
clean, neat, tidy	sauber	net/-te, propre	pulito/-a	limpio/-a
clear	deutlich	distinct/-e, évident/-e	chiaro/-a,distinto/-a	articulado/-a, claro/-a
cleft, crevice, gap	Spalte *f*	crevasse *f*, fente *f*	crepa *f*	fisura *f*, resquicio *m*
cleft, gully	Geländenarbe *f*	stigmate *m* dans le sol	strato *m* erboso	capa *f* de hierba
climate	Klima *n*	climat *m*	clima *m*	clima *m*
climatic	klimatisch	climatique	climatico/-a	climático/-a
climatic conditions	Klimaverhältnisse	conditions *f pl* climatiques	condizioni *f pl* climatiche	condiciones *f pl* Climáticas
cline/ kline	Kline *f*	klinê *f*	kline *f*	kline *m*
clip	Klammer *f*	pince *f*	graffetta *f*	grapa *f*, laña *f*
clipboard	Klemmbrett *n*	porte-bloc *m*	cartellina *f* con pinza	tablilla *f* con sujetapapeles
closed, completed	geschlossen	fermé/-ée	chiuso/-a	cerrado/-a
clothes	Kleidung *f*	vêtement *m*	abbigliamento *m*	indumento *m* , ropa *f*
cloth, fabric	Gewebe *n*	tissage *m*	tessuto *m*	tejido *m*
cloudiness	Trübung *f*	opacification *f*	intorbidamento *m*	enturbiamiento *m*
club, cudgel	Keule *f*	massue *m*	clava *f*	clava *f*
clump, cluster	Klumpen *m*	agglomérat *m*	zolla *f*	pella *f*
cluster, heap, pile	Haufen *m*	tas *m*	mucchio *m*	montón *m*
coal	Kohle *f*	charbon *m*	carbone *m*	carbón *m*
coarse clay	Schluff *m*	limon *m*	limo *m*	limo *m*
coarsely porous	grobporig	lâche	poroso/-a	poroso/-a
coarse sand	Grobsand *m*	gravillon *m*	pietrisco *m*	arena gruesa *f*
coarse ware	Grobkeramik *f*	céramique *f* commune/ grossière	ceramica *f* ad impasto	cerámica *f* bronca/ gruesa
coast	Küste *f*	côte *f*, littoral *m*	costa *f*, riva *f*	costa *f*
coat, coating	Überzug *m*	engobe *m* , revêtement *m*	ingobbio *m*	capa *f*
coin	Münze *f*	monnaie *f*	moneta *f*	moneda *f*
cold	kalt	froid/-e	freddo/-a	frío/-a
collapse	Einsturz *m*	écroulement *m*	crollo *m*	derrumbamiento *m* , derrumbe *m*
collapse	Versturz *m*	écroulement *m*	crollo *m*	derrumbe *m*
collection	Sammlung *f*	collection *f*	raccolta *f*	colección *f*
collection vessel, reservoir	Sammelbehälter *m*	réservoir *m*	serbatoio *m*	colector *m* , depósito *m*
colonnade street	Kolonnadenstraße *f*	rue *f* à colonnade	strada *m* colonnata	arcadas *pl*

Greek		Turkish	Arabic	
πλινθότοιχος *m*	plinthotoichos	kerpiç duvar	حائط من الطوب الطيني	haet men eltub eltienie
πηλός *m*	pilos	balçık	طين	tien
πηλοσφραγίδα *f*	pilosfragida	kil mühür	ختم صلصال	chetm selsaal
πηλώδες έδαφος *n*	pilodes edafos	balçıklı zemin	تربة طينية	turba tieneia
άψητος	apsitos	çiğ, pişmemiş	غير محترق	geer mohtarek
πήλινο σκεύος *n*	pilino skevos	çanak çömlek	آنية فخارية	anija fucharija
καθαρισμός *m*	katharismos	arıtma, temizleme	تنظيف	tanzief
καθαρός	katharos	düzgün, temiz	نظيف	nazief
σαφής	safis	açık, belirgin	واضح	wadeh
ρήγμα *f*	rigma	kolon, sütun	عمود	amud (fi gadwal)
εδαφικό ρήγμα *n*	edafiko rigma	arazi izi	ندبة الموقع	nadbet elmawkea
κλίμα *n*	klima	iklim, klima	مناخ	munach
κλιματικός	klimatikos	iklimsel, klimatik	مناخي	munachi
κλιματικές συνθήκες *f pl*	klimatikes sinthikes	iklim koşulları	أحوال المناخية	ahwal munachija
κλίνη *f*	klini	kline	أريكة	arika
συνδετήρας *m*	sindetiras	ataç, bağlama çenesi	مِشبك	mischbak
πρόχειρο σημειωματάριο *n*	procheiro simeiomatario	çizim tahtası	لوحة بمشبك فى أعلاها	loha bemaschbak fi aalaha
κλειστός	kleistos	kapalı	مغلق	moglak
ενδυμασία *f*	endimasia	elbise, giyim, kıyafet	ملابس	malabes
ιστός *m* , ύφασμα *n*	istos, ifasma	doku, dokuma	نسيج	nasieg
θολότητα *f*	tholotita	bulanıklık	تَعتيم	taatiem
λέσχη *f*	leschi	çomak, topuz	هراوة	herawa
συστάδα *f*	sistada	topak	كتلة	kotla
σωρός *m*	soros	küme, yığın	كومة	koma
κάρβουνο *n*	karvouno	kömür	فحم	fahm
ακατέργαστος πηλός *n*	akatergastos pilos	alüvyon	رمل طفيلي	raml tofailie
έντονα πορώδης	entona porodis	iri gözenekli	ذو مسام كبيرة	zo masam kabiera
αδρή άμμος *f*	adri ammos	iri kum	رمل خشن	raml cheschen
αδρή κεραμική *f*	adri keramiki	kaba cidarlı seramik	فُخار خشن	fuchar cheschen
ακτή *f*	akti	sahil	ساحل	sahel
επένδυση *f* , επίχρισμα *n*	ependisi, epichrisma	kap, kılıf	طلاء	tilaa
νόμισμα *n*	nomisma	sikke	عملة معدنية	umla madineja
κρύος, ψυχρός	krios, psichros	soğuk	بارد	bared
κατάρρευση *f*	katarrefsi	çökme, yıkılma	انهيار	enhiyar
συντρίμμια *n pl* , μπάζα *n pl* , χαλάσματα *n pl*	sintrimmia, baza, chalasmata	döküntü	انهيارمفتعل لسد فراغات الصخور	enhijar moftaal lesad fragaat elsochur
συλλογή *f*	sillogi	koleksiyon, müze	مجموعة	magmua
αποταμιευτήρας *m* , συλλέκτης *m*	apotamieftiras, sillektis	biriktirme havuzu, biriktirme kabı	خزان	chazan
οδός με κιονοστοιχίες *f*	odos me kionostoichies	sütunlu cadde	شارع محاط بالأعمدة	scharea mohat belaameda

English	German	French	Italian	Spanish
colony	Kolonie *f*	colonie *f*	colonia *f*	colonia *f*
colour	Farbe *f*	couleur *f*	colore *m*	color *m*
colourant, pigment	Farbstoff *m*	colorant *m*	colorante *m* , pigmento *m*	colorante *m*
colouration	Färbung *f*	coloration *f*	tintura *f*	tendencia *f,* teñido *m*
coloured	farbig	coloré/-ée	colorato/-a	colorido/-a, de color
colour-fast	farbecht	grand teint	indelebile	indeleble
colouring	Farbgebung *f*	coloris *m*	colorazione	colorido *m*
colour shade	Farbton *m*	teinte *f*	tinta *f*	tonalidad *f*
column	Säule *f*	colonne *f*	colonna *f*	columna *f*
column drum	Säulentrommel *f*	tambour *m* de colonne	tamburo *m* della colonna	bloques *m* cilíndricos, tambores
comb	Kamm *m*	peigne *m*	pettine *m*	peine *m*
common/cooking ware	Gebrauchskeramik *f*	céramique commune *f*	ceramica comune *f*	cerámica de uso *f*
community	Gemeinschaft *f*	communauté *f*	comunità *f*	comunidad *f*
compass	Kompass *m*	boussole *f*	bussola *f*	brújula *f*
competent, expert, specialised	fachkundig	compétent, expert	competente, esperto	pericial, competente
complete	vollständig	complet/-ète, entier/-ière	completo/-a, intero/-a	completo/-a, entero/-a
complex	Komplex *m*	ensemble *m*	complesso *m*	complejo *m*
complex of discovery	Fundkomplex *m*	ensemble *m* (d'objets)	complesso *m* di reperti	conjunto *m* de hallazgos
component, part	Bestandteil *m*	élément *m*	elemento *m* , parte *f*	componente *m* , parte *f*, elemento *m*
composite capital	Kompositkapitell *n*	chapiteau *m* composite	capitello *m* composito	capitel *m* compuesto
composition	Zusammensetzung *f*	remontage *m*	composizione *f*	composición *f*
computer	Computer *m*	ordinateur *m*	computer *m*	ordenador *m*
concave	konkav	concave	concavo/-a	cóncavo/-a
concentric	konzentrisch	concentrique	concentrico/-a	concéntrico/-a
concept, draft	Entwurf *m*	ébauche *f*, esquisse *f*	progettazione *f*	borrador *m*
conchate, shell-shaped	muschelförmig	conchoïdal/-e	concoide	conquiforme
conclusion	Rückschluss *m*	déduction *f*	deduzione *f*	conclusión *f*
concrete	Beton *m*	béton *m*	calcestruzzo *m*	hormigón *m*
condition	Bedingung *f*	condition *f*	condizione *f*	condición *f*
condition, state	Zustand *m*	condition *f*, état *m*	condizione *f*, stato *m*	condición *f,* estado *m*
cone	Kegel *m*	cône *m*	cono *m*	cono *m*
conglomerate	Konglomerat *n*	conglomérat *m*	conglomerato *m*	conglomerado *m*
conifer	Nadelbaum *m*	conifère *f*	conifera *f*	conífera *f*
connector, middle section	Zwischenstück *n*	pièce *f* intermédiaire	frammento *m* / tratto intermedio	pieza *f* intermedia
consecutive, continous	fortlaufend	continu/-e	continuo/-a	continuo/-a
conservation	Erhaltung *f*	conservation *f*	conservazione *f*	conservación *f*

Greek		Turkish	Arabic	
αποικία *f*	apoikia	koloni	مستعمرة	mostamara
χρώμα *f*	chroma	renk	لون	lown
βαφή *f*, χρωστική *f*	vafi, chrostiki	boyar madde	مادة مُلونة	mada mulawena
χρωματισμός *m*	chromatismos	boyama, renk verme	تلوين	talwien
έγχρωμος	egchromos	renkli	متعدّد الألوان	motaaded elalwan
ανεξίτηλος	anexitilos	kök boyalı	لون أصلى	lown asli
βαφή *f*, χρωματισμός *m*	vafi, chromatismos	renk kullanımı	تلوين	talwien
απόχρωση *f*, τόνος *n* χρώματος	apochrosi, tonos chromatos	renk tonu	درجة اللون	daraget ellown
κίονας *m*	kionas	kolon, sütun	عمود	amud mastadier
σπόνδυλος κίονα *m*	spondilos kiona	sütun tamburu	أسطوانة عمود	hagar estiwanie kagoza men amud
χτένα *f*	chtena	dağ sırtı, tarak	مشط	mescht
χρηστική κεραμική *f*	chrisriki keramiki	günlük kullanım kapları	فخّارمستخدم	fuchar mostachdam
κοινότητα *f*	koinotita	cemiyet, topluluk	مجتمع	mogtamaa
πυξίδα *f*	pixida	pusula	بوصلة	bosla
εξειδικευμένος, ειδικός	exeidikevmenos, eidikos	uzman	خبير	chabier
πλήρης	pliris	eksiksiz, tam	كامل	kamels
σύμπλεγμα *n*	siblegma	bütünlük, karışık	مجمع	mogamaa
σύμπλεγμα *n* εύρεσης	siblegma evresis	buluntu kompleksi	محتوى الإكتشافات	muhtawa elektischafat
συστατικό στοιχείο *n*	sistatiko stoicheio	parça	جُزء	guza
σύνθετο κιονόκρανο *n*	sintheto kionokrano	kompozit başlık	تاج عامود مركب	tag amud murakab
σύνθεση *f*	sinthesi	bileşim, bir araya gelme	تجميع	tagmea
ηλεκτρονικός υπολογιστής *m*	ilektrinikos ipologistis	bilgisayar	كمبيوتر	computer
κοίλος	koilos	konkav, içbükey	مقعر	mokaar
ομόκεντρος	omokentros	tek merkezli	متمركز	motamarkez
σχέδιο *n*, σύλληψη *f*	schedio, sillipsi	kroki, taslak	تصميم	tasmiem
κογχοειδής	kogchoeidis	konkoidal	صدفي	sadafie
συμπέρασμα *n*	siberasma	çıkarsama, netice	استنتاج	estentag
σκυρόδεμα *n*	skirodema	beton	خرسانة	charasana
περίσταση *f*	peristasi	koşul, şart	شرط	schart
κατάσταση *f*	katastasi	durum, konum	حالة	hala
κώνος *m*	konos	koni	مخروط	machrut
συσσωμάτωση *f*	sossomatosi	çakıl kayaç	خليط	chaliet
κωνοφόρο *n*	konoforo	çam ağacı, karaçam	شجرة صنوبرية	schagara sanubareia
ενδιάμεσο/ συνδετικό τμήμα *n*	endiameso/ sindetiko tmima	ara parçası, zincir halkası	قطعة وصل	ketet wasl
συνεχής	sinechis	birbirini izleyen	متصل	motasel
διατήρηση *f*	diatirisi	koruma, saklama	صيانة	sijana

English	German	French	Italian	Spanish
conservation	Konservierung *f*	conservation *f*	conservazione *f*	conservación *f*
conservation agent	Konservierungsmittel	agent *m* de conservation	mezzo *m* di conservazione	medio *m* de conservacíon
conservation, restoration	Restaurierung *f*	conservation *f*	restauro *m*	restauración *f*
conservator, restoration worker	Restaurator *m*	conservateur *m*	restauratore *m*	restaurador *m*
consistence	Konsistenz *f*	consistence *f*	consistenza *f*	consistencia *f*
consistent	konsistent	consistant	consistente	consistente
constancy, durability	Beständigkeit *f*	constance *f*	continuità *f*, riserva *f*	fondo *f*
constancy, durability	Dauerhaftigkeit *f*	durabilité *f*	durevolezza *f*, resistenza *f*	durabilidad *f*, estabilidad *f*, resistencia *f*
constant	konstant	constant/-e	costante	constante
constant	Konstante *f*	constante *f*	costante *f*	constante *f*
constant, steady	beständig	constant, durable	costante, durevole	constante, estable
construction plan	Bauplan *m*	plan *m* de construction	piano *m* di costruzione	plano *m* de construcción
construction, structure	Aufbau *m*	construction *f*, édification *f*, structure *f*	costruzione *f*	construcción *f*, estructura *f*
constructive	konstruktiv	constructif/-ve	costruttivo/-a	constructivo/-a
container	Behältnis *n*	récipient *m*	contenitore *m*	contenedor *m*, envase *m*,
contaminated	verunreinigt	contaminé/-e	contaminato/-a	contaminado/-a
contamination	Kontamination *f*, Verunreinigung *f*	contamination *f*	contaminazione *f*	contaminación *f*
contemporary	zeitgenössisch	contemporain/-e	contemporaneo/-a	contemporáneo/-a
content	Inhalt *m*	contenu *m*	contenuto *m*	contenido *m*
Content-wise	inhaltlich	qui concerne le contenu	contenutistico/-a	en cuanto al contenido
context	Kontext *m*	contexte *m*	contesto *m*	contexto *m*
continent	Kontinent *m*	continent *m*	continente *m*	continente *m*
continental	kontinental	continental	continentale	continental
continent, mainland	Festland *n*	continent *m*, terre ferme *f*	terra *f* ferma	continente *m*, tierra firme *f*
contour, outline	Kontur *f*	contour *m*, délinéation *f*	contorno *m*, profilo *m*	contorno *m*
contour, outline, profile	Umriss *m*	contour *m*, silhouette *f*	contorno *m*	contorno *m*, silueta *f*
contract archaeology	Kontraktarchäologie *f*	archéologie *f* contractuelle	archeologia *f* a contratto	arqueología *f* contractual
control	Kontrolle *f*	contrôle *m*	controllo *m*	control *m*
convergent	konvergierend	convergent	convergente	convergente
convex	konvex	convexe	convesso/-a	convexo/-a
cool, frigid	kühl	frais/ fraîche	fresco/-a	fresco/-a
coordinate	Koordinate *f*	coordonnée *f*	coordinata *f*	coordenada *f*
coordinate system	Koordnatensystem *n*	système *m* de coordonées	sistema *f* di coordinate	sistema *f* de coordenadas
copper	Kupfer *n*	cuivre *m*	rame *m*	cobre *m*

Greek		Turkish	Arabic	
συντήρηση f	sintirisi	konservasyon	حفظ	hefz
συντηρητικό n	sintiritiko	koruyucu (madde)	مواد حافظة	mawad hafiza
συντήρηση f, αποκατάσταση f	sintirisi, apokatastasi	restorasyon	ترميم	tarmiem
συντηρητής m, συντηρήτρια f	sintiritis, sintiritria	restoratör	مرمم	moramem
συνοχή f	sinochi	dayanıklılık, kıvam	كثافة	kasafa
συνεκτικός	sinektikos	dayanıklı	كثيف	kasief
σταθερότητα f	statherotita	elde bulunan	إستمرار	istemraar
αντοχή f	avtochi	süreklilik	قوة التحمل	kuwat eltahamol
διαρκής, σταθερός	diarkis, statheros	değişmez, sabit	ثابت	sabet
σταθερότητα f	statherotita	değişmez değer, sabit	قيمة ثابتة	kima sabeta
σταθερός	statheros	daimi, sürekli	مستديم	mostadiem
οικοδομικό σχέδιο n	oikodomiko schedio	yapı planı	خطة البناء	chutat elbinaa
δομή f	domi	inşa, yapı	تشييد	taschjed
εποικοδομητικός	epoikodomitikos	kurucu, yapıcı	بنّاء	banaa
δοχείο n	docheio	kap	وعاء	weaa
μολυσμένος	molismenos	kirlenmiş, kirletilmiş	ملوث	mulawas
μόλυνση f	molinsi	bulaşma	مزج بين الكلمات	mazg beina elkalemat
σύγχρονος	sigchronos	çağdaş	معاصر	moaser
περιεχόμενο n	periechomeno	içerik, kapsam	محتوى	mohtawa elmaalumat
όσον αφορά το περιεχόμενο	oson afora to periechomeno	içeriksel, kapsamsal	من حيث المحتوى	men heis elmohtawa
συμφραζόμενα n pl	simfrazomena	bağlam	سياق	sijak
ήπειρος f	ipeiros	kıta	قارة	kara
ηπειρωτικός	ipeirotikos	karasal	قاري	karie
ξηρά f, στεριά f	xira, steria	kara	بر	bar
περίγραμμα n, ισοϋψής f	perigramma, isoupsis	kontur	خطوط تحدد المعالم	chotut tuhded elmamalem
περίγραμμα n	perigramma	kontur, taslak	معالم	maalem
αρχαιολογία του ιδιωτικού τομέα f	archaiologia tou idotikou tomea	sözleşmeli arkeoloji	علم آثار العقود	elm asar elukud
έλεγχος m	elegchos	denetim	مراقبة	morakaba
συγκλίνων	sigklinon	yakınsak	متطابق	motatabek
κυρτός	kirtos	dışbükey	محدب	mohadab
δροσερός, ψυχρός	droseros, psichros	serin	بارد	bared
συντεταγμένη f	sintetagmeni	koordinat	تنسيق	tansiek
σύστημα συντεταγμένων n	sistima sintetagmenon	koordinat sistemi	نظام تنسيق	nizam tansiek
χαλκός m	chalkos	bakır	نحاس أحمر	nahas ahmar

English	German	French	Italian	Spanish
copper chloride	Kupferchlorid *n*	chlorure *m* de cuivre	cloruro *m* di rame	cloruro *m* de cobre
copy	Kopie *f*	copie *f*, réplique *f*	copia *f*	copia *f*
copy, replication	Nachbildung *f*	réplique *f*	imitazione *f*	copia *f*, imitación *f*
cord, string	Schnur *f*	cordon *m*, ficelle *f*	cordino *m*	cordón *m*
core	Kern *m*	noyau *m*, nucléus *m*	seme *m*	núcleo *m*
Corinthian order	korinthische Ordnung *f*	ordre *m* corinthien	ordine *m* corinzio	orden *m* corintio
cork	Kork *m*	liège *m*	sughero *m*	corcho *m*
cornerstone	Grundstein *m*	première pierre *f*	prima pietra *f*	primera piedra *f*
cornice	Gesims *n*	corniche *f*	cornicione *m*	cornisa *f*, moldura *f*
coronet, diadem, tiara	Diadem *n*	diadème *m*	diadema *m*	diadema *f*
correction	Korrektur *f*	correction *f*	correzione *f*	corrección *f*
correlation	Korrelation, Wechselbeziehung *f*	corrélation *f*	correlazione *f*	correlación *f*
corroded	korrodiert	corrodé/-ée	corroso/-a	corrosivo/-a
corrosion	Korrosion *f*	corrosion *f*	corrosione *f*	corrosión *f*
cotton	Baumwolle *f*	cotton *m*	cotone *m*	algodón *m*
cottonwood, poplar	Pappel *f*	peuplier *m*	pioppo *m*	álamo *m*
courtyard, inner court	Innenhof *m*	cour *f* intérieure	cortile *m* interno	patio *m* interior
cover	abdecken	découvrir, recouvrir	scoprire	cubrir algo, tapar
cover	bedecken	couvrier, recouvrir	coprire	cubrir, tapar
covering	Abdeckung *f*	couverture *f*	copertura *f*	cubierta *f*
cover plate	Deckplatte *f*	dalle *f* de couverture	pannello *m* di copertura	losa *f* de coronación, placa *f* de cubierta
cracked, split	rissig	fêlé/ée, fissuré/-ée	crepato/-a	agrietado/-a
craft	Handwerk *n*	artisanat *m*	artigianato *m*	artesanía *f*
craftsman	Handwerker *m*	artisan *m*	artigiano/-a *m/f*	artesano *m*
crane	Kran *m*	grue *f*	gru *f*	grúa *f*
crayon	Buntstift *m*	crayon *m* de couleur	matita *f* colorata	lápiz *m* de color
cremated remains	Leichenbrand *m*	crémation *f*, incinération *f*	ceneri *pl*	cenizas *pl*
cremation	Einäscherung *f*	incinération *f*	cremazione *f*	cremación *f*
cremation	Feuerbestattung *f*	crémation *f*	cremazione *f*	cremación *f*
cremation burial	Brandbestattung *f*	sépulture *f* à incinération	cremazione *f*	incineración *f*
cremation remains	Brandreste *m pl*	restes *m pl* d'incinération	residuo *m* di cremazione	quemados *m pl* incinerados
cro-magnon	Cro-Magnon-Mensch *m*	homme *m* de Cro-Magnon!	Uomo *m* di Cro-Magnon	hombre *m* de Cro-Magnon
cropland, farmland	Ackerland *n*	terrain *m* agricole, terre *f* cultivée	campagna *f*, terreno *m* coltivato	campagna *f*, terreno *m* cultivo
cross	Kreuz *n*	croix *f*	croce *f*	cruz *f*
crossbeam	Querbalken *m*	poutre *f* transversale, traverse *f*	trave *f* trasversale	travasaño *m*
cross-section	Querschnitt *m*	coupe *f*, section *f*	sezione *f* trasversale	sección *f* transversal
crude	unbearbeitet	brut/-e	non lavorato/-a	bruto/-a, no labrado/-a

Greek		Turkish	Arabic	
χλωριούχος χαλκός *m*	choriouchos chalkos	bakır klorürü	كلوريد النحاس الأحمر	klurid elnahas elahmar
αντίγραφο *n*	antigrafo	kopya	نسخة	nuscha
απομίμηση *f*	apomimisi	kopya, taklit eser	نسخة / تقليد	nuscha / taklied
ιμάντας *n* , κορδόνι *n*	imantas, kordoni	ip	دُبارة	dubara
πυρήνας *m*	pirinas	meyve çekirdeği	لب / نواة	lob/ nawah
κορινθιακός ρυθμός *m*	korinthiokos rithmos	Korinth Düzeni	نظام كورنتى	nizam kuranti
φελλός *m*	fellos	mantar	فلين	fellien
ακρογωνιαίος λίθος *m* , αγκωνάρι *n*	akrogoniaios lithos, agkonari	temel taşı	حجر الأساس	hagar elasas
σίμη *f* , κορνίζα *f*	simi, korniza	pervaz	حافة بارزة	hafa bareza
διάδημα *n*	diadima	diadem	تاج	tag
διόρθωση *f*	diorthosi	düzeltme	تصحيح	tashih
συσχετισμός *m*	sischetismos	bağlılaşım, ilişki	ارتباط	ertibat
διαβρωμένος	diavromenos	aşınmış	متآكل	motaakel
διάβρωση *f*	disvrosi	aşınma	تآكل	taakul
βαμβάκι *n*	vamvaki	pamuk	قطن	kotn
λεύκα *f*	lefka	kavak	شجر الحور	schagar elhor
εσωτερική αυλή *f*	esoteriki avli	iç avlu	فناء داخلى	finaa dacheli
καλύπτω	kalipto	üstünü açmak	يغطي	yugati
καλύπτω	kalipto	gizlemek, kapamak, örtmek	يغطي	yugati
κάλυψη *f*	kalipsi	üstünü açma	تغطية	tagtija
καλυπτήρια πλάκα *f*	kaliptiria plaka	sütun başlığı	لوح غطاء	loh gitaa
ραγισμένος, σπασμένος	ragismenos, spasmenos	çatlamış, yarık	متصدع	motasdea
τέχνη *f* , χειροτεχνία *f*	techni, cheirotechnia	el sanatı, zanaat	صناعة يدوية	sinaa jadawija
τεχνίτης *m* , χειροτέχνης *m*	technitis, cheirotechnis	el işçisi, sanatkar	صاحب حرفة	saheb herfa
γερανός *m*	geranos	vinç	ونش	winsch
ξυλομπογιά *f*	xilobogia	renkli kalem	قلم للتلوين	kalam leltlwin
αποτεφρωμένα λείψανα *n pl*	apotefromena leipsana	ölü külü	حرق الجثث	hark elgosas
αποτέφρωση *f*	apotefrosi	ölünün yakılması	إحراق جثث الموتى	ihrak gosas elmawta
καύση (νεκρού) *f*	kafsi (nekrou)	ölünün yakılması	إحراق جثث الموتى	ihrak gosas elmawta
ταφή καύσης *f*	tafi kafsis	kremasyon	حرق الجثث	hark elgusas
ίχνη *n pl* καύσης	ichni kafsis	yangın artıkları	رواسب الحريق	rawasib elharik
(Άνθρωπος *m*) Cro-Magnon *m*	('Anthropos) Cro-Magnon	Cro-Magnon	إنسان كرو مجنون	insan kro-magnon
καλλιεργίσιμη έκταση *f*	kalliergisimi ektasi	tarıma elverişli toprak	أرض زراعية	arad zeraaja
σταυρός *m*	stavros	çarmıh, haç	صليب	salib
οριζόντιο δοκάρι *n*	orizontio dokari	kiriş	عماد أفقى	imad ufukie
διατομή *f*	diatomi	enine kesit	مقطع عرضي	maktaa ardie
ακατέργαστος	akatergatos	ham, işlenmemiş	خام	chaam

English	German	French	Italian	Spanish
crumbly, fragile	brüchig	cassant/-e, friable	fragile	fragil, quebradizo
crust	Kruste *f*	croûte *f*	crosta *f*	costra *f*
crypt, grave	Gruft *f*	caveau *m*	cripta *f*	fosa *f*, sepulcro *m*
crystal	Kristall *n*	cristal *m*	cristallo *m*	cristal *m*
crystalline	kristallin	cristallin/-e	cristallino/-a	cristalino/-a
cult	Kult *m*	culte *f*	culto *m*	culto *m*
cult building	Kultbau *m*	édifice *m* de culte, structure *f* réligieuse	edificio di culto *m*	arquitectura *f* religiosa
cult complex	Kultanlage *f*	complexe *m* cultuel	complesso *m* di culto	lugar *m* de culto
cult district	Kultbezirk *m*	aire *f* sacrée	distretto *m* di culto	recinto *m* de culto
cultic	kultisch	cultuel/-elle	cultuale	cultual, del culto
cultivation	Kultivierung *f*	culture *f*	coltivazione *f*	cultivación *f*
cult of the dead	Totenkult *m*	culte *m* funéraire	culto *m* dei morti	culto *m* de los muertos
cult site	Kultstätte *f*	lieu *m* de culte	luogo *m* di culto	templo *m*
cultural	kulturell	culturel	culturale	cultural
cultural assets	Kulturgut *n*	biens culturels!, patrimoine *m* culturel	beni culturali *m* *pl*	patrimonio *m* cultural
cultural heritage preservation	Denkmalpflege *f*	conservation *f* des monuments historiques	tutela *f* dei monumenti	conservación *f* de monumentos
cultural history	Kulturgeschichte *f*	histoire *f* des civilisations	storia *f* culturale, storia *f* della civiltà	historia *f* cultural
cultural science	Kulturwissenschaft *f*	étude *f* des civilisations	scienza *f* della civiltà, scienza *f* della cultura	ciencias *f* de la cultura, humanidades
cuneiform	keilförmig	cunéiforme	cuneiforme	cuneiforme
cup	Tasse *f*	tasse *f*	tazza *f*	taza *f*
cupola	Kuppel *f*	coupole *f*	cupola *f*	cúpula *f*, domo *m*
cut	Schnitt *m*	coupe *f*	taglio *m*	corte *m*, incisión *f*
cyclopean masonry	Zyklopenmauer *f*	mur *m* cyclopéen	mura *f* ciclopiche	muralla *f* ciclópea
cylinder	Zylinder *m*	cylindre *m*	cilindro *m*	cilindro *m*
cylinder seal	Rollsiegel *n*	sceau-cylindre *m*	sigillo *m* cilindrico	sello *m* cilíndrico
cylindrical	zylindrisch	cylindrique	cilindrico/-a	cilíndrico/-a
dagger	Dolch *m*	poignard *m*	pugnale *m*	daga *f*, puñal *m*
damage	Schaden *m*	dommage *m*	danno *m*	daño *m*
damage, damaging	Beschädigung *f*	endommagement *m*	danneggiamento *m*, danno *m*	desperfecto *m*, deterioro *m*
danger	Gefahr *f*	danger *m*, péril *m*	pericolo *m*	peligro *m*
dangerous	gefährlich	dangereux/-euse	pericoloso/-a	peligroso/-a
dark	dunkel	obscure, sombre	oscuro/-a, sordo/-a	oscuro/-a
data	Daten *f* *pl*	données *m* *pl*	dati *m* *pl*	datos *m* *pl*
database	Datenbank *f*	banque *f* de données	banca *f* dati	banco *m* de datos
database	Datensammlung *f*	recueil *m* de données	raccolta *f* di dati	recopilación *f* de datos

Greek		Turkish	Arabic	
εύθραστος, εύθριπτος	efthrastos, efthriptos	kırılgan	هش	hasch
φλοιός *m*	floios	kabuk	قشرة صلبة	kischra salba
κρύπτη *f*	kripti	mezar odası, türbe	لحد	lahd
κρύσταλλος *m*	kristallos	kristal	بلّور / كرستال	ballur/ kristal
κρυσταλλικός	kristallikos	kristalleşmiş	بلوري	balluri
λατρεία *f*	latreia	kült	عبادة	ibada
λατρευτικό κτίσμα *n*	latreftiko ktisma	kült yapısı	بناء للعبادة	binaa lelibada
λατρευτικό σύμπλεγμα *n*	laktreftiko siblegma	kült tesisi	معبد	maabd
λατρευτικός περίβολος *m*	latreftikos perivolos	kült alanı, kült yeri	منطقة العبادة	manteket elibada
λατρευτικός	latreftikos	kült ile ilgili	تعبّدى	tabudi
καλλιέργεια *f*	kalliergia	toprağı ekip biçme	استصلاح	esteslah
νεκρική λατρεία *f*	nekriki latreia	ölü kültü	طقوس الدفن	tokus eldafn
τόπος λατρείας *m*	topos latreias	kült yeri	معبد	mabad
πολιτιστικός, πολιτισμικός	politistikos, polotismikos	kültürel	حضارى	hadari
πολιτιστικά αγαθά *n pl*	politistika agatha	kültürel varlık	التراث الحضارى	elturas elhadari
Συντήρηση *f* Μνημείων	Sintirisi Mnimeion	anıt bakımı	العناية بالتراث	elinaia belturas
ιστορία *f* του πολιτισμού	istoria tou politismou	uygarlık tarihi	التاريخ الحضارى	eltarich elhadari
επιστήμη του πολιτισμού *f*	epistimi tou politismou	Kültür Bilimi	علم الحضارة	elm elhadara
σφηνοειδής	sfinoeidis	kama şeklinde	إسفينى الشكل	esfini elschakl
φλυτζάνι *f*	flitzani	fincan	فنجان	fengaan
τρούλος *m*	troulos	kubbe	قبة	kuba
τομή *f*, εγκοπή *f*	tomi, egkopi	açma, kesit	مقطع	maktaa
κυκλώπειο τείχος *n*	kiklopeio teichos	kiklop duvar	سور بأحجار غير مستوية	sur beahgar geer mostawija
κύλινδρος *m*	kilindros	silindir	اسطوانة	estiwana
κυλινδρικός σφραγιδόλιθος *m*	kilindrkos sfragidolithos	silindir mühür	ختم إسطوانى	chetm estwanie
κυλινδρικός	kilindrikos	silindirik	اسطواني	estiwanie
εγχειρίδιο *n*, μαχαίρι *n*	egcheiridio, machairi	hançer, kama	خنجر	chengar
βλάβη *f*	vlavi	hasar, zarar	ضرر	darar
βλάβη *f*, φθορά *f*, ζημιά *f*	vlavi, fthora, zimia	hasar	إتلاف	itlaf
κίνδυνος *m*	kindinos	tehlike	خطر	chatar
επικίνδυνος	epikindinos	rizikolu, tehlikeli	خطير	chatier
σκοτεινός	skoteinos	karanlık, koyu	مظلم	muzlem
δεδομένα *n pl*	dedomena	bilgiler, veriler	بيانات	bianat
βάση *f* δεδομένων	basi dedomenon	databank, veri bankası	قاعدة بيانات	kaedat bianat
συλλογή *f* δεδομένων	sillogi dedomenon	veri toplama	مجموعة بيانات	magmoaat bianat

English	German	French	Italian	Spanish
date	Datum *n*	date *f*	data *f*	fecha *f*
dating	Datierung *f*	datation *f*	datazione *f*	cronología *f,* datación *f*
datum point, site datum	Nullpunkt *m*	point zero *m*	zero *m*	punto cero *m*
debris	Schutt *m*	décombres *m pl*	macerie *f pl*	escombros *m pl*
debris, ruins	Trümmer	ruines *f pl* , décombres *m pl*	rovine *pl*	escombros *pl* , ruinas *pl*
debris, sedimentation	Ablagerung *f*	dépôt *m*	sedimentazione *f*	sedimento *m*
decay, decomposition	Verwesung *f*	décomposition *f*	decomposizione *f*	descomposición *f*
decay, ruin	Zerfall *m*	déclin *m*	degrado *m* , rovina *f*	desmoronamiento *m* , ruina *f*
decomposition	Zersetzung *f*	décomposition *f*	disaggregazione *f*	descomposición *f*
decoration	Dekoration *f*	décoration *f*	decorazione *f*	decoración *f*
decoration	Dekor *n*	décor *m*	decorazione *f*	adorno *m*
decoration, ornament	Verzierung *f*	décor *m, d* écoration *f*	decorazione *f*	decoración *f,* ornamento *m*
decoration technique	Verzierungstechnik *f*	technique *f* ornementale/ décorative	tecnica di decorazione *f*	técnica de la decoración *f*
dedication place	Weihestätte *f*	lieu *m* sacré, sanctuaire *m*	luogo *m* di consacrazione	lugar *m* sagrado, sagrado *m*
deforestation	Abholzung *f*	abattage *m*	diboscamento *m*	desforestación *f,* tala *f*
degradation	Abtrag *m* , Erosion *f*	nivellement *m*	asportazione *f*	ablación *f*
degree, grade	Grad *m*	degré *m*	grado *m*	grado *m*
delicate, filigree	filigran	filigrane	filigrana *f*	de filigrana
delicate, sensitive	empfindlich	sensible	fragile	frágil
delta	Delta *n*	delta *m*	delta *m*	delta *m*
demography	Demographie *f*	démographie *f*	demografia *f*	demografía *f*
dendrite	Dendrit *m*	dendrite *f*	dendrite *f*	dendrita *f*
dendrochronology	Dendrochronologie *f*	dendrochronologie *f*	dendrocronologia *f*	dendrocronología *f*
dendrology	Dendrologie *f*	dendrologie *f*	dendrologia *f*	dendrología *f*
dense, thick	dicht	compact/-e, dense	fitto/-a, folto/-a	compacto/-a, denso/-a
density	Dichte *f*	densité *f*	fittezza *f* , foltezza *f*	densidad *f* , espesor *m*
dent	Delle *f*	creux *m* , cupule *f*	ammaccatura *f* , cuppella *f*	abolladura *f*
dent decoration	Dellenverzierung *f*	décor *m* de cupules	decorazione *f* a cuppelle	ornamento *m* con abolladuras
departement	Abteilung *f*	département *m*	ripartizione *f*, ufficio *m*	departamento *m*
deposit	Depot *n*	dépôt *m*	deposito *m*	depósito *m*
deposit, fill	Auffüllung *f*	remplissage *m*	riempimento *m*	relleno *m* , reposición *f*
deposition	Ausschlämmung *f*	curage *m,* débourbage *m,*	sfangamento *m*	vaciado *m* de posos
depth	Tiefe *f*	profondeur *f*	profondità *f*	profundidad *f*

Greek		Turkish	Arabic	
χρονολογία f	chronologia	tarih	تاريخ	tariech
χρονολόγηση f	chronologisi	tarihleme	تأريخ	taariech
σημείο μηδέν n	simeio miden	nötr nokta, sıfır noktası	نقطة الصفر	noktat elsefr
μπάζα n pl	baza	döküntü, moloz	رديم	rediem
χαλάσματα n pl	chalasmata	moloz, döküntü	أنقاض	ankaad
συσσώρρευση f	sissorrefsi	çökelti, tortu	ترسيب	tarsieb
αποσύνθεση f	aposinthesi	çürüme	تحلل	tahalol
παρακμή f, πτώση f, κατάπτωση f	parakmi, ptosi, kataptosi	dağılma	إنهيار	enhijar
αποσύνθεση f	aposinthesi	ayrışım, erime	تحلل	tahalol
διακόσμηση f	diakosmisi	dekorasyon	زينة	zina
διάκοσμος m	diakosmos	dekor	ديكور	dikor
διακόσμηση f	diakosmisi	bezeme, süs	زخرفة	zachrafa
διακοσμητική τεχνική f	diakosmitiki techniki	bezeme tekniği, süsleme tekniği	تقنية الزخرفة	teknija elzachrafa
καθαγιασμένος χώρος m	kathagiasmenos choros	kutsal alan	مكان مقدس	makan mukadas
αποψίλωση f δάσους	apopsilosi dasous	ormansızlaştırma	إزالة الأشجار	izalet elaschgar
ανάλωση f	analosi	heyelan	تآكل	taakol
βαθμός m	vathmos	derece	درجة	daraga
συρματερός, φιλιγκράν	sirmateros, filigkran	ince, narin	مزخرف بالتثقيب	mozachraf beltaskieb
ευαίσθητος	evaisthitos	hassas	حساس	hasaas
δέλτα n	delta	delta	دلتا	delta
δημογραφία f	dimografia	Demografi	علم السكان	elm elsukan
δενδρίτης m	dendritis	dandrit	التغصنات الشجرية	eltgasonat elschagareiea
δενδροχρονολόγηση f	dendrochronologisi	dendrokronoloji	تعيين سن الشجرة	taeiin sen elschagara
δενδρολογία f	dentrologia	Ağaç Bilimi	علم الشجر	elm elschagar
πυκνός	pinkos	katı, sıkı	كثيف	kasif
πυκνότητα f	piknotita	sıkılık, yoğunluk	كثافة	kasafa
οδόντας m, δόντι n	odontas, donti	hafif derinlik, yayvan çukurluk	إسم مدينة فرنسية	ism madinah fransija
οδοντωτό κόσμημα n	odontoto kosmima	çukur bezeme	زخرفة ديل	zachrafit del
τμήμα n	tmima	bölüm	قسم	kesm
αποθήκη f	apothiki	depo	مستودع	mustawda
γέμισμα n	gemisma	doldurma	تعبئة	tabiaa
απόθεση f	apothesi	ayırma, tasfiye etme, yıkayıp	إزالة الطمى	izalet eltami
βάθος n	vathos	derinlik	عمق	umk

English	German	French	Italian	Spanish
descent, origin	Abstammung *f*	filiation *f*, lignage *m*, origine *f*	derivazione *f*, discendenza *f*, filazione *f*,	derivación *f*, filiación *f*, *or* igen *m*
describe	beschreiben	décrire	descrivere	describir
description	Beschreibung *f*	description *f*	descrizione *f*	descripción *f*
desert	Wüste *f*	désert *m*	deserto *m*	desierto *m*
design, form, shape	Formgebung *f*	façonnement *m*	formatura, modellatura *f*	formación *f*, modelación *f*
destruction	Zerstörung *f*	destruction *f*	distruzione *f*	destrucción *f*
destruction horizon	Zerstörungshorizont *m*	horizon *m* de destruction	fase *f* di distruzione	nivel *m* de destrucción
detail	Detail *n*	détail *m*	dettaglio *m*	detalle *m*
detailed	detailliert	détaillé/-ée	dettagliato/-a	detallado/-a
detail, section	Ausschnitt *m*	détail *f*, partie *m*	dettaglio *m*, settore *m*	detalle *m*, recorte *m*, sector *m*
determination of origin	Herkunftsbestimmung *f*	détermination *f* de l'origine	deteminazione *f* della provenienza	determinación *f* de la procedencia
development	Entwicklung *f*	développement *m*	sviluppo *m*	desarrollo *m*
diachronic	diachron	diachronique	diacrono	diacrónico
diagonal	diagonal	diagonal	diagonale	diagonal
diagonal	schräg	biais/-e, oblique	obliquo/-a, sbieco/-a	oblicuo, transversal
diameter	Durchmesser *m*	diamètre *m*	diametro *m*	diámetro *m*
difference in altitude	Höhenunterschied *m*	différence *f* de niveau	differenza *f* di altitudine	desnivel *m*
digger, dredger	Bagger *m*	pelle *f* mécanique, pelleteuse *f*	escavatore *m*	draga *f*, excavadora *f*
digital	digital	digital	digitale	digital
dilluvium	Dilluvium *n*	diluvium *m*	diluvio *m*	diluvio
dimension, measurement	Abmessung *f*	dimensions *f pl*, mesurage *m*	misurazione *f*	dimensión *f*, medidas *f*
dimension, size	Größe *f*	dimension *f*, taille *f*	estensione *f*, taglia *f*	tamaño *m*
diorite	Diorit *m*	diorite *f*	diorite *f*	diorita *f*
dipper, scoop	Grabungskelle *f*	truelle *f*	cazzuola *f*, trowel *f*	llana *f*, paleta *f*
dipylon	Dipylon *n*	Dipylon *m*	Dipylon *m*	dípilo, dípilon *m*
direction, orientation	Himmelsrichtung *f*	direction *f*, point *m* cardinal	punto *m* cardinale	punto *m* cardinal
dirty	schmutzig	sale	sporco/-a	sucio/-a
discoid	scheibenförmig (diskoidal)	discoïde	discoidale	discoidal
discolouration	Verfärbung *f*	altération *f* de la couleur	cambiamento *m* di colore	cambio *m* de color
discontinuity, interruption	Unterbrechung *f*	interruption *f*	interruzione *f*	interrupción *f*
discus	Diskus *m*	disque *m*	disco *m*	disco *m*
disinfectant	Desinfektionsmittel *n*	désinfectant *m*	disinfettante *m*	desinfectante *m*
disinfection	Desinfizierung *f*	désinfection *f*	disinfezione *f*	desinfección *f*

Greek		Turkish	Arabic	
καταγωγή *f*, προέλευση *f*	katagogi, proelefsi	asıl, köken	نسب	nasab
περιγράφω	perigrafo	tanımlamak	يصف	yasef
περιγραφή *f*	perigrafi	tanımlama	وصف	wasf
έρημος *f*	erimos	çöl	صحراء	sahraa
διαμόρφωση *m*	dismorfosi	kalıplama işi, şekillendirme	تصميم	tasmiem
καταστροφή *f*	katastrofi	tahrip, yıkım	تدمير	tadmier
στρώμα καταστροφής *n*	stroma katastofis	tahrip tabakası	أفق الدمار	ufok eldamaar
λεπτομέρεια *f*	leptomereia	detay	تفاصيل	tafasil
λεπτομερής	leptomeris	detaylı	تفصيلى	tafsili
απόσπασμα *n*	apospasma	kesit	مقطع	maktaa
καθορισμός προέλευσης *m*	kathorismos proelefsis	köken belirleme	تحديد الأصل	tahdied elasl
ανάπτυξη *f*	anaptixi	gelişme, ilerleme,	تطور	tatawor
διαχρονικός	diachronikos	bir dilin tarihi gelişimi ile ilgili	تاريخيا	taricheian
διαγώνιος	diagonios	diyagonal	قطري	kitrie
διαγώνιος	diagonios	eğik, eğimli	مائل	mael
διάμετρος *f*	diametros	çap	قطر الدائرة	kotr eldagira
διαφορά υψομέτρου *f*	diafora ipsometrou	seviye farkı	فرق شاسع	fark schasea
εκσκαφέας *m*	ekskafeas	kepçe	حفارة	hafarah
ψηφιακός	psifiakos	dijital	رقمي	rakami
πλημμυρική απόθεση *f*	plimmiriki apothesi	dilüviyum	عصر الطوفان	aser eltufan
μέτρηση *f*	metrisi	boyut	قياس	kijas
μέγεθος *n*	megethos	büyüklük	حجم	hagm
διορίτης *m*	dioritis	diyorit	ديوريت	dejureit
σέσουλα *f*	sesoula	mala	مغرفة الحفر	magrafet elhafr
Δίπυλο(ν) *n*	Dipilo(n)	dipylon	صرح مُزدوج	sarh muzdawag
προσανατολισμός *m*	prosanatolismos	yön	اتجاه	itegah
βρώμικός, ρυπαρός	vromikos, riparos	kirli	متسخ	motasech
δισκοειδής	diskoeidis	disk biçiminde	قرصي الشكل	kursi elschakl
αποχρωματισμός *m*	apochromatismos	rengini değiştirme	تغيير اللون	tagjier elloon
ασυνέχεια *f*	asinecheia	ara, kesilme	انقطاع	enkitaa
δίσκος *m*	diskos	diskos	قرص الرمي	kurs elramei
απολυμαντικό *n*	apolimantiko	dezenfeksiyon maddesi	مطهر	mutaher
απολύμανση *f*	apolimansi	dezenfekte	تطهير / تعقيم	takim, tathier

English	German	French	Italian	Spanish
dispersal (area)	Verbreitungsgebiet n	aire f de distribution	zona f di diffusione	área f de distribución
dispersed habitat/ settlement	Streusiedlung f	habitat m dispersé	insediamento m disperso	asentamiento m en dispersión
(dis-) solvable	löslich	soluble	solubile	soluble
distance	Abstand m	distance f	distanza f	distancia f
distance	Entfernung f	distance f, éloignement m	distanza f	distancia f
distance, range	Strecke f	distance f	distanza f, tratto m	distancia f
distilled water	destilliertes Wasser n	eau f distillée	acqua f distillata	agua f destilada
distribution	Verteilung f	distribution f, répartition f	distribuzione f	distribución f
distribution map	Verbreitungskarte f	carte f de distribution	mappa f di distribuzione	mapa f de distribución
distribution, spread	Verbreitung f	distribution f	diffusione f	circulación f, difusión f
disturbance, perturbation	Störung f	perturbation f	disturbo m	estiorbo m
disturbed	gestört	perturbé (-ee)	disturbato/-a	perturbado/-a
distylos	distylos	distyle	distilo	dístilo m
ditch, fosse	Graben m	fossé m	fossato m	fosa f
documentation	Dokumentation f	documentation f	documentazione f	documentación f
dog whelk	Purpurschnecke f	coquillage m à pourpre, murex m	murice m	cañadilla f, concha f
dolerite	Dolerit m	dolérite f	dolerite f	dolerita f
dolmen, megalithic chamber tomb	Dolmen m, Großsteingrab n	dolmen m	dolmen m, tomba f megalitica	dolmen m
domestic animal, pet	Haustier n	animal m domestique	animale m domestico	animal m doméstico
domestication	Domestikation f	domestication f	domesticazione f	domesticación f
door	Tür f	porte f	porta f	puerta f
door lintel	Türsturz m	linteau m	architrave m	dintel m
doorpost, -jamb	Türpfosten m	jambage m	stipite m della porta	jamba f
doorsill, threshold	Türschwelle f	seuil m	soglia della porta f	umbral m
Doric order	dorische Ordnung f	ordre m dorique	ordine m dorico	orden m dórico
dot	Punkt (Verzierung) m	point m	punto m	punto m
dotted row	Punktreihe f	trait m pointillé	linea f punteggiata	línea f de puntos
dotting	Punktierung f	décor m pointillé	punteggiatura f	punteo m
downspout	Traufe f	chéneau m, gouttière f	gronda f	canalón m
drain	Abflussrohr n	déchargeoir m, détritus m pl	tubo m di scarico	tubo m de desagüe
drainage	Trockenlegung f	assèchement m, drainage m	bonifica f, prosciugamento m	desecación f
drawing pad	Zeichenunterlage f	planche f à dessin	tavola f da disegno	carpeta f de dibujo
drawing pin	Reißnagel m	punaise f	puntina f	chinche f, chincheta f
drawing, sketch	Zeichnung f	dessin m	disegno m	dibujo m

Greek		Turkish	Arabic	
περιοχή διάδοσης *f*	periochi diadosis	yayılım alanı	منطقة الإنتشار	manteket elentischar
αραιή εγκατάσταση *f*	araii egkatastasi	dağınık yerleşim	مستوطنة مبعثرة	mostawtana mobasara
διαλυτός	dialitos	erir, çözünür	قابل للذوبان	kabel lelzawaban
απόσταση *f*	apostasi	ara, mesafe	مسافة	masafah
απόσταση *f*	apostasi	çıkarma, mesafe, uzaklaştırma, uzaklık	إزالة	izalah
απόσταση *f*	apostasi	hat, mesafe, yol	مسافة	masafa
αποσταγμένο νερό *n*	apostagmeno nero	damıtılmış su, saf su,	ماء مقطر	maa mokatar
κατανομή *f*, μοιρασιά *f*	katanomi, moirasia	dağıtım, paylaşım	توزيع	tawziea
χάρτης κατανομής *m*	chartis katanomis	yayılma haritası	التوزيع خرائط	chraet eltawzia
διάδοση *f*	diadosi	genişleme, yayılma	توسع	tawasoa
διατάραξη *f*	diataraxi	kesinti, tahribat	اضطراب	itiraab
διαταραγμένος	diataragmenos	tahrip edilmiş	مُتضرر	motaderer
δίστυλος	distilos	distylos	واجهة معبد بعامودين	wagehat mabad beamudein
τάφρος *f*	tafros	hendek, uçurum	حُفرة	hufra
καταγραφή *f*	katagrafi	belgeleme	توثيق	tawsik
πορφύρα *f*, όστρα κο πορφύρας *n*	profira, ostrakoporfiras	purpura pansa	حلزون أرجواني	halazon argiwanie
δολερίτης *m*	doleritis	dolantaşı, dolerit	حجر الدُلوريت	hagar eldulorit
μεγαλιθικό ταφικό μνημείο *n*, ντολμέν *n*	megalithiko tafiko mnimeio, ntolmen	dolmen, megalitik mezar	مقبرة صخرية كبيرة	makbara sachreia kabira
οικόσιτο/ ήμερο ζώο *n*	oikosito/ imero zoo	evcil hayvan	حيوان أليف	hajawan alief
εξημέρωση *f*	eximerosi	evcilleştirme	استئناس	estenas
θύρα *f*, πόρτα *f*	thira, porta	kapı	باب	bab
ανώφλι *n*	anofli	atkı, üst eşik	عتب الباب	atab elbab
παραστάδα πόρτας *f*	parastada portas	kapı sövesi	عضادة الباب	udadet elbab
κατώφλι *n*	katofli	kapı eşiği	عتبة الباب	ataba elbab
δωρικός ρυθμός *m*	dorikos rithmos	Dor Düzeni	نظام دوريسي	nizam durisi
στιγμή *f*, κουκκίδα *f*	stigmi, koukkida	benek, nokta	نقطة	nukta
κοκκιδωτή γραμμή *f*	kokkidoti grammi	nokta dizisi	مجموعة نقط متصلة	magmuat nukat mutasila
στίξη *f*, κοκκίδωση *f*	stixi, kokkidosi	noktalama	تنقيط	tankit
γείσο *n*	geiso	saçak	ماسورة نصفيّة لتصريف مياة الأمطار	masura nesfija letasrief mijah elamtar
αποχετευτικός αγωγός *m*	apocheteftikos agogos	atık su borusu, künk	أنبوب التصريف	anbubet eltasrief
αποξήρανση *f*, αποστράγγιση *f*	apoxiransi, apostraggisi	drenaj, kanal açma	تجفيف	tagfief
επιφάνεια σχεδίασης *f*	epifaneia schediasis	çizim tahtası	لوحة رسم	lohet rasm
πινέζα *f*	pineza	raptiye	دبّوس مكتب	dabus maktab
σχεδίαση *f*, σχέδιο *n*	schediasi, schedio	çizim	رسم	rasm

English	German	French	Italian	Spanish
dressing material	Verbandszeug *f*	pansements *m pl*	materiale *m* di pronto soccorso	material *m* de apósito
dried	getrocknet	séché	secco/-a	curado/-a, secado/-a
dried up	ausgetrocknet	desséché/-e	secco/-a	árido/-a
drift, process	Verlauf *m*	cours *m*	corso *m*, svolgimento *m*	curso *m*, desarrollo *m*
drill bit	Bohrer *m*	foret *m*, perçoir *m*	trapano *m*	barrena *f*
drill machine	Bohrmaschine *f*	foreuse *f*	trapano *m* meccanico	taladradora *f*
drinking horn	Trinkhorn *n*	corne *f* à boire	rython *m*	cuerna *f*
dromos	Dromos *m*	dromos	dromos *m*	dromos *m*
drop-shaped	tropfenförmig	en forme de goutte *f*	a goccia *f*	en forma de gota *f*
dry	trocken	sec/-èche	secco/-a	seco/-a
dune	Düne *f*	dune *f*	duna *f*	duna *f*
duplicate	Duplikat *n*	duplicata *m*	duplicato *m*	duplicado *m*
durability	Haltbarkeit *f*	durabilité *f*, solidité *f*	durevolezza *f*	durabilidad *f*
durable, lasting	haltbar	résistant/e, solide	durevole	duradero/-a, sostenible
duration	Dauer *f*	durée *f*	durata *f*	duración *f*
dust	Staub *m*	poussière *f*	polvere *f*	polvo *m*
dusty	staubig	poussiéreux/-euse	polveroso/-a	polvoriento *m*
dwelling, settlement	Siedlung *f*	habitat *m*	insediamento *m*	asentamiento *m*, poblado *m*
earthenware, stoneware	Steingut, -zeug *n*	grès *m*	terraglia *f*	loza *f*
earth grave	Erdgrab *n*	tombe *f* plate	sepoltura *f* in terra	sepultura *f* de tierra
earthquake	Erdbeben *n*	séisme *m*, tremblement *m* de terre	terremoto *m*	seísmo *m*, terremoto *m*
east	Osten *m*	est *m*	est *m*, oriente *m*	este *m*, oriente *m*
eastern	östlich	oriental/-e	dell'est, orientale	oriental
ebony	Ebenholz *n*	(bois d') ébène *f*	ebano *m*	(madera de) ébano *m*
ecclesiasterion	Ekklesiasterion *n*	ecclésiasterion *m*	ekklesiasterion *m*	ekklesiasterion *m*
economic	wirtschaftlich	économique	economico/-a	económico/-a
ecosystem	Ökosystem *n*	écosystème *m*	ecosistema *f*	ecosistema *f*
edge	Ecke *f*	angle *m*, coin *m*	angolo *m*	ángulo *m*, esquina *f*
edged, polygonal	kantig	à arête(s) vive(s)	angoloso/-a	anguloso
egg and dart	Eierstab *m*	rang *m* d'oves	baccello *f*	gallonado *m*
egg-shaped	eiförmig	ovale	ovale	ovoide
eggshell	Eierschale *f*	coquille *f* d'oeuf	guscio *m* d'uovo	cáscara *f* de huevo
Egyptian	ägyptisch	égytien, -ne	egizio/-a	egipcio/-a
Egyptology	Ägyptologie *f*	égyptologie *f*	egittologia *f*	egiptología *f*
einkorn	Einkorn *n*	engrain *m* ·	piccolo farro *m*	espelta *f*
element	Element *n*	élément *m*	elemento *m*	elemento *m*

Greek		Turkish	Arabic	
υλικό περιτυλίγματος *n*	iliko peritiligmatos	ilk yardım malzemesi	مواد التضميد	mawaad eltadmied
αποξηραμένος	apoxiramenos	kurumuş	مجففة	mogafafa
αποξηραμένος	aposiramenos	kurumuş	جاف	gaaf
διαδικασία *f*	diadikasia	gelişme, seyir süreç	مسار	masar
τρυπάνι *n*	tripani	matkap	مثقب / حفار	miskab, hafar
τρυπάνι *n* , δράπανο *n*	tripani, drapano	matkap makinesi	آلة حفر	alet hafr
κέρας πόσης *n*	keras posis	içki boynuzu	قدح على شكل قرن	kadah ala schakl karn
δρόμος *m*	dromos	dromos	ممر الدخول للمعبد	mamar eldochul lelmaabad
σταγονόσχημος	stagonoschimos	damla şeklinde	على شكل قطرة	als schakl katra
στεγνός, ξηρός	stegnos, xiros	kurak, kuru	جفاف	gaaf
αμμόλοφος *m*	ammolofos	kumlu, kumul	كثبان رملية	kusban ramleja
αντίγραφο *n*	antigrafo	kopya, suret	نسخة	nuschah
αντοχή *f*	antochi	dayanıklılık, sağlamlık	متانة / صلاحية	matanah / salahija
ανθεκτικός	anthektikos	çürümez, dayanıklı, sağlam	متين	matien
διάρκεια *f*	diarkeia	süre	مُدَّة	moudda
σκόνη *f*	skoni	toprak, toz	تراب	turaab
σκονισμένος	skonismenos	tozlu	متّرب	mutarab
εγκατάσταση *f*, οικισμός *m*	egkatastasi, oikismos	yerleşme, yerleşim yeri	مستوطنة	mostawtana
πήλινα σκεύη *n pl*	pilina skevi	kilden yapılma çanak-çömlek	خزف	chazaf
λακκοειδής τάφος *m*	lakkoeidis tafos	basit toprak mezar	قبر	kabr
σεισμός *m*	seismos	deprem	زلزال	zelzal
ανατολή *f*	anatoli	doğu	شرق	schark
ανατολικός	anatolikos	doğuda, doğusunda	شرقي	scharkie
έβενος *m*	evenos	abanoz	خشب الأبنوس	chaschab elabanos
εκκλησιαστήριο(ν) *n*	ekklisiastirio(n)	ekklesiasterion	قاعة إجتماعت لمجلس الشعب	kaat egtimaat limagles elschab
οικονομικός	oikonomikos	ekonomik, iktisadi	اقتصادي	ektesadie
οικοσύστημα *n*	oikosistima	ekolojik sistem	نظام البيئي	nizam biie
γωνία *f*	gonia	kenar, köşe	زاوية	zawia
γωνιώδης	goniodis	keskin kenarlı	حاد الحواف	had elhawaf
ιωνικό κυμάτιο *n*	ioniko kimatio	Kymation, yumurta dizisi	شريط زخرفى من بيض وأسهم	schariet zochrofie men beed wi ashom
ωοειδής	ooeidis	oval, yumurta biçiminde	بيضاوى الشكل	bajdawi elschakl
κέλυφος *n* αυγού	kelifos avgou	yumurta kabuğu	قشر البيض	keschr elbeid
αιγυπτιακός	aigiptiakos	Mısır'a ait, Mısırlı	مصري	mesri
αιγυπτιολογία *f*	aigiptiologia	Ejiptoloji, Mısırbilim	علم الآثار المصرية	elm elasar elmasrjeh
μονόκοκκο σιτάρι *n*	monokokko sitari	küçük kızılca buğday	نوع من القمح	noa men alkamh
στοιχείο *n*	stoicheio	element	عنصر	unsor

English	German	French	Italian	Spanish
elevation	Ansicht *f*	vue *f*	veduta *f*	vista *f*
elevation	Bodenerhöhung *f*	élévation *f* de terrain	elevazione *f* del terreno	elevación *f* del terreno
elevation	Erhebung *f*	élévation *f*	elevazione *f*	elevación *f*
embalming	Einbalsamierung *f*	embaumement *m*	imbalsamazione *f*	embalsamamiento *m*
embossing	Prägung *f*	estampage *m* , frappe *f*	monetazione *f*	acuñación *f*
embroidery	Stickerei *f*	broderie *f*	ricamo *m*	bordado *m*
emmer	Emmer *m*	ammidonnier *m*	farro *m*	farro *m*
empire	Reich *n*	empire *m*	impero *m*	imperio *m*
emporium	Emporion *n*	emporion *m*	emporion *m*	emporio *m*
enamel	Email *n*	courriel *m*	smalto *m*	esmalte *m*
encaustic	Enkaustik *f*	encaustique *f*	encaustica *f*	encáustica *f*
enchased	gefasst (Schmuck)	enchâssé/-ée	incastonato/-a	engastado/-a
enclosure wall	Umfassungsmauer *f*	enceinte *f* , mur *m* de clôture	muro *m* di cinta	muralla *f*, muro *m* de cerramiento
engobe, slip	Überzug (Engobe) *m*	enduit *m* , engobe *m*	ingobbio *m*	capa *f*, engobe *m*
engobe, slip-glaze	Schlicker *m*	barbotine *f*	argilla *f* umida	cieno *m*
engraving	Gravur *f*	gravure *f*	incisione *f*	grabado
entomology	Entomologie *f*	entomologie *f*	entomologia *f*	entomología *f*
entrance	Eingang *m* , Zugang *m*	accès *m*, entrée *f*	entrata *f*, ingresso *m*	acceso *m* , entrada *f*
environment	Umwelt *f*	environnement *m*	ambiente *m*	ambiente *m*
environment, milieu, setting	Millieu *n*	millieu *m*	ambiente *m*	medio *m*
environment, surroundings	Umfeld *n*	environnement *m*	milieu *m*	ambiente *m* , entorno *m*
epidemic	Epidemie *f*	épidémie *f*	epidemia *f*	epidemia *f*
epigraph	Epigraph *m*	épigraphe *f*	epigrafe *f*	epígrafe *m*
epigraphic	Epigrafik *f*	épigraphie *f*	epigrafia *f*	epigrafía *f*
epoxy resin	Epoxydharz *n*	résine *f* époxyde	resina *f* di epossido	resina *f* epoxi
equipment	Ausrüstung *f*	équipement *m*	equipaggiamento *m*	equipo *m*
equipment, tools	Geräte *n pl*	instruments *m pl* , outils *m pl*	attrezzi *m pl*	instrumento *m*, utensilio *m*
era	Epoche *f*	époque *f*	epoca *f*	época *f*
era	Zeitalter *n*	âge *m*, époque *f*	era *f*, età *f*	época *f*, era *f*
era, epoch, period	Zeitraum *m*	période *f*	periodo *m*	período *m*
erosion	Erosion *f*	érosion *f*	erosione *f*	erosión *f*
eruption	Eruption *f*	éruption *f*	eruzione *f*, sfogo *m*	erupción *f*
eruption	Vulkanausbruch *m*	éruption *f*	eruzione *f*	erupción *f*
eruptive rock	Eruptivgestein *n*	roches *f pl* éruptives	roccia *f* eruttiva	roca *f* volcánica
estuary, river mouth	Flussmündung *f*	embouchure *f*	foce *f*	estuario *m*
ethno-archaeology	Ethnoarchäologie *f*	ethnoarchéologie *f*	etnoarcheologia *f*	etnoarqueología *f*
ethnography	Ethnographie *f*	ethnographie *f*	etnografia *f*	etnografía *f*

Greek		Turkish	Arabic	
όψη *f*	opsi	düşünce, fikir	منظر / رأى	manzar, raai
έξαρμα *n*	exarma	tümsek	رفع الأرض	rafa elard
ανύψωση *f*	anipsosi	tümsek, yükselti, çıkıntı	مُرتفع / تل	murtafaa/ tall
βασάμωμα *f*	vasamoma	tahnit etme	تحنيط	tahniet
αποτύπωμα *n*	apotipoma	basılmış resim, nitelik	سك	sak
κέντημα *n*	kentima	elişi, nakış	تطريز	tatriz
δίκοκκο σιτάρι *n*	dikokko sitari	kızılca buğday	نوع من القمح	noa men alkamh
Αυτοκρατορία *f*	Aftokratoria	İmparatorluk	إمبراطورية	embraturejah
εμπόριο(ν) *n*	eborio(n)	pazar yeri, ticaret merkezi	سوق	suk
σμάλτο *n*	smalto	emay, mine	البريد الإلكتروني	elbarid eleliktroni
εγκαυστική *f*	egkafstiki	enkaustik	الرسم بألوان شمعية	elrasm bialwan schameya
εγκιβωτισμένος	egkivotismenos	sakin	مُتزن	motazen
περίβολος *m*	perivolos	çevre duvarı	سورمُحيط	suur mohiet
γάνωμα *n*	ganoma	astar	طلاء	tilaa
γάνωμα *n*	ganoma	çömlek hamuru	الطينة المُعدّة لصناعة الفُخّار	eltina elmoada lesinaet elfochar
χαρακτικό *n*	charaktiko	gravür	نقش	naksch
εντομολογία *f*	entomologia	Etimoloji	علم الحشرات	elm elhascharat
είσοδος *f*	eisodos	antre, giriş	مدخل	madchal
περιβάλλον *n*	perivallon	çevre, doğa	بيئة	bieaa
περιβάλλον *n*	perivallon	çevre, ortam	بيئة	biaa
περιβάλλον *n*	perivallon	çevre, etraf	المناطق المحيطة	elmanatek elmohieta
επιδημία *f*	epidimia	epidemi, salgın	وباء	wabaa
επιγραφολόγος *m*	epigrafologos	epigraf	نقش	naksch
επιγραφική *f*	epigrafiki	Epigrafi/ Yazıtbilim	دراسة النقوش	derasat elnokosch
εποξική ρητίνη *f*	epoxiki ritini	epoksi	صمغ إيوكسي	hokba/fatra
εξοπλισμός *m*	exoplismos	donanım	تجهيز	taghiez
εξοπλισμός *m*	exoplismos	aletler, takımlar	معدات	moedat
εποχή *f*	epochi	çağ, devir	حقبة	hokbah
εποχή *f*	epochi	çağ, yüzyıl	عصر	asr
χρονική περίοδος *f*	chroniki periodos	müddet, süre	فترة زمنية	fatra zamanija
διάβρωση *f*	diavrosi	erozyon	تآكل	taakul
έκρηξη *f*	ekrixi	püskürme	ثوران	sawaran
ηφαιστειακή έκρηξη *f*	ifaisteiaki ekrixi	yanardağ püskürmesi	انفجار بركاني	enfigar borkanie
ηφαιστιακό πέτρωμα *n*	ifaistiako petroma	püskürük taş	الصخور النارية	elsuchor elnarija
εκβολές *f pl* ποταμού	ekvoles potamou	nehir ağzı	مصب النهر	mesab elnahr
εθνοαρχαιολογία *f*	ethnoarchaiologia	Etnoarkeoloji	علم آثار الشعوب	elm asar elschuub
εθνογραφία *f*	ethnografia	Etnografya	وصف منهجى للشعوب	wasf manhagi lelschuub

English	German	French	Italian	Spanish
ethnology	Ethnologie *f*	ethnologie *f*	etnologia *f*	etnología *f*
Etruscan	etruskisch	étrusque	etrusco/-a	etrusco/-a
Etruscology	Etruskologie *f*	Étruscologie *f*	etruscologia *f*	etruscología *f*
eustylos	Eustylos *m*	eustyle *m*	eustilio	éustilo *m*
even, flat, plane	eben	plan, plat	livellato/-a, piano/-a	llano/-a, plano/-a
even, smooth	glatt	lisse	liscio/-a	liso/-a
evolution	Evolution *f*	évolution *f*	evoluzione *f*	evolución *f*
examination	Untersuchung *f*	examen *m*	analisi *f*	investigación *f*
examination, treatment	Behandlung *f*	traitement *m*	trattamento *m*	tratamiento *m*
excavation	Ausgrabung *f*	fouille *f*	scavo *m*	excavación *f*
excavation house	Grabungshaus *n*	maison *f* de fouilles	casa *f* di scavo	casa *f* de excavación
excavation journal	Grabungstagebuch *n*	journal *m* de fouilles	diario *m* / giornali *m* *pl* di scavo	diario *m* de excavación *m*
excavation office	Grabungsbüro *n*	bureau *m* de fouilles	ufficio *m* di scavo	oficina *f* de excavación
excavation tools	Grabungswerkzeug *n*	outils *m pl* de fouilles	attrezzi *m pl* di scavo	herramienta *f* de excavación
excavator	Ausgräber *m*	fouilleur *m*	scavatore *m* /-trice *f*	excavador *m*
exemplary	exemplarisch	exemplaire	esemplare	ejemplar
exhibit	Exponat *n*	pièce *f* d'exposition	pezzo *m* d'esposizione	objeto *m* expuesto
exhibition, display	Ausstellung *f*	exposition *f*	esposizione *f*	exposición *f*
experimental archaeology	experimentelle Archäologie *f*	archéologie *f* expérimentale	archeologia *f* sperimentale	arqueología *f* experimental
exploitation	Abbau *m*	décapage *m*, exploitation *f*	estrazione *f*	explotación *f*
export	Export *m*	exportation *f*	esportazione *f*	exportación *f*
export goods	Exportware *f*	merchandise *f* d'exportation	merce *f* esportata	género *m* de exportación
extension, spread	Ausdehnung *f*	étendue *f*, extension *f*	estensione *f*	extensión *f*
extensive, large scale	großflächig	étendu/-e	ampio	vasto
external, outer	außen	(au) dehors, à l'extérieur	fuori, allesterno	exterior
extinct	ausgestorben	éteint/-e	scomparato/-a	extinto/-a
facade	Fassade *f*	façade *f*	facciata *f*	fachada *f*
factor	Faktor *m*	facteur *m*	fattore *m*	factor *m*
faience	Fayence *f*	faïence *f*	fayence *f*	fayenza *f*
faint, indistinct	undeutlich	indistinct/-e	indistinto/-a	indistinto/-a
fake, forgery	Fälschung *f*	contrefaçon *f*, faux *m*	falsificazione *f*, falso *m*	falsificación *f*
fallow land, wasteland	Brachland *n*	terre *f* en friche	campo *m* a maggese	baldío *m*
family	Familie *f*	famille *f*	famiglia *f*	familia *f*
farmer	Bauer *m*	paysan *m*, -anne *f*	contadino *m*	campesino *m*
fastener	Fixiermittel *n*	fixateur *m*	fissativo *m*	fijador *m*
fat	Fett *n*	graisse *f*	grasso *m*	grasa *f*
feature drawing	Befundzeichnung *f*	dessin *m* de la structure	disegno *m* del reperto	dibujo *m* del hallazgo/ del perfil

Greek		Turkish	Arabic	
εθνολογία *f*	ethnologia	Etnoloji	علم الأعراق البشرية	elm elaarak elbaschareja
ετρούσκος	etrouskos	Etrüsk	اتروسكاني	itruskanie
Ετρουσκολογία *f*	Etrouskologia	Etrüskoloji	علم الإتروسكانيات	elm elitruskanijat
εύστυλος	eistilos	eustylos	طراز من الأعمدة	traaz men elaameda
επίπεδος	epipedos	düz, engebesiz, yassı	مُمهد	mumahad
λείος	leios	düz, kaygan	أملس	amlas
εξέλιξη *f*	exelixi	evrim	نظرية التطور	nasariet eltatawor
εξέταση *f*	exetasi	araştırma	فحص	fahs
διερεύνηση *f*, επεξεργασία *f*	dierevnisi, epexergasia	ele alma, işlem	معالجة	mualaga
ανασκαφή *f*	anaskafi	arkeolojik kazı	حفريات	hafrijat
σπίτι ανασκαφών *n*	spiti anaskafon	kazı evi	بيت الحفريات	beit elhafreijat
ημερολόγιο *n* ανασκαφής	imerologio anaskafis	kazı günlüğü	مذكرات الحفريات	muzakerat elhafrijat
γραφείο *n* ανασκαφών	grafeio anaskafon	kazı ofisi	مكتب الحفريات	maktab elhafrijat
ανασκαφικά εργαλεία *n* *pl*	anaskafika ergaleia	kazı aleti	أداة الحفر	adat elhafr
ανασκαφέας *m/f*	enaskafeas	arkeolojik kazı yapan	حفريين	hafrieen
υποδειγματικός	ipodeigmatikos	numunelik, örneklik	مثالي	misali
έκθεμα *n*	ekthema	sergilenen eser	قطعة متحفية	kitea mathafeia
έκθεση *f*	ekthesi	sergi, teşhir	معرض	maarad
πειραματική αρχαιολογία *f*	peiramatiki archaiologia	Deneysel Arkeoloji	علم الآثار التجريبي	elm elasar eltagribi
εξόρυξη *f*	exorixi	kazanma, tasfiye etme, yıkayıp ayırma	تنقيب	tankieb
εξαγωγή *f*	exagogi	ihracat	تصدير	tasdir
εξαγώγιμο προϊόν *n*	exagogimo proion	ihraç malı	البضائع المصدّرة	elbadaae elmusadara
εξάπλωση *f*	exaplosi	genişleme	توسيع	tawsiea
εκτεταμένος	ektetamenos	geniş alanlı	واسع المساحة	wasea elmisaha
εξωτερικός	exoterikos	dış, dışarı, dışarıda	خارج	chareg
εκλιπών	eklipon	nesli tükenmiş	منقرض	monkarid
πρόσοψη *f*	prosopsi	yapının ön cephesi	واجهة	wageha
παράγοντας *m*	paragontas	faktör	عامل / سبب	amel/ sabab
φαγεντιανή *f*	fagentiani	fayans	قيشاني	kischani
ασαφής, θολός	asafis, tholos	belirsiz	غير واضح	geer wadeh
παραχάραξη *f*, παραποίηση *f*	paracharaxi, parapoiisi	sahte, taklit	تزوير	tazwier
ακαλλιέργητη γη *f*	akalleirgiti gi	verimsiz toprak	أرض بور	ard bur
οικογένεια *f*	oikogeneia	aile	أسرة / عائلة	usra/ aila
αγρότης *m* , γεωργός *m*	agrotis, georgos	çiftçi	فلاح	falah
στερεωτικό μέσο *n*	stereotiko meso	fiksatör	مادة مُثبتة	mada musabeta
λίπος *n*	lipos	semiz, yağlı, verimli	دهن	dehn
σχέδιο *n* ευρήματος	schedio evrimatos	buluntu çizimi	رسم نتيجة البحث	rasm natigat elbahs

English	German	French	Italian	Spanish
felt	Filz *m*	feutre *m*	feltro *m*	fieltro *m*
felt-tip pen, marker	Filzstift *m*	stylo-feutre *m*	pennarello *m*	rotulador *m*
female, feminine	weiblich	femelle, féminin/-e	femminile	femenino/-a
fence, grid	Gitter *n*	grille *f*, quadrillage *m*	grata *f*, griglia *f*	barandilla *f*, reja *f*
fermentation	Fermentation *f*	fermentation *f*	fermentazione *f*	fermentación *f*
ferric/ iron oxide	Eisenoxid *n*	oxyde *m* de fer	ossido *m* ferroso	óxido *m* de hierro
fibre	Faser *f*	fibre *f*	fibra *f*	fibra *f*
field	Feld *n*	champ *m*	campo *m*	campo *m*
field, ground	Gelände *n*	terrain *m*	terreno *m*	terreno *m*
field mapping	Kartierung *f*	cartographie *f*, relevé *m*	mappatura *f*	mapeo *m*
fieldwork	Feldarbeit *f*	travail *m* des champs	lavoro *m* del campo	trabajo *m* de campo
fieldwork	Geländearbeit *f*	travail *m* de terrain	lavoro *m* del campo	trabaro *m* de campo
figurative	figurativ	figuratif/-ve	figurativo/-a	figurativo/-a
figurative	figürlich	figuré/-ée	figurato/-a	figurado/-a
figure	Figur *f*	figure *f*	figura *f*	figura *f*
figure	Gestalt *f*	figure *f*	figura *f*	forma *f*
figured capital	Figuralkapitell *n*	chapiteau *m* figuré	capitello *m* figurato	capitel *m* figurado
figurine, statuette	Figurine *f*, Statuette *f*	figurine *f*	figurina *f*, statuetta *f*	figurita *f*
filed	gefeilt	limé/-e	limato/-a	limado/-a
file, rasp	Feile *f*	lime *f*	lima *f*	lima *f*
filled brick-/stonework	Füllmauerwerk *n*	massif *m* de blocage, mur *m* de remplage	muratura *f* di riempimento	aparejo *m*
filling	Verfüllung *f*	remplissage *m*	imbottitura *f*	relleno *m*
filter	Filter *m*	filtre *m*	filtro *m*	filtro *m*
find	Fund *m*	trouvaille	reperto *m*, scoperta *f*	hallazgo *m*
find bag	Fundtüte *f*	sac *m*	busta *f*, sacchetto *m* per i reperti	bolsa *f* de plástico para hallazgos
find box	Fundkiste *f*	boîte *f*, caisse *f*	scatola *f* dei reperti	caja *f* de hallazgos
finding, result	Befund *m*	contexte *m*, état *m*, structure *f*	reperto *m*	evidencia *f*
find location	Fundort *m*	lieu *m* de trouvaille	luogo *m* di scoperta	lugar *m* del hallazgo, procedencia *f*
find processing	Fundaufarbeitung *f*	étude *f* du matériel	restauro *m* del reperto	estudio *m* análisis *m* de los hallazgos arqueológicos
finds(s) scatter	Fundstreuung *f*	disperion *f* des trouvailles	dispersione *f* di reperti	dispersión *f* de hallazgo
fine ceramic	Feinkeramik *f*	céramique *f* fine	ceramica *f* fina	cerámica *f* fina
fine gravel	Feinkies *m*	gravier *m* fin	ghiaia *f*	garbancillo *m*
fine tools	Feinwerkzeug *n*	outils *m pl* fins	strumenti *m pl* di precisione	herramienta *f* de precisión
fingerprint	Fingerabdruck *m*	empreinte *f* digitale	impronta *f* digitale	huella *f* dactilar
finishing coat	Feinputz *m*	enduit *m* fin	intonaco *m* fino	revoque *m* fino
finish, polish	Politur *f*	polissage *m*	lucidatura *f*, vernice *f*	pulimento *m*

Greek		Turkish	Arabic	
τσόχα *f*	tsocha	keçe	لبّاد	lubad
μαρκαδόρος *m*	markadoros	keçeli kalem	قلم فولومستر	kalam folomaster
θηλυκός	thilikos	kadın, kadınsı, dişi	أنثى, مؤنث	moanas
κάγκελο *n* , κάναβος *m*	kagkelo, kanavos	parmaklık	شبكة من الأسياخ	schabaka men elasjach
ζύμωση *f*	zimosi	fermantasyon	تخمر	tachamor
οξείδιο *n* του σιδήρου	oxeidio tou sidirou	demir oksit	أكسيد الحديد	uksid elhadid
ίνα *f*	ina	elyaf, lif	وبرة	wabrah
επιτόπιος	epitopios	arazi	حقل	hakl
έκταση *f*, πεδίο *n*	ektasi, pedio	arazi	موقع	mawkea
χαρτογράφηση *f*	chartografisi	harita yapma	رسم خرائط	rasm charaet
επιτόπια έρευνα *f*	epitopia erevna	arazi çalışması	عمل ميداني	amal meidani
εργασία *f* πεδίου	ergasia pediou	arazi çalışması	عمل ميدانى	amal maidani
εικονιστικός	eikonistikos	biçimsel, figüratif	شكلى	schakli
εικονιστικός	eikonistikos	tasviri, temsili	رمزي	ramzi
μορφή *f*	morfi	figür	تمثال	temsal
μορφή *f*	morfi	form	شكل	schakl
ζωομορφικό κιονόκρανο *n*	zoomorfiko kionokrano	figürlü sütun başlığı	تاج عامود على شكل تمثال	tag amud ala schakl temsal
ειδώλιο *n*	eidolio	figürin, heykelcik	تمثال صغير	temsal sagier
λιμαρισμένος	limarismenos	törpülenmiş	مبرود	mabruud
ράσπα *f*	raspa	törpü	مبرد	mebrad
γέμισμα *n* με αργολιθοδομή	gemisma me argolithodomi	kaba duvar örgüsü	حائط حشو	haet haschw
γέμισμα *n* , πλήρωση *f*	gemisma, plirosi	doldurma, dolgu	تعبئة	tabiaa
φίλτρο *n*	filtro	filtre	مصفاة	misfah
εύρημα *n*	evrima	buluntu	اكتشاف	ekteschaf
σάκκος *m* ευρημάτων	sakkos evrimaton	buluntu torbası	كيس المكتشفات	kies elmoktaschafat
κιβώτιο *n* ευρημάτων	kivotio efrimaton	buluntu kasası	صندوق المكتشفات	sunduk elmuktaschafat
αποτέλεσμα *n* , εύρημα *n*	apotelisma, efrima	buluntu	نتيجة البحث	natigat elbahs
θέση *f* εύρεσης	thesi efresis	buluntu yeri	مكان الإكتشاف	makan elektischaf
επεξεργασία *f* ευρήματος	epexergasia efrimatos	buluntu incelemesi	توثيق الإكتشافات	tawsik elektischafat
διασπορά *f* ευρημάτων	diaspora evrimaton	buluntu dağılımı	تناثر الإكتشاف	tanahsur elektischaf
καλή κεραμική *f*	keli keramiki	ince cidarlı seramik	فخار أملس	fuchar amls
(λεπτό) χαλίκι *n*	(lepto) chaliki	ince çakıl	حصى صغير	hasa sagier
λεπτό εργαλείο *n*	lepto ergaleio	ince alet	أداة يدوية دقيقة	adat yadwija dakika
δακτυλικό αποτύπωμα *n*	daktiliko apotipoma	parmak izi	بصمة الأصابع	basmet elasabea
τελείωμα *n*	teleioma	ince sıva	طبقة جص ناعمة	tabaket ges naema
στίλβωση *f*	stilvosi	cila, vernik	ملمع	molamea

English	German	French	Italian	Spanish
fire pit/ hearth	Herdgrube f	foyer m en cuvette	fossa f terragna	hogar m
fireplace, hearth	Feuerstelle f, Kamin m	cheminée f, foyer m	camino m	hogar m
fireproof	feuerfest	incombustible, ininflammable	refrattario/-a	ignífugo/-a
fire protection	Brandschutz m	protection f contre l'incendie	protezione f antincendio	protección f antiincendios
firewood	Brennholz n	bois m de chauffage/ à brûler m	legna f da ardere	leña f
firmness	Festigkeit f	fermeté f, solidité f	solidità f	dureza f, estabilidad f
firm, solid	fest	ferme, solide	fermo/-a	firme, sólido
fir tree	Tanne f	sapin m	abete m	abeto m
fish	Fisch m	poisson m	pesce m	pescado m
fishbone	Fischgräte f	arête f	lisca f	espina f
fishbone/ herringbone pattern	Fischgrätmuster n	motif m en arête de poisson	motivo m a spina di pesce	motivo m en espiga/ espina de pescado
fitting, fixture	Befestigung (tech.) f	attache f, fixation f	fissagio m	fijación f
fitting, mount	Fassung (Schmuck) f	enchâssure f, sertissure f, monture f	incastonatura f	montura f
fixation	Fixierung f	fixation f	fissaggio m	fijación m
fixative	Fixativ n	fixatif m	fissativo m	fijador m
flagstone, slab	Steinplatte f	dalle f	lastra f di pietra	placa f (de piedra)
flake	Abschlag m	éclat m	abbattimento m , taglio m	lasca f
flaking technique	Abschlagtechnik f	technique f d'éclatement	tecnica f di abbattimento	tecnología f lítica
flashlight	Taschenlampe f	torche f	lampada tascabile f, torcia f	linterna f
flat	flach	plat	piano/-a, piatto/-a	llano/-a, plano/-a
flat roof	Flachdach n	toit m plat/ en terrasse	tetto m piano	azotea f
flaw, mark	Fehlstelle f (Keramik)	défaut	imperfezione f	defectos pl
flax	Flachs n	lin m	lino m	lino m
flint	Feuerstein m , Flint m , Silex m	pierre à feu f, silex m	pietra f focaia, selce f	pedernal m , sílex m
flood	Flut f	marée f haute	alta f marea	marea f
flooding, inundation	Überschwemmung f	inondation f	inondazione f	inundación f
floor	Etage f, Stockwerk	étage m	piano m	planta f
floor jack	Wagenheber m	cric m	cric m	gato m
floor screed	Estrichboden m	sol m constitué d'une chape	battuto m pavimentale	suelo m de arganasa
floor slab	Bodenplatte f	dalle f	piastra f	placa f de base
fluvial	fluvial	fluviatile	fluviale	fluvial
foil, tarpaulin	Folie f (Plane)	feuille f	telone m	lona f para cubir
folding rule	Zollstock m	mètre m pliant	metro m pieghevole	metro m
fold, pleat	Falte f	pli m , ride f	piega f	pliegue m

Greek	Turkish	Arabic	
εσχάρα *f* esachra	ocak	حفرة فرن	hofret forn
εστία *f* estia	ocak, şömine	موقد	mawked
αντιπυρικός antipirikos	ateşe dayanıklı, yanmaz	مضادة للاشتعال	modada leleschtial
αντιπυρική προστασία *f* antipiriki prostasia	yangın koruma	الوقاية من الحريق	elwikeia men elharik
καυσόξυλα *n pl* kafsoxila	odun	حطب	hatab
σταθερότητα *f* statherotita	dayanıklılık	ثبات	sabat
στερεός, σταθερός stereos statheros	sıkı, sağlam	ثابت	sabet
έλατο *n* elato	çam	شجرة التنوب	schagaret eltanuub
ψάρι *n* psari	balık	سمك	samak
ψαροκόκαλο *n* psarokokalo	kılçık	شوك السمك	schok elsamk
σχήμα *n* ψαρο κόκαλου schima psaro kokalou	balık kılçığı motifi	صورة شوك السمك	surat schok elsamak
στερέωση *f* stereosi	sağlamlaştırma	تثبيت	tasbiet
εξάρτημα *n* , τόρμος *m* , υποδοχή *f* exartima, tormos, ipodochi	kaş, kenar süsü, söve pervazı	إطار	itar
στερέωση *f* stereosi	sabitleştirme	تثبيت	tasbiet
συγκολλητική ουσία *f* sigkollitiki ousia	sabitleştirici	مثبت	musabet
λίθινη πλάκα *f* lithini plaka	döşeme taşı, plakası	لوح حجرى	loh hagari
φολίδα *f* folida	yonga	إزالة	izala
τεχνική *f* κατασκ ευής φολίδων techniki kataskevis folidon	taş yontma tekniği	تكنولوجيا التنقيب	toknologja el tankieb
φακός *m* fakos	el feneri, el lambası	كشاف	kaschaaf
επίπεδος epipedos	alçak, düz	مسطح	musatah
επίπεδη στέγη *f* epipedi stegi	düz çatı	سقف مسطح	sakf musatah
έλλειψη *f* elleipsi	boşluk, hata	عيب	eeb
λινάρι *n* linari	keten	كتان	kitan
πυριτόλιθος *f* piritolithos	çakmak taşı, çört	حجر صوان	hagar sawan
πλημμύρα *f* plimmira	sel	فيضان	fajadan
πλημμύρα *f* plimmira	su baskını	فيضان	faidaan
δάπεδο *f* dapedo	kat	طابق	tabek
γρύλος *m* grilos	kriko	رافعة / كُريك	rafea/ koriek
επιστρωμένο δάπεδο *n* epistromeno dapedo	beton taban	أرضية ملساء	ardeja malsaa
πλάκα δαπέδου *f* plaka dapedou	taban plakası	مُسطح	musatah
ποτάμιος potamios	nehirle ilgili	نهري	nahri
φύλλο *n* fillo	folyo	مشمع	mischama
χάρακας *m* charakas	katlanır metre	متر للقياس قابلة للطي	metr lelkijas kabel leltei
πτυχή *f* ptichi	büküm, kıvrım	طية	tajah

English	German	French	Italian	Spanish
food, provisions	Lebensmittel *pl*	aliments *m pl*, denrées *f pl* alimentaires	alimenti *pl*	alimentos *m*, víveres *pl*
food remains	Nahrungsreste *pl*	restes *pl* de nourriture	residuo *m* di alimenti	residuos *m* alimenticos
forceps	Pinzette *f*	pincette *f*	pinzetta *m*	pinzas *pl*
forest	Wald *m*	bois *m*, forêt *m*	bosco *m*	bosque *m*, selva *f*
forge	Schmiedefeuer *n*	feu *m* de forge	fuoco *m* di fucina	fuego *m* de forja
form	Form *f*	forme *f*	forma *f*	forma *f*, molde *m*
formation	Formation *f*	formation *f*	formazione *f*	formación *f*
former/ profile gauge	Profil- (Scherben-)kamm *m*	conformateur *m*	profilometro *m*	perfilómetro *m* metálico
fortification	Befestigung (Bau) *f*	fortification *f*	fortificazione *f*	fortificación *f*
forum	Forum *n*	forum *m*	foro *m*	foro *m*
fossil	Fossil *n*, Petrefakt *n*	fossile *m*	fossile *m*	fósil *m*
fossil bed	fossiler Boden *m*	sol *m* fossile	suolo *m* fossile	suelo *m* fósil
fossilisation, petrification	Versteinerung *f*	pétrification *f*	fossilizzazione *f*, petrificazione *f*	petrificación *f*
foundations	Fundament *n*	fondations *f pl*, soubassement *m*	fondamento *m*	basamento *m*
fracture	Fraktur *f*	fracture *f*	frattura *f*	fractura *f*
fragile	fragil	fragile	fragile	frágil
fragility, frailty	Zerbrechlichkeit *f*	fragilité *f*	fragilità *f*	fragilidad *f*
fragment	Fragment *n*	fragment *m*	frammento *m*	fragmento *m*
fragment, piece	Bruchstück *n*	fragment *m*, morceau *m*	frammento *m*	fragmento *m*, ripio *m*
framework	Verschalung (techn.) *f*	coffrage *m*	rivestimento *m*	encofrado *m*
framework, scaffolding	Gerüst *n*	échafaudage *m*	impalcatura *f*	andamiaje *m*
Free-formed	freigeformt	non tournée	formato a mano libera	hecha sin moldes
friable, tender	mürbe	friable	friabile	degastado/-a
frigidarium	Frigidarium *n*	frigidarium *m*	frigidario *m*	frigidario *m*
front	Front *f*	front *m*	facciata *f*	frente *m*
frontal	frontal	frontal	frontale	frontal
frost zone	Frostzone *f*	zone *f* de gel	zona *f* di congelamento	zona *f* helada
fruit remains	Fruchtreste *f pl*	reste *m* de fruit	resti *m pl* di frutti	restos *m pl* de frutas
function	Funktion *f*	fonction *f*	funzione *f*	función *f*
functional	funktional	fonctionnel/-le	funzionale	funcional
funeral	Bestattung *f*	sépulture *f*	sepoltura *f*	sepultura *f*, tumba *f*
funeral feast	Totenmahl *n*	banquet *m* funéraire	banchetto *m* funebre	ágape *m* funerario
funeral pile, pyre	Scheiterhaufen *m*	bûcher *m*	rogo *m*	hoguera *f*

Greek		Turkish	Arabic	
τρόφιμα *n pl*	trofima	gıda maddesi	مواد غذائية	mawad gizaeia
υπολείμματα τροφής *n pl*	ipoleimmata trofis	yiyecek atıkları	فضلات الطعام	fadalat eltaam
λαβίδα *f*	lavida	cımbız	ملقط	malkat
δάσος *n*	dasos	orman	غابة	gaba
μεταλλευτική κάμινος *f*	metalleftiki kaminos	demirci ocağı	كُور الحدّاد	kuur elhadad
μορφή *f*	morfi	form	شكل	schakl
διαμόρφωση *f*	diamorfosi	oluşum	تشكيل	taschkiel
προφιλόμετρο *n*	profilometro	konformatör, çömlek parçası sırtı	أداة كالمشط بأسنان متحركة, مشط مكسور	adah kalmescht beasnan muthareka
οχύρωση *f*	ochirosi	kale	تدعيم	tadiem
φόρουμ *n*	foroum	forum	منتدى	montada
απολίθωμα *n*	apolithoma	fosil	تحجر	tahgor
απολιθωμένο έδαφος *n*	apolithomeno edafos	fosilli toprak	تربة متحجرة	torbah motahagerah
απολίθωση *f*	apolithosi	fosilleşme, taşlaşma	تحجر	tahador
θεμέλιο *n*	themelio	temel	أساس	asas
ρήξη *f*	rixi	kemik kırılması	تصدع	tasadua
εύθραυστος	efthrafstos	ince, narin	هش	hasch
εύθραυστο *n* , θραυστότητα *n*	efthrafsto, thrafstotita	kırılganlık	هشاشة	haschascha
απόσπασμα *n*	apospasma	parça	قطعة	ketaa
θραύσμα *n*	thrafsma	kırık parça, kırıntı	شظية	schesia
σανίδωση *f*	sanidosi	kaplama	تجليد بالألواح	taglied belalwaah
ικρίωμα *n* , σκαλω σιά *f*	ikrioma, skalosia	iskele	سقالة	saalah
ελεύθερα διαμορφωμένος	eleftera diamorfomenos	kalıpsız şekillendirilmiş	مُشكل بإبداع	moscakal beebdaa
εύθραυστος, ευαίσθητος, εύθριπτος	efthrafstos, evaisthitos, efthriptos	aşınmış, yıpranmış	لَيِّن	lajen
frigidarium *m*	frigidarium	soğukluk odası	حمام ماء بارد	hamam maa bared
μέτωπο *n*	metopo	cephe, ön taraf	جبهة	gabha
μετωπικός	metopikos	cepheden, önden	أمامي	amami
παγωμένη ζώνη *f*	pagomeni zoni	don bölgesi	منطقة صقيع	mantekat sakia
υπολείμματα *n pl* καρπών	ipoleimmata karpon	meyve artığı	بقايا الثمار	bakaja elsemar
λειτουργία *f*	leitourgia	işlev	مهمة / وظيفة	mohema/ wazifa
λειτουργικός	leitourgikos	fonksiyonel, işlevsel	وظيفي	wazifie
κηδεία *f* , ταφή *f*	kideia, tafi	defnetme, gömme	دفن	dafn
νεκρόδειπνο *n*	nekrodeipno	ölü yemeği	وليمة الجنازة	walimat elganaza
νεκρική πυρά *f*	nekriki pira	odun yığını (ölü yakmak için)	كومة المحرقة	komet elmahraka

English	German	French	Italian	Spanish
funeral type	Bestattungsform *f*	forme *f* de sépulture	tipo *m* di sepoltura	tipo *m* de sepultura
fur	Fell *n*	peau *f*, pelage *m*	pelo *m*	pellejo *m*, piel *m*
fur	Pelz *m*	fourrure *f*, peau *f*	pelliccia *f*	piel *f*
fusion	Versinterung *f*	concrétion *f*	sinterizzazione *f*	sinterización *f*
Gallic	gallisch	gaulois/-e	gallico/-a	gálico/-a
gap	Lücke *f*	espace *m*, vide *m*	lacuna *f*, vuoto *m*	brecha *f*, vacío *m*
gap, joint	Fuge *f*	joint *m*, jointure *f*	crepa *f*	junta *f*
gargoyle, waterspout	Wasserspeier *m*	gargouille *f*	doccione *m*	gárgola *f*
gas chromatography	Gaschromatographie *f*	chromatographie *f* en phase gazeuse	gascromatografia *f*	cromatografía de gases *f*
geison	Geison *n*	geison *m*	geison *m*	geison *m*
gemstone	Edelstein *m*	pierre *f* précieuse	gemma *f*	joya *f*, piedra *f* preciosa
gender	Geschlecht *n*	sexe *m*	sesso *m*	sexo *m*
genetic	Genetik *f*	génétique *f*	genetica *f*	genética *f*
geography	Geografie *f*	géographie *f*	geografia *f*	geografía *f*
geology	Geologie *f*	géologie *f*	geologia *f*	geología *f*
geomagnetic	geomagnetisch	géomagnétique	geomagnetico/-a	geomagnético/-a
geomagnetism	Geomagnetismus *m*	géomagnétisme *m*	geomagnetismo *m*	geomagnetismo *m*
geomorphology	Geomorphologie *f*	géomorphologie *f*	geomorfologia *f*	geomorfología *f*
geophysical	geophysikalisch	géophysique	geofisico/-a	geofisico
geophysical prospection	Geophysikalische Prospektion *f*	prospection *f* géophysique	prospezione *f* geofisica	prospección *f* geofísica
geophysics	Geophysik *f*	géophysique *f*	geofisica *f*	geofísica *f*
German	germanisch	germain/-e	germanico/-a	germanico/-a
glacial epoch/ stage, glaciation	Vergletscherung *f*	glaciation *f*	glaciazione *f*	glaciación *f*
glacier	Gletscher *m*	glacier *m*	ghiacciaio *m*	glaciar *m*
glass	Glas *n*	verre *m*	vetro *m*	vidrio *m*
glass corrosion	Glaskorrosion *f*	corrosion *f* du verre	corrosione *m* del vetro	Irisación *f*
glass painting	Glasmalerei *f*	peinture *f* sur verre, vitrail *m*	pittura *f* del vetro	pintura *f* sobre cristal
glazed tile	Kachel *f*	carreau *m* (de faïence)	piastrella *f* di maiolica	azulejo *m*
glazed/ varnished ware	glasierte Ware *f*	céramique *f* glaçurée	ceramica *f* invetriata	cerámica *f* esmaltada
glaze, varnish	Glasur *f*	glaçure *f*, vernis *m*	smaltatura *f*	esmalte *m*
glimmer	Glimmer *m*	mica *m*	mica *f*	mica *f*
gloss, polish	Glanz *m*	lustré *m*	lucentezza *f*	brillo *m*, lustre *m*
glue, paste	Leim *m*	colle *f*	colla *f*	cola *f*, pegamento *m*
glyptic	Siegelkunst *f*	glyptique *f*	arte *f* dei sigilli	arte *m* de sellos
glyptothek	Glyptothek *f*	glyptothèque *f*	gliptoteca *f*	gliptoteca *f*
god	Gott *m*	dieu *m*	dio *m*	dios *m*
goddess	Göttin *f*	déesse *f*	dea *f*	diosa *f*
gold	Gold *n*	or *m*	oro *m*	oro *m*
gold foil/ leaf	Blattgold *n*	or battu/ en feuilles *m*	lamina *m* d'oro	pan *m* de oro

Greek		Turkish	Arabic	
τύπος *m* ταφής	tipos tafis	gömme şekli	شكل الجنازة	schakl elganaza
γούνα *f*	gouna	kürk, post	فرو	faro
γούνα *f*	gouna	post, kürk	فرو	farw
σχηματισμός αποθέσεων αλάτων *m*	schimatismos apotheseon alaton	cüruflaşma	تكلس	takalos
γαλλικός	gallikos	Galya ile ilgili, Galyalı	غالي	galie
κενό *n*	keno	ara, boşluk	فجوة	fagwa
αρμός *m*	armos	aralık, birleşme yeri	شق	schak
υδρορρόη *f*	idrorroi	çörten	مرزاب	merzab
χρωματογραφία *f* αερίων	chromatografia aerion	gaz kromatografi	الفصل اللوني للغاز	elfasl ellanie lelgas
γείσο *n*	geiso	geison	إفريز من الأقواس	ifriez men elakwas
πολύτιμος λίθος *f*	politimos lithos	değerli taş, mücevher	حجر كريم	hagar karim
φύλο *n*	filo	cinsiyet	جنس	gens
γενετική *f*	genetiki	genetik	علم الوراثة	elm elwerasa
γεωγραφία *f*	geografia	coğrafya	جغرافيا	gografja
γεωλογία *f*	geologia	Jeoloji	جيولوجيا	gejologja
γεωμαγνητικός	geomagnitikos	jeomanyetik	مغناطيسي أرضى	magnatisi ardi
γεωμαγνητισμός *m*	geomagnitismos	Jeomanyetizm	المغنطيسية الأرضية	elmagnatisija elardija
γεωμορφολογία *f*	geomorfologia	Jeomorfoloji	علم أشكال الأرض	elm aschkal elard
γεωφυσικός	geofisikos	jeofiziksel	فيزيائي أرضى	fizjaie ardi
γεωφυσική διασκόπηση *f*	geofisiki diaskopisi	jeofiziksel prospeksiyon	مسح فيزيائى أرضى	mash fizjaie ardi
γεωφυσική *f*	geofisiki	Jeofizik	الفيزياء الأرضية	elfisija elardija
γερμανικός	germanikos	cermen, germen	جرماني	germanie
παγετώνια φάση *f*	pagetonia fasi	buz kesme, buzullaşma	تجلد	tagalod
παγετώνας *m*	pagetonas	buzul, buzullar	مجرى جليدي	magra galidi
γυαλί *n*	giali	cam	زجاج	zogag
διάβρωση γυαλιού *f*	diavrosi gialiou	cam korozyonu	النحت الزجاجى	elnaht elzogagi
υαλογραφία *f*	ialografia	cam resim sanatı	رسم على الزجاج	rasm ala elzogag
εφυαλωμένη κεραμίδα *f*	efialomeni keramida	çini, fayans	بلاط	balat
εφυαλωμένη κεραμική *f*	efialomeni keramiki	cilalı ürün	سلعة بطلاء زجاجى	selaa betilaa zogagi
εφυάλωση *f*	efialosi	cila, sır, vernik	طلاء زجاجى	tilaa zogagi
μαρμαρυγία *f*	marmarigia	mika	مادة مُلمعة	madah molameah
στίλβη *f*	stilvi	parlaklık, pırıltı	لمعان	lamaahn
κόλλα *f*	kolla	tutkal, yapışkan	غراء	giraa
σιγιλλογραφία *f*	sigillografia	mühür sanatı	فن الأختام	fan elachtam
γλυπτοθήκη *f*	gliptothiki	Glyptothek	مجموعة أحجار مقطعة	magmuet ahgar mokataa
θεός *m*	theos	tanrı	إله	ilah
θεά *f*	thea	ilahe, tanrıça	آلهة	aleha
χρυσός *m*	chrisos	altın	ذهب	zahab
φύλλο *n* χρυσ ού	fillo chrisou	yaprak altın	طبقة ذهب رقيقة	tabakat zahab rakika

English	German	French	Italian	Spanish
gradation	Abstufung *f*	gradation *f*, nuance *f*	graduazione *f*	gradación *f*
graded, stepped	gestuft	en escalier	a gradini	graduado/-a
graffito	Graffito *n*	graffiti *m*	graffito *m*	grafito *m*
grained, granular	körnig	granuleux (-euse)	granulare	granulado/-a
grain, texture	Maserung *f*	nervures du bois *f pl*	marezzatura *f*, venatura	vetas *pl*
granary, magazine	Speicher *m*	grenier *m*, magasin *m pl*, silo *m*	deposito *m*, magazzino *m*	almacén *m*, granero *m*
granite	Granit *n*	granit *m*	granito *m*	granito *m*
grape sugar	Traubenzucker *m*	dextrose *m*	glucosio *m*	glucosa *f*
graphic	grafisch	graphique	grafico/-a	gráfico/-a
graphite	Graphit *n*	graphite *m*	grafite *f*	grafito *m*
grass	Gras *n*	herbe *f*	erba *f*	hierba *f*
grater, scraper	Schaber *m*	grattoir *m*	raschietto *m*	raspador *m*
grattoir, mark, scratch	Kratzer *m*	grattoir *m*	graffio *m*, raschiatoio *m*	arañazo *m*
grave chamber	Grabkammer *f*	chambre *f* funéraire	camera *f* sepolcrale	cámara *f* sepulcral
grave good	Grabbeigabe *f*	offrande *f* funéraire	oggetto *m* di corredo	ajuar *m* funerario
gravel	Kies *m*	gravier *m*	ghiaia *f*	casquijo *m*, grava *f*
gravel sand	Kiessand *m*	gravier *m*	ghiaia *f*	gravilla *f*
gravesite, sepulchre	Grabstätte *f*	(lieu de) sépulture *f*	sepolcro *m*	lugar *m* funerario
grave stele	Grabstele *f*	stèle *f* funéraire	stele *f* funeraria	estela *f*
gravestone	Grabstein *m*	pierre *f* tombale	pietra *f* tombale	lápida *f*
grave, tomb	Grab *n*	tombe *f*, tombeau *m*	tomba *f*, sepultura *f*	fosa *f*, sepulcro *m*, tumba *f*
greasy, smeary	schmierig	graisseux/-euse	grasso/-a, unto/-a	grasoso/-a
Greco-Roman	griechisch-römisch	gréco-romain/-e	greco-romano/-a	grecorromano/-a
Greek	griechisch	grec/-que	greco/-a	griego/-a
grid system	Gittersystem *n*	système *m* de grille	sistema *f* di grata	sistéma *f* de barandilla
grime, soot	Ruß *m/n*	suie *f*	fuliggine *f*, nerofumo *m*	hollín *m*
grinding	Schliff *m*	polissage *m*	affilatura *f*, molatura *f*	filo *m*, talla *f*
grindstone	Schleifstein *m*	pierre *f* à aiguiser/ affûter, polissoir *m*	cote *f*, mola *f*	piedra *f* de afilar
grindstone, whetstone	Wetzstein *m*	pierre *f* à affûter/ aiguiser *f*	pietra *f* per affilare	piedra *f* de afilar/ amolar *f*
gripper	Zange *f*	tenailles *pl*	tenaglie *f*	tenazas *pl*
groove	Rille *f*	cannelure *f*, rainure *f*	scanalatura *f*	ranura *f*
groove, trench	Furche *f*	sillon *m*	scanalatura *f*, solco *m*	ranura *f*, surco *m*
ground-based radar	Georadar *m*	géoradar *m*	georadar *m*	georradar
ground plan, outline	Grundriss *m*	plan *m*	pianta *f*	plano *m*, planta *f*
ground, powdered	gemahlen	broyé/-e, moulu/-e	macinato/-a	molido/-a
ground, terrain	Terrain *n*	terrain *m*	terreno *m*	terreno *m*

Greek		Turkish	Arabic	
διαβάθμιση *f*	diavathmisi	basamak, kademe	تدرج	tadarog
κλιμακωτός	klimakotos	kademeli	متدرج	motadareg
γκράφιτι *n pl*	gkrafiti	duvar yazısı	نقش تذكارى	naksch tezkarie
σπυρωτός	spirotos	tanecikli	على شكل حبيبات	ala schakl hubeibat
υφή *f*	ifi	dalgalı olma, damarlı	شكل تموج	schakl tamawog
αποθήκη *f*	apothiki	ambar, depo, hafıza	مخزن	machzan
γρανίτης *m*	granitis	granit	حجر الجرانيت	hagar elgraniet
σταφυλοσάκχαρο *n*	stafilosakcharo	glikoz, nişasta şekeri	سكر العنب	sukar elenab
γραφικός, σχεδιαγραμματικός	grafikos schediagrammatikos	çizgesel, grafiksel	مرسوم بالتصوير	marsum beltaswir
γραφίτης *m*	grafitis	grafit	كربون الرصاصى	karbon rosasi
χόρτο *n*	chorto	çim, çimen	عشب	uschb
ξύστρα *f*	xistra	kazıma bıçağı, kazıyıcı, raspa	مكشطة	mekschata
χάραγμα *n*	charagma	çizik	خدش	chadsch
ταφικός θάλαμος *m*	tafikos thalamos	mezar odası	حجرة الدفن	hograt eldafn
κτέρισμα *n*	kterisma	gömü hediyesi	محتوى المقبرة	muhtawa elmakbara
χαλίκι *n*	chaliki	çakıl	حصى	hasa
αμμοχάλικο *n*	ammochaliko	çakıllı kum	خليط من الرمل والحصى	chaliet men elraml wi elhasa
χώρος *m* ταφής	choros tafis	mezar, mezarlık	مدفن	madfan
επιτύμβια στήλη *f*	epitimvia stili	mezar steli	لوحة جنائزية	loha ganaizeia
επιτύμβιος λίθος *m* , ταφόπετρα *f*	epitimvios lithos, tafopetra	mezar taşı	شاهد القبر	schahed elkabr
τάφος *m*	tafos	kabir, mezar, türbe	مقبرة	makbara
λιπαρός	liparos	balçıklı, yağlı	مدهن	medahan
ελληνορωμαϊκός	ellinoromaikos	Grek-Roma	يوناني روماني	yunani rumani
ελληνικός	ellinikos	Yunanlı	يوناني	yunanie
σύστημα κανάβου *n*	sistima kanavou	kafes sistemi	منظومة من الأسياخ	manzoma men elasjach
αιθάλη *f*	aithali	is	سناج	senag
άλεση *f*	alesi	cilalandırma, perdahlatma	تنعيم	taniem
(λίθινος) τριπτήρας *m*	(lithinos) triptiras	bileğitaşı, bileme taşı	حجر للتنعيم	hagar leltaniem
ακονόπετρα *f*	akonopetra	bileme taşı	حجر للسن	hagar lelsan
πένσα *f*	pensa	kerpeten, maşa, pense	كماشة	kamascha
αύλακα *f* , ράβδωση *f*	aflaka, ravdosi	olu, oyuk, yiv	أخدود	uchdud
αύλακα *f* , ράβδωση *f*	avlaka, ravdosi	yiv	أخدود	uchdud
υπεδάφειο ραντάρ *n*	ipedafeio rantar	jeoradar	رادار الاختراق الأرضي	radar elechtirak elardi
σκαρίφημα *n*	skarifima	ana hat	تصميم	tasmiem
κονιορτοποιημένος	koniortopoiimenos	öğütülmüş	مطحون	mathun
έδαφος *n*	edafos	arazi, toprak	تضاريس	tadaries

64

English	German	French	Italian	Spanish
groundwater	Grundwasser n	nappe f phréatique	acqua freatica f	agua subterránea f
grub, larva	Larve f	larve f	larva f	larva f
guideline	Richtlinie f	directives f pl	direttiva f	directivas f pl
gymnasium	Gymnasium n	gymnase m	ginnasio m	gimnasio m
gypsum	Gips m	gypse m , plâtre m	gesso m	emplaste m , yeso m
gypsum mortar, plaster	Gipsmörtel m	enduit m de plâtre, gâchis m	stucco m	enlucido m
hair	Haar n	cheveu m	capello m	cabello m , pelo m
half-life	Halbwertzeit f	demi-vie f	tempo m di dimezzamento	período m de semidesintegración
hall	Halle f , Saal m	salle f	sala f	sala f
hallmark	Punzierung f	estampage m	punzonatura f	cicelado m, repujado m
hammer	Hammer m	marteau m	maglio m, martello m	martillo m
hammered	gehämmert	bouchardé/-eé, martelé/-e	martellato/-a	martilleado/-a
hammered/ worked copper	gehämmertes Kupfer n	cuivre m martelé	rame m martellato	cobre m martilleado
handicrafts	Kleinkunst f	art m mobilier	arte itinerante m/f	arte mueble m
handle, knob	Griff m	manche m, poignée f	manico m , pomo m	asa f
handle, knob	Henkel m	anse f	ansa f	asa f
handmade	handgemacht	fait à la main	fatto al mano	hecho a mano
Hand-shaped/ formed	handgeformt	modelé à la main	formato a mano	moldeado a mano
harbour, port	Hafen m	port m	porto m	puerto m
hardness	Härte f (Festigkeit f)	dureté f, solidité f	durezza f	dureza f
hardwood	Hartholz n	bois m dur	legno m duro	madera f dura
hart	hart	dur	duro/-a	duro/-a
hatching	Schraffur f	hachure f	tratteggio m	rayado m
headdress	Kopfbedeckung f	couvre-chef m	copricapo m	sombrero m
head of excavation	Grabungsleitung f	direction f des fouilles	direzione f di scavo	dirección f de excavación
heap/ pile of stones	Steinhaufen, -hügel m	cairn m	cumolo m di pietra	hormazo m
heat treatment	Hitzebehandlung f	traitement m thermique	trattamento m termico	tratamiento m de calor
hellenism	Hellenismus m	hellénisme m, période f hellénistique	ellenismo m	helenismo m
Hellenistic	hellenistisch	hellénistique	ellenistico/-a	helenístico/-a
helmet	Helm m	casque m	elmo m	casco m
hematite	Hämatit n	hématite f	ematite f	hematita f
hemp	Hanf n	chanvre m	canapa f	cáñamo m
herb	Kraut n	herbe f	erba f	hierba f
heritage	Erbe n	héritage m	eredità f	patrimonio m
heroon	Heroon n	hérôon m	heroon m	heroo, heróon m
heterogeneous	heterogen	hétérogène	eterogeneo/-a	heterogéneo/-a
hieroglyph	Hieroglyphe f	hiéroglyphe m	geroglifico m	jeroglífico m

Greek		Turkish	Arabic	
υπόγεια ύδατα *n pl*	ipogeia idata	kaynak suyu	مياة جوفية	mijah gawfija
κάμπια *f*	kabia	larva	يرقة	yaraka
κατευθυντήρια γραμμή *f*	katefthintiria grammi	esas, yönerge, yönetmelik	توجيهات	tawgihat
γυμνάσιο *n*	gimnasio	gymnasion	مدرسة ثانوية	madrasa sanawija
γύψος *m*	gipsos	alçı	جبس	gebs
γυψοκονίαμα *n*	gipsokoniama	alçı harcı, sahte memer	مونة جبس	monat gebs
μαλλιά *n pl* , τρίχα *f*	mallia, tricha	saç	شعر	schar
χρόνος ημιζωής *m*	chronos imizois	radyoaktif periyod, yarılanma süresi	مُدَة نصف العُمر	modet nesf elumr
αίθουσα *f*	aithousa	hol, salon	قاعة	kaah
εμπίεση *f*, εμπίεστη τεχνική *f*	ebiesi, ebiesti techniki	değerli madene basılmıs ayar damgası	دمغ	damg
σφυρί *n*	sfiri	çekiç	شاكوش	schakusch
σφυρήλατος	sfirilatos	dövülmüş	مطروق	matruk
σφυρήλατος χαλκός *m*	sfirilatos chalkos	dövülmüş bakır	نحاس مطروق	ṇahas matruk
μικροτεχνία *f*	mikrotechnia	kabare	فن المحمول	fan mahmul
λαβή *f*	lavi	kulp, sap	مقبض	makbad
λαβή *f*	lavi	kulp, sap, tutacak	مقبض	makbad
χειροποίητος	cheiropoiitos	el işi, elle yapılmış	مصنوعة يدوياً	masnuah jadawijan
χειρόπλαστος	cheiroplastos	elle şekillendirilmiş	مشكلة يدوياً	muschkala jadawijan
λιμάνι *n*	limani	liman	ميناء	minaa
σκληρότητα *f*	sklirotita	çetinlik, dayanıklılık, tav	صلابة	salaba
σκληρό ξύλο *n*	skliro xilo	sert ağaç	خشب صلب	chaschab salb
σκληρός	skliros	dayanıklı, sert	صلب / جامد	salb/ gamed
επώαση *f*	epoasi	tarama	خطوط متوازية	chotut motawazija
κάλυμμα κεφαλής *n*	kalimma kefalis	başlık , baş örtüsü	غطاء الرأس	gitaa elraas
διεύθυνση *f* ανασκαφής	diefthinsi anaskafis	kazı yönetimi	إدارة الحفريات	idaret elhafrijat
λιθοσωρός *m*	lithosoros	taş yığını	كوم من الأحجار	koom men elahgar
θερμική επεξεργασία *f*	thermiki epexergasia	ısıl işlem	معالجة حرارية	mualaga hararija
Ελληνισμός *m* , Ελληνιστική Περίοδος *f*	Ellinismos, Ellinistiki Periodos	Hellenizm	هلينية	hilinija
ελληνιστικός	ellinistikos	hellenistik	هليني	hilinie
κράνος *n* , περικεφαλαία *f*	kranos, perikefalia	kask, miğfer	خوذة	choza
αιματίτης *m*	aimatitis	hematit, kantaşı	حجر الهيماتيت	hagar elhimateit
κάνναβη *f*	kannavi	kendir, kenevir	قنب	kinab
βότανο *n*	votano	bitki, ot	نبات عشبى	nabat uschbi
κληρονομιά *f*	klironomia	miras	تراث	toras
ηρώο *n*	iroo	heroon	مقبرة ومعبد لبطل	makbara we maabad lebatal
ετερογενής	eterogenis	ayrışık, heterojen	غير متجانس	geer motaganes
ιερογλυφικό *n*	ieroglifiko	hiyeroglif	هيروغليفية	hieroglifija

English	German	French	Italian	Spanish
hieroglyphic	hieroglyphisch	hiéroglyphique	geroglifico/-a	jeroglífico/-a
high quality	hochwertig	de grande valeur	pregiato/-a	de alta calidad
high relief	Hochrelief *n*	haut-relief *m* , ronde-bosse *f*	altorelievo *m*	alto relieve *m*
hill	Hügel *m*	colline *f*	collina *f*	cerro *m* , colina *f*
hill-top settlement	Höhensiedlung *f*	habitat *m* de hauteur	insediamento *m* su altura	asentamiento *m* de altura
hilltop settlement	Siedlungshügel *m*	tell *m*	collina *f* di insediamento	colina *f* de ocupación humana, tell *f*
hinge	Scharnier *n*	charnière *f*	cerniera *f*	bisagra *f*
hinterland	Hinterland *n*	arrière-pays *m*	retroterra *f*	hinterland *m*
hint, trace	Spur *f*	piste *f*, trace *f*	traccia *f*	huella *f*
historic	historisch	historique	storico/-a	histórico
historic monument	Baudenkmal *n*	monument *m*	monumento *m* architettonico	monumento *m*
historic preservation agency	Denkmalamt/ Landesamt *n*	Service *m* des monuments historiques	soprintendenza *f* dei beni culturali	servicio *m* de patrimonio histórico
Hittite	hethitisch	hittite	ittita	hitita
Hittitology	Hethitologie *f*	hittitologie *f*	Ittitologia *f*	estudio *m* de las hititas
hoard	Depotfund *m* , Hort *m*	trésor *m*	tesoro *m*	tesoro *m*
hoard	Hortfund *m*	dépôt *m*	ripostiglio *m*	hallazgo *m* de un tesorillo
hock	Hacke *f*	binette *f*, houe *f*	zappa *f*	azada *f*
hole	Loch *n*	trou *m*	buco *m*	agujero *m*
holocene	Holozän *n*	Holocène	olocene *m*	holoceno *m*
homogeneous	homogen	homogène	omogeneo/-a	homogéneo/-a
hoofed animal, ungulate	Huftier *n*	ongulé *m*	ungulato *m*	ungulado *m*
horizontal	horizontal, waagerecht	horizontal/-e	orizzontale	horizontal
horn	Horn *n*	corne *f*	corno *m*	cuerno *m*
horticulture	Gartenbau *m*	horticulture *f*	orticultura *f*	horticultura *f*
hot	heiß	(très) chaud (-e)	caldo/-a	caliente
human being	Mensch *m*	être humain *m*	essere umano *m*, uomo	hombre *m*
humanoid	menschenähnlich	humanoïde	antropomorfo/-a	antropomorfo/-a
human remains	Menschenreste *pl*	restes humains *m pl*	ossa umane *pl*	restos *m pl* humanos
humide	feucht	humide	umido/-a	húmedo/-a
humidity	Feuchtigkeit *f*	humidité *f*	umidità *f*	humedad *f*
humus, top soil	Humus *m*	humus *m*	humus *m*	humus *m*
hunt	Jagd *f*	chasse *f*	caccia *f*	caza *f*
hunter-gatherer	Jäger und Sammler *m pl*	chasseur-cueilleur *m*	cacciatori e raccoglitori	cazadores-recolectores *pl m*
hut	Hütte *f*	cabane *f*	capanna *f*	cabaña *f*
hypocaust	Hypokaustum *n*	hypocauste *m*	ipocausto *m*	hipocausto *m*

Greek		Turkish	Arabic	
ιερογλυφικός	ieroglifikos	hiyeroglif	هيروغليفي	hieroglifie
υψηλής αξίας	ipsilis axias	değerli, kaliteli	عالي الجودة	alie elgawda
έκτυπο/ υψηλό ανάγλυφο n	ektipo/ipsilo anaglifo	yüksek kabartma	نحت بارز	naht barez
λόφος m	lofos	tepe, toprak yığını	تل	tal
οικισμός σε ύψωμα m	oikismos se ipsoma	yüksek yerleşim yeri	مستوطنة مرتفعة	mostawtana mortafia
λόφος οικισμού m , τούμπα f	lofos oikismou, touba	höyük	تلة المستوطنة	tal elmostawtana
μεντεσές m	menteses	menteşe	مفصلة	mefasala
ενδοχώρα f	endochora	iç bölge	مناطقة نائية	manteka naija
ίχνος n	ichnos	belirti, iz	أثر	asar
ιστορικός	istorikos	tarihi, tarihsel	تاريخي	tarichie
αρχιτεκτονικό/ ιστορικό μνημείο n	architektoniko/ istoriko mnimeio	mimari anıt	نصب تذكاري	nusb tezkari
Εψρεία f , Υπηρεσία f Μνημείων □	Epsreia, Ipiresia Mnimeion	Anıtlar Yüksek Kurulu	مكتب التراث	maktab elturas
χαττικός	chattikos	hitit	حيثيّ	heisie
Χατταιολογία f	Chattaiologia	Hititoloji	علم الحثيين	elm elhajsijien
θησαυρός m	thisavros	define, gömü	وديعة, كنز	kinz, wadia
θησαυρός m	thisavros	toplu buluntu	إكتشاف كنز	ikteschaf kanz
σκαλιστήρι n	skalistiri	çapa, kazma	فأس	faas hagari kalchabur
τρύπα f , οπή f	tripa, opi	delik, oyuk, yarık	ثقب	sukb
ολόκαινο n	olokaino	holosen	عصر الهولوسين	asr elholosien
ομοιογενής	omoiogenis	homojen	متجانس	mutaganes
οπληφόρο n	opliforo	toynaklı	حيوان ذو حوافر	hajwan zo hawafer
οριζόντιος	orizontios	soldan sağa, yatay	أفقي	ufokie
κέρατο n , κέρας n	kerato, keras	boynuz	قرن	karn
κηπουρική f , κηποκαλλιέργεια f	kipouriki, kipokalliergeia	bahçecilik, bahçıvanlık	زراعةالحدائق	ziraet elhadaek
ζεστός, θερμός	zestos, thermos	kızgın, sıcak, yakıcı	ساخن	sachen
άνθρωπος m	anthropos	birey, fert, insan	إنسان	ensan
ανθρωποειδής	anthropoeidis	insana benzeyen	شبيه بالإنسان	schabieh belensan
ανθρώπινα λείψανα n pl	anthropina leipsana	insan kalıntısı	رفات بشرية	rufat bascharija
υγρός	igros	nemli	مبلل	mobalal
υγρασία f	igrasia	nem	رطوبة	rotuba
χούμος m , φυλλόχωμα n	choumos, fillochoma	humus	دبال / تربة الخصبة	dobal/ torbah chesbah
κυνήγι n	kinigi	av	صيد	seed
τροφοσυλλέκτης-κυνηγός m	trofosillektis-kinigos	avcı-toplayıcı toplum	صياد وجامع	sajad we gamea
καλύβα f	kaliva	kulübe	كوخ	kuch
υπόκαυστο n	ipokafto	hipokaust	نظام تدفئة	nizam tadfiaa

68

English	German	French	Italian	Spanish
hypogaeum	Hypogäum *n*	hypogée *m*	ipogeo *m*	hipogeo *m*
Iberian	iberisch	ibère	iberico/-a	ibérico/-a
ice age	Eiszeit *f*, Eiszeitalter *n*	période *f* glaciaire	era *f* glaciale	época *f*/ período *m* g lacial
icon	Ikone *f*	icône *f*	icona *f*	icono *m*
iconography	Ikonografie *f*	iconographie *f*	iconografia *f*	iconografia *f*
icy	vereist	gelé/-e	congelato/-a	congelado/-a
identification	Identifikation *f*	identification *f*	identificazione *f*	identificación *f*
ideogram/-graph	Ideogramm *n*	idéogramme *m*	ideogramma *m*	ideograma *m*
idol	Götterbild *n*	idole *f*	idolo *m*	ídolo *m*
illicit excavation/ digging	Raubgrabung *f*	fouilles *f pl* clandestines	scavo clandestino *m*	excavación *f* de expolio, saqueo *f* arqueológico
illumination	Beleuchtung *f*	illumination *f*	illuminazione *f*	alumbrado *m*, iluminación *f*
illustration, image	Abbildung *f*	figure *f*, image *m*	figura, illustrazione *f*	figura *f*, ilustración *f*
illustrator	Zeichner *m*	dessinateur *m*	disegnatore *m*	debujante *m/f*
image	Bild *n* / Bildnis *n*	image *m*	immagine *f*	imagen *m*, retrato *m*
impasto	Impasto *n* (Keramik)	céramique *f* d'impasto	impasto *m*	impasto *m*
impenetrable	undurchlässig	imperméable	impermeabile	impermeable
imperial	kaiserzeitlich	de l'époque impériale, impérial/-e	imperiale	imperial
impluvium	Impluvium *n*	impluvium *m*	impluvio *m*	impluvium *m*
import	Import *m*	importation *f*	importazione *f*	importación *f*
imported ware	Importware *f*	article *m* d'importation	ceramica *f* di importazione	producto *m* importado
impression, mark, stamp	Eindruck *m*	empreinte *f*, impression *f*	impressione *f*	impresión *f*, impronta *f*
imprint	Abdruck *m*	empreinte *f*	impronta *f*	impresión *f*, impronta *f*
incense burner	Räucherständer *m*	brûle-parfum *m*	portaincenso *m*	incensario *m*, timiaterio *m*
incipient, incomplete	unvollendet	inachevé/-ee	incompleto/-a	incompleto/-a
incline, slope	Gefälle *n*	déclivité *f*, pente *f*	discesa *f*	declive *m*
inclusion	Einschluss *m*	pièce *f* incluse	inclusione *f*	inclusión *f*
incrustation	Inkrustation *f*	décor *m* incrusté, incrustation *f*	incrostazione *f*	incrustación *f*
incrustation	Verkrustung *f*	encroûtement *m*	incrostazione *f*	incrustación *f*
index fossil	Leitfossil *n*	fossile *m* directeur	fossile guida *m*	fósiles característicos *pl*
indication	Angabe *f*	indication *f*	indicazione *f*	indicación *f*
indication	Hinweis *m*	indication *f*	indicazione *f*	indicio *m*

Greek		Turkish	Arabic	
υπόγειο *n*	ipogeio	hypogeum	مقبرة تحت الأرض	makbara taht elard
ιβηρικός	ivirikos	İberlerle ilgili, İberyalı	ايبيري	ibierie
Εποχή *f* των Παγετώνων, Παγετώνια Περίοδος *f*	Epochi ton Pagetonon, Pagetonia Periodos	Buzul Çağı	العصر الجليدي	elasr elgalidi
εικόνα *f*	eikona	ikon, simge	أيقونة	aikona
εικονογραφία *f*	eikonografia	ikonografi, resmetme	وصف الشكل والمضمون	wasf elschakl we elmadmun
παγωμένος	pagomenos	buzla örtülü, buzlu	مُجمّد	mogamad
ταύτιση *f*	taftisi	tanıma, tespit, teşhis	تحديد الهوية	tahdied elhawija
ιδεόγραμμα *n*	ideogramma	ideogram	علامة تصويرية توحى معناها	alama taswirija tuhi manaha
είδωλο *n* , εικόνα *f* θεότητας	eidolo, eikona theotitas	put	صنم	sanam
λαθρανασκαφή *f*	lathranaskafi	kaçak kazı	حفريات غير قانونية	hafreijat geer kanuneja
φωτισμός *m*	fotismos	aydınlatma	إضاءة	idaa
εικόνα *f*	eikona	resim	منظر	manzar
σκεδιαστής *m*	skediastis	çizimci	رسّام	rasaam
εικόνα *f*	eikona	portre, resim, tasvir	صورة	sura
impasto *n*	impasto	koyu renk boya	تقنية رسم بإستخدام ألوان كثيفة	taknijet rasm bestechdam alwan kasiefa
αδιαπέραστος	adiaperastos	hava ve su geçirmez	غير منفذ	geer monfez
αυτοκρατορικών χρόνων	aftokratorikon chronon	Roma İmparatorluk Dönemi	من العهد القيصرى	men elahd elkaisarie
impluvium *n*	impluvium	impluvium	حوض لتخزين مياه الأمطار	hog letachzien mijah elamtar
εισαγωγή *f*	eisagogi	dış alım, ithal	استيراد	istirad
επείσακτη κεραμική *f*	epeisakti keramiki	ithal malı	سلعة مستوردة	sela mostawrada
εντύπωση *f*, σφράγισμα *n* , εμπίεστο κόσμημα *n*	entiposi, sfragisma, ebiesto kosmima	etki, görünüm, izlenim	انطباع	intebaa
αποτύπωμα *n*	apotipoma	baskı, kopya	أثر	asar
θυμιατήρι *n*	thimiatiri	tütsü kabı	مبخرة	mebchara
ημιτελής	imitelis	tamamlanmamış	غير مكتمل	geer moktamel
κλίση *f*	klisi	eğim, meyil	إنحدار	inhedar
πρόσμιξη *f*	prosmixi	dahil olma	إدراج	edrag
επένδυση *f*	ependisi	kaplama	زخرفة الجدار بالأحجار	zachrafet elgidar belahgar
σχηματισμός φλοιού *m*	schimatismos floiou	kabuklanma	تقشّر	takaschor
ενδεικτικό απολίθωμα *n*	entheiktiko apolithoma	kılavuz fosil	مؤشر تحجر	moascher tahagor
δεδομένο *n*	dedomeno	beyan, ifade	ذكر	zekr
ένδειξη *f*	endeixi	bildirim, ipucu	إشارة	ischara

English	German	French	Italian	Spanish
indigenous, native	eingeboren	indigène, natif/-ve	indigeno/-a, nativ/-a	indígena, nativo/-a
industrial	industriell	industriel/-le	industriale	industrial
industry	Industrie *f*	industrie *f*	industria *f*	industria *f*
industry, trade	Gewerbe *n*	industrie *f,* métier *m*	industria *f*	comercio *m* , industria *f*
influence	Einfluss *m*	influence *f*	influenza *f*	influencia *f*, influjo *m*
information	Information *f*	information *f*	informazione *f*	información *f*
information content	Informationsgehalt *m*	contenu *m* informatif	quantità *f* di informazione	contenido *m* de información
infrared	Infrarot *n*	infrarouge	infrarosso *m*	infrarrojo *m*
in front	vorne	à l'avant	avanti, devanti	adelante, (por) delante
ingot	Barren *m*	lingot *m*	lingotto *m*	barra *f* , lingote *f*
inlaid work, marquetry	Einlegearbeit *f*	incrustation *f,* marqueterie *f*	intarsio *m*	incrustación *f,* marquetería *f*
inlay	Einlage *f*	chose incluse *f*	inserezione *f*	taracea *f*
inlay	einlegen	incruster, marqueter	intarsiare	incrustar
inner	innen	intérieur/-e	all'interno, dentro	dentro, en el interior
inorganic	anorganisch	anorganique	anorganico/-a	inorgánico/-a
inscription	Inschrift *f*	inscription *f*	epigrafe *f*, iscrizione *f*	inscripción *f*
insect	Insekt *n*	insecte *m*	insetto *m*	insecto *m*
instrument, tool	Werkzeug *n*	outil *m*	arnesi *m* , attrezzo *m*	herramienta *f,* instrumento *m*
insula	Insula *f*	insula *f*	insula *f*	insula *f*
intercolumniation	Interkolumnium *n*	entrecolonnement *m*	intercolunnio *m*	intercolumnio *m*
interlayer	Zwischenschicht *f*	couche *f* intermédiaire	strato *m* intermedio	capa *f* intermedia
interpretation	Interpretation *f*	interprétation *f*	interpretazione *f*	interpretación *f*
intransparent, obscure	undurchsichtig	louche, opaque	opaco/-a	opaco/-a
intra-urban	innerstädtisch	local/-e	intra-urbano/-a	urbano/-a
inventory	Bestand *m* (Inventar *n*)	inventaire *m*	inventario *m*	inventario *m*
inverted rim	eingezogener Rand *m*	bord *m* rentrant	labbro *m* rientrante	borde *m* entrante
Ionic order	ionische Ordnung *f*	ordre *m* ionique	ordine *m* ionico	orden *m* jónico
iron	Eisen *n*	fer *m*	ferro *m*	hierro *m*
iron age	Eisenzeit *f*	âge *m* du Fer	età *f* del ferro	Edad *f* de Hierro
iron ore	Eisenerz *n*	minerai *m* de fer	minerale *m* di ferro	mineral *m* de hierro
irregular	unregelmäßig	irrégulier/-ère	irregolare	irregular
irrigation	Bewässerung *f*	irrigation *f*	irrigazione *f*	irrigación *f*, riego *m*
island	Insel *f*	île *f*	isola *f*	isla *f*
isodomic	isodom	isodome	isodomo/-a	isódom/-a
isotope	Isotop *n*	isotope *m*	isotopo *m*	isótopo m
ivory	Elfenbein *n*	ivoire *m*	avorio *m*	marfil *m*

Greek		Turkish	Arabic	
εκ γενετής	ek genetis	yerli	أصلى	asli
βιομηχανικός	viomichanikos	endüstriyel	صناعي	sinaie
βιομηχανία f	viomichania	endüstri	صناعة	sinaa jadawija
βιοτεχνία f, εμπόριο n	viotechnia, eborio	meslek, zanaat	مشروع تجارى	maschrua togari
επίδραση f	epidrasi	etki	تأثير	taasier
πληροφορία f	pliroforia	bilgi	معلومات	maalumat
πληροφοριακό περιεχόμενο n	pliroforiako periechomeno	bilgi içeriği	محتوى المعلومات	mohtawa elmaalumat
υπέρυθρος	iperithros	kızılötesi	أشعة تحت الحمراء	aschea taht elhamraa
εμπρός, μπροστά	ebros, brosta	başta, önde	في الأمام	fi elamam
ράβδος f	ravdos	külçe	سبيكة	sabika
ενθετική τεχνική f	entheiki techniki	kakma, kakmacılık, oymacılık	ترصيع	tarsiea
ένθεμα n	enthema	taban	حشوة	haschwa
ενθέτω, τοποθετώ με την ενθετική τεχνική	entheto, topotheto me tin enthetiki techniki	içine koymak, yerleştirmek	يُرصع	yurasea
εσωτερικός (adj.), εσωτερικά (adv.)	esoterikos, esoterika	içerde, içerisinde	في الداخل	fi eldachel
ανόργανος	anorganos	inorganik	غير عضوي	geer udwi
επιγραφή f	epigrafi	kitabe, yazıt	نقش	naksch
έντομο n	entomo	böcek	حشرة	haschara
εργαλείο n	ergaleio	alet, araç gereç	أداة	adah
νησίδα f	nisida	insula	عمارة سكنية	imara sakanija
μετακιόνιο n	metakionio	interkolumnium	مسافة بين عمودين	masafa bein amudein
ενδιάμεσο στρώμα n	enthiameso stroma	ara tabaka	طبقة وسطى	tabaka wusta
ερμηνεία f	ermineia	yorum, yorumlama	تفسير	tafsier
αδιαφανής	adiafanis	saydam olmayan	غير شفاف	geer schafaf
ενδοαστικός	endoastikos	şehir içi	فى داخل المدينة	fi dachel elmadina
ευρετήριο n , κατάλογος m	evretirio, katalogos	envanter	رصيد	rasieed
εσωστρεφές χείλος n	esostrefes cheilos	içe çekik ağız kenarı	حافة ملمومة	hafa malmuma
ιωνικός ρυθμός m	ionikos rithmos	İon Düzeni	نظام أيوني	nezam ayonie
σίδερο n , σίδηρος m	sidero, sidiros	demir	حديد	hadid
Εποχή f του Σιδήρου	Epochi tou Sidirou	Demir Çağı	العصر الحديدى	elasr elhadidi
σιδηρομετάλλευμα n	sidirometallevma	ham demir madeni	خام الحديد	cham elhadid
ακανόνιστος	akanonistos	düzensiz	غير منتظم	geer muntazem
ύδρευση f	idrefsi	sulamak	ري	rei
νησί n	nisi	ada	جزيرة	gazira
ισόδομος	isodomos	isodom	سور من الكتل الحجرية	sur men elkotal elhagarija ?
ισότοπο n	isotopo	izotop, yerdeş	نظير مُشع	nazier moschea
ελεφαντοστό n , ελεφαντόδοντο n	elefantosto, elefantodonto	fildişi	عاج	aag

English	German	French	Italian	Spanish
jagged, serrated	gezackt	denté/-ée, dentelé/-ée	dentato/-a	dentado/-a
jar, jug	Krug *m*	cruche *f*	brocca *f*	botijo *m* , jarra *f*
jewellery	Schmuck *m*	bijoux *m pl,* parure *f*	gioiello *m*	joyas *pl*
journal	Tagebuch *n*	journal *m*	diario *m*	diario *m*
jute	Jute *f*	jute *m*	iuta *f*	yute *m*
kerbstone, orthostat	Orthostat *m* , Randstein *m*	orthostate *m*	ortostato *m*	ortostato *m*
kiln	Brennofen *m*	fourneau *m*	fornace *f*, forno *m*	horno *m* de calcinación
kiln	Töpferofen *m*	four *m* de potier	fornace *f*	horno *m* de alfarero
kind, species, type	Art *f*	espèce *f,* sorte *f*	categoria *f,* modo *m* , tipo *m*	especie *f*, manera *f* , tipo *m*
king	König *m*	roi *m*	re *m*	rey *m*
kingdom	Königreich *n*	règne *m,* royaume *m*	regno *m*	reino *m*
kitchenware	Küchenware *f*	céramique *f* culinaire	ceramica *f* di cucina	cerámica *f* de cocina
knee pad	Knieschützer *m*	genouillère *f*	ginocchiera *f*	rodillera *f*
knife	Messer *n*	couteau *m*	coltello *m*	cuchillo *m*
knot	Knoten *m*	noeud *m*	nodo *m*	nudo *m*
krater	Krater (Gefäß) *m*	cratère	cratere *m*	crátera *f*
laboratory	Labor *n*	laboratoire *f*	laboratorio *m*	laboratorio *m*
labyrinth	Labyrinth *n*	labyrinthe *f*	labirinto *m*	laberinto *m*
labyrinthine	labyrinthisch	labyrinthique	labirintico/-a	laberíntico/-a
lacquer, varnish	Lack *m*	laque *m*	vernice *f*	barniz *m* , laca *f*
ladder	Leiter *f*	échelle *f*	scala *f*	escalera *f*
lake	See *m*	lac *m*	lago *m*	lago *m*
lake dwelling	Seesiedlung *f*	habitat *m* lacustre	insediamento *m* lacustre	asentamiento *m* en el lago
lake dwelling/ pile	Pfahlbau *m*	construction *f* sur pilotis	palafitta *f*	construcción lacustra *f*
lamp	Lampe *f*	lampe *f*	lampada *f*	lámpara *f*
lance	Lanze *f*	lance *f*	lancia *f*	lanza *f*
land surveying	Landvermessung *f*	arpentage *m* , géodésie *f*	agrimensura *f*	agrimensura *f*
lapis lazuli	Lapislazuli *m*	lapis-lazuli *m*	lapislazuli *m*	lapislázuli *m*
lateral	lateral	latéral	laterale	lateral
lateral	seitlich/ lateral	latéral/-e	laterale	lateral
latrine	Latrine *f*	latrines *pl*	latrina *f*	letrina *f*
lattice framework	Fachwerk *n*	cloisonnage *m* , pans *m pl* de bois	intelaiatura *f*, traliccio *m*	armadura *f* , entramado *m*
layer	Schicht *f*	couche *m*	strato *m*	estrato *m*
layer of sand	Sandschicht *f*	couche *f* de sable	strato *m* di sabbia	estrato *m* de arena
lead	Blei *n*	plomb *m*	piombo *m*	plomo *m*
lead oxid	Bleioxid *n*	oxyde *m* de plomb	ossido *m* di piombo	óxido *m* de plomo
leaf	Blatt *n*	feuille	foglio *m*	hoja *f*
leaky	undicht	perméable	permeabile	permeable
leather	Leder *n*	cuir *m*	cuoio *m*	cuero *m*
legend	Legende *f*	légende *f*	leggenda *f*	leyenda *f*

Greek		Turkish	Arabic	
οδοντωτός	odontotos	dişli, tırtıllı	مسنن	mosanan
οινοχόη f, κανάτα f	oinochoi, kanata	testi	إبريق	ebrik
κοσμήματα n pl	kosmimata	dekor, takı	حلي	hulei
ημερολόγιο n	imerologio	günlük	مذكرات	mozakiraat
γιούτα f	giouta	hint keneviri	جوت	got
ορθοστάτης m	orthostatis	bordür taşı, kenar taşı, orthostat	حجر الرصيف	hagar elrasief
κλίβανος m	klivanos	fırın	فرن	furn
κεραμικός κλίβανος m	keramikos klivanos	çömlekçi fırını	فرن لحرق الفخار	forn lehark elfuchar
είδος n	eidos	biçim, çeşit, tür	نوع	noa
βασιλιάς m	vasilias	kral	ملك	malek
βασίλειο n	vasileio	kraliyet, krallık	مملكة	mamlaka
μαγειρική κεραμική f	mageiriki keramiki	mutfak kabı	أدوات المطبخ	adawat elmatbach
επιγονατίδα f	epigonatida	dizlik	واقى للركبة	wakie lelrokba
μαχαίρι n	machairi	bıçak, saat, sayaç	سكين	sekien
κόμπος m, κόμβος m	kobos, kobos	deniz mili, düğüm	عقدة	ukda
κρατήρας m	kratiras	krater	فوهة البركان	fuwahat elburkan
εργαστήριο n	ergastirio	laboratuvar	معمل	mamal
λαβύρινθος m	lavirinthos	labirent	متاهة	mataha
λαβυρινθώδης	lavirinthodis	dolambaçlı	متاهي	matahi
βερνίκι n, λούστρο n	verniki, loustro	cila, lak, vernik	طلاء	tilaa
σκάλα f	skala	merdiven	سلم	selem
λίμνη f	limni	deniz, göl	بحيرة	bohajra
λιμναίος οικισμός m	limnaios oikismos	göl yerleşmesi	مستوطنة بحرية	mostawtana bahrija
πασσαλόπυκτο οίκημα n	passalopikto oikima	kazık temelli yapı	ركائز	rakaez
λυχνάρι n	lichnari	kandil, lamba	مصباح	mesbah
λόγχη f	logchi	kargı, mızrak	رمح	rumh
τοπογράφηση f	topografisi	arazi ölçme	قياس الأراضي	kiejas elaradi
λαζουρίτης m	lazouritis	lacivert taşı	لازورد	lazurd
πλευρικός	plevrikos	yanal	جانبي	ganebi
πλευρικός	plevrikos	eğik, yan, yanal,	جانبي	ganebie
αποχωρητήριο n	apochoritirio	latrine	مرحاض	merhad
πλέγμα n	plegma	kafes yapı	نوع من البناء	nua men elbinaa
στρώμα n	stroma	tabaka	طبقة	tabaka ramlija
στρώμα άμμου n	stroma ammou	kum tabakası	طبقة رملية	tabaka ramlija
μόλυβδος m	molivdos	kurşun	رصاص	rasas
οξείδιο n του μολύβδου	oxeidio tou molivdou	kurşun oksit	أكسيد رصاص	uksid resas
φύλλο n	fillo	yaprak	ورقة	waraka
διαπερατός	diaperatos	hava veya su geçirgen	غير مُحكم	geer mohkam
δέρμα n	derma	deri	جلد	geld
θρύλος m, υπόμνημα n	thrilos, ipomnima	efsane	أسطورة	ustura

English	German	French	Italian	Spanish
legend, myth	Legende *f*, Mythos *m*	légende *f*, mythe *m*	mito *m*	mito *m*
length	Länge *f*	longitude *f*	lunghezza *f*	largo *m*, longitud *f*
lenticular, lentoid	linsenförmig	lenticulaire	lenticolare	lenticular
level, elevation	Niveau *n*	niveau *m*	livello *m*	nivel *m*
level(l)ed soil	abgeflachter Boden *m*	fond *m* aplati	terreno *m* spianato	suelo *m* aplanado
levelling	Nivellement *n*	nivellement *m*	livellamento *m*	nivelación *f*
level plane	Planum *n*	plan *m*	taglio *m* artificiale	plano *m*
libation	Libation *f*, Trankopfer *n*	libation *f*	libagione (libazione) *f*	libación *f*
library	Bibliothek *f*	bibliothèque	biblioteca *f*	biblioteca *f*
lid	Deckel *m*	couvercle *m*	coperchio *m*	tapa *f*
light	Licht *n*	lumière *f*	luce *f*	luz *f*
lime	Kalk *m*	calcaire *m*, chaux *f*	calce *f*	cal *f*
lime soil	Kalkboden *m*	sol *m* crayeux	terreno *m* calcareo	suelo *m* de cal
limestone	Kalkstein *m*	calcaire *m*, pierre *f* à chaux	pietra *f* calcarea	caliza *f*, piedra *f* calcárea
line	Linie *f*	ligne *f*	linea *f*	línea *f*
linear	linear	linéaire	lineare	lineal
lip	Lippe *f*	lèvre *f*	labbro *m*	labio *m*
lithic technology	Steinbearbeitungstechnik *f*	technique *f* de débitage/ de taille	tecnologia *f* litica	técnica de *f* labrar/ tallar piedras
loading gauge	Messrahmen *m*	grille *f* de relevé	cornice da disegno *f*	encuadre *m* de medición
loam coating/ grout	Lehmbewurf *m*	crépi *m* d'argile	intonaco *m* di argilla	camisa *f* de barro
loamy sand	Tonsand *m*	sable *m* argileux	sabbia *f* argillosa	arena *f* arcillosa
local	lokal, örtlich	local	locale	local
localisation	Lokalisation *f*	localisation *f*	localizzazione *f*	localización *f*
location	Ort *m*	lieu *m*, localité *f*	località *f*	localidad *f*, sitio *m*
location, position	Lage *f*	emplacement *m*, position *f*	posizione *f*, situazione *f*	posición *f*
longitudinal section	Längsschnitt *m*	section *f* longitudinale	sezione *f* longitudinale	sección *f* longitudinal
loom weight	Webgewicht *n*	poids *m pl* de métier à tisser	peso *m* da telaio	fusayola *f*, pesa de barro *f*
lost-wax casting	Wachsausgussverfahren *n*	coulée *f* à la cire perdue	fusione *f* a cera persa	técnica *f* de la cera perdida
lowlands, plain	Ebene *f*	plaine *f*	pianura *f*	llano *m*, llanura *f*
lumber, timber	Bauholz *n*	bois *m* de construction	legname *m* da costruzione	madera *f* de construcción
luminescence	Lumineszenz *f*	luminescence *f*	luminescenza *f*	luminescencia *f*
lustre coating	Glanztonüberzug *m*	enduit *m* brillant, lustré *m*	rivestimento *m* a vernice lucida	engobe *m*
luxury goods	Luxusgüter	produits *pl* de luxe	beni *f* di lusso	bienes *f pl* de lujo
macroorganism	Makroorganismus *m*	macroorganisme *m*	macroorganismo *m*	macroorganismo *m*
magnetic	magnetisch	magnétique	magnetico	magnético/-a
magnetometer	Magnetometer *m*	magnétomètre *m*	magnetometro *m*	magnetómetro *m*

Greek		Turkish	Arabic	
μύθος *m*	mithos	efsane, mitos	أسطورة	ustura
μήκος *n*	mikos	uzunluk	طول	tul
φακοειδής	fakoeidis	mercek şeklinde	شكل عدسي	schakl adasie
επίπεδο *n*	epipedo	seviye	مستوى	mustawa
ισοπεδωμένο έδαφος *n*	isopedomeno edafos	düzleştirilmiş zemin	أرض مستوية	ard mustauja
υψομέτρηση *f*	ipsometrisi	nivelman	تسوية	taswija
πάσα *f*	pasa	düzlem, tesfiye	قاعدة ممهدة	kaeda momahada
χοή *f*	choi	libasyon, sıvı adağı	تقديم مشروب كقربان	takdiem maschrub kakurban
βιβλιοθήκη *f*	vivliothiki	kütüphane	مكتبة	maktaba
κάλυμμα *n* , καπάκι *n*	kalimma, kapaki	kapak	غطاء	gitaa
φως *n*	fos	aydınlatma, ışık	ضوء	doea
ασβέστης *m*	asvestis	kireç	جير	gir
ασβεστώδες έδαφος *n*	asvestodes edafos	kireçli taban	أرض جيرية	ard gireia
ασβεστόλιθος *m*	asvestolithos	kireç taşı	حجر جيري	hagar giri
γραμμές *f pl*	grammes	çizgiler	خطوط	chutut
γραμμικός	grammikos	çizgisel, uzunlamasına	خطي / مستقيم	chatie/ mostakiem
χείλος *n*	cheilos	dudak, kap ağzı	شفة	schefa
επεξεργασία του λίθου *f*	epexergrasia tou lithou	taş işleme tekniği	تقنية إعداد الأحجار	taknejet eadad elahgar
καρότσα *f*	karotsa	ölçüm çerçevesi	إطار القياس	itar elkijas
χυτή πηλοδομή *f*	chiti pilodomi	balçık sıva	مونة طينية	muna tienija
αργιλώδης άμμος *f*	argilodis ammos	killi kum	رمل طيني	raml tienie
τοπικός	topikos	yerel	محلي	mahali
εντοπισμός *f*	entopismos	lokalizasyon, yer belirleme	تحديد الموضع	tahdied elmawdia
τόπος *m* , τοποθεσία *f*	topos, topothesia	alan, konum, yer	مكان	makan eltadhija
θέση *f*	thesi	konum, yer	موقع	mawkea
τομή κατά μήκος *f*	tomi kata mikos	yanal kesit	قطع طولي	kataa tuli
αγνύθα *f*, υφαντικό βάρος *n*	agnitha, ifantiko varos	ağırşak, tezgah ağırlığı	مثقال النول	meskaal elnool
τεχνική *f* του χαμένου κεριού	techniki tou chamenou keriou	balmumu döküm işlemi	عملية صب الشمع	amalijet sab elschama
πεδιάδα *f*	pediada	alan, düzlem, ova	مستوى	mustawi
οικοδομική ξυλεία *f*	oikodomiki xileia	inşaat kerestesi	خشب البناء	chaschab elbinaa
φωταύγεια *f*	fotavgeia	gazışı, ışılışıma	تلألؤ	talalua
στιλβωτικό επίχρισμα *n*	stilvotiko epichrisma	parlak astar kaplama	طلاء لامع	tilaa lamea
προϊόντα πολυτελείας *n pl*	proionta politeleias	lüks eşyalar, lüks mallar	بضائع فاخرة	badaea fachera
μακροοργανισμός *m*	makroorganismos	makroorganizma	الكائنات الكبيرة	elkainat elkabira
μαγνητικός	magnitikos	manyetik	مغناطيسي	magnatiesie
μαγνητόμετρο *n*	magnitometro	manyetometre	جهاز فحص الأجسام المعدنية	gihaz fahs elagsam elmadinija

English	German	French	Italian	Spanish
magnifying glass	Lupe *f*, Vergrößerungsglas *n*	loupe *f*	lente *f* d'ingrandimento	lupa *f*
main component	Hauptkomponente *f*	composante *f* principale	componente *m* principale	componente *m* principal
malachite	Malachit *m*, Kupferspat	malachite *f*	malachite *f*	malaquita *f*
male	männlich	mâle, masculin	maschile	masculino
mammal	Säugetier *n*	mammifère *m*	mammifero *m*	mamífero *m*
mammoth	Mammut *n*	mammouth *m*	mammut *m*	mamut *m*
manual	manuell	manuel/-elle	manuale	manual
map	Landkarte *f*	carte *f*	carta (geografica) *f*	mapa *m*
maple	Ahorn *m*	érable *m*	acero *m*	arce *m*
map, plan	Plan *m*	plan *m*	pianta *f*	plano *m*
marble	Marmor *m*	marbre *m*	marmo *m*	mármol *m*
marbled, marmorate	marmoriert	marbré/-e	marmorizzato/-a	marmóreo/-a
marine/ sea sand	Meeressand *m*	sable *m* de mer	sabbia *f* marina	arena *f* de mar
marking	Markierung *f*	marquage *m*, repère *m*	marcatura *f*	señalización *f*
marsh, wetland	Marsch (Gelände) *f*	marais *m* (z.B. Marais poitevin)	polder *m*	marisma *f*
mask	Maske *f*	masque *m*	maschera *f*	máscara *f*
masonry bond	Mauerverband *m*	appareil *m*	commessura *f*	aparejo *m* de construcción
mass burial	Massengrab *n*	sépulture *f* collective	fossa *f* comune	fosa *f* común
massive	massiv	massif/-ve	massiccio/-a	macizo/-a
mass spectrometry	Massenspektrometrie *f*	spectrométrie *f* de masse	spettrometria *f* di massa	espectrómetro *m* de masas
material	Material *n*	matière *f*	materiale *m*	material *m*
mat, matting	Matte *f*	natte *f*, paillasson *m*	stuoia *f*	estera *f*
matriarchy	Matriarchat *n*	matriarchat *m*	matriarcato *m*	matriarcado *m*
matte	matt	mat	smorto/-a, spento/-a	apagado/-a, opaco/-a
matting cast	Mattenabdruck *m*	impression *f* de vannerie	impronta *f* della stuoia	impresión *f* de estera
mausoleum	Mausoleum *n*	mausolée *m*	mausoleo *m*	mausoleo *m*
meadow	Wiese *f*	prairie *f*, pré *m*	prato *m*	prado *m*
meander (pattern)	Mäander *m*	méandre *m*	meandro *m*	meandro *m*
measurement	Vermessung *f*	mesurage *m*	misurazione *f*	agrimensura *f*
measuring point	Messpunkt *m*	point *f* de mesure	punto *m* di misura	punto *m* de medida
measuring tape	Maßband *n*	ruban *m* métrique	metro *m* a nastro	cinta *f* métrica
medal	Medaille *f*	medaille *f*	medaglia *f*	medalla *f*
medieval age	Mittelalter *n*	Moyen Âge *m*	medioevo *m*	Edad media *f*
mediterranean	mediterran	méditerranéen/-enne	mediterraneo/-a	mediterráneo/-a
megalith	Megalith *m*	mégalithe *m*	megalite *m*	megalito *m*
megalithic grave	Megalithgrab *n*	tombe *f* mégalithique	tomba *f* megalitica	tumba *f* megalítica
megaron	Megaron *n*	mégaron *m*	megaron *m*	mégaro, mégaron *m*

Greek		Turkish	Arabic	
μεγεθυντικός φακός *m*	megethintikos fakos	büyüteç, mercek	عدسة مكبرة	adasa mukabera
κύριο συστατικό *n*	kirio sistatiko	anabileşen	عنصر أساسى	unsor asasie
μαλαχίτης *m*	malachitis	bakır taşı, malakit	الملكيت	elmalkiet
ανδρικός, αρσενικός	andrikos, arsenikos	eril	مُذكَّر	muzakar
θηλαστικό *n*	thilastiko	memeli hayvan	حيوان ثديي	hajawan sadie
μαμούθ *n*	mamouth	mamut	حيوان الماموث	hayawa elmamus
χειρωνακτικός	cheironaktikos	elle yapılan, manüel	يدوي	yadawi
χάρτης *m*	chartis	harita	خريطة	charita
σφεντάμι *n*	sfentami	akçaağaç	خشب القيقب	chaschab elkajkab
σχέδιο *n*	schedio	plan	خطة	chota
μάρμαρο *n*	marmaro	mermer	رخام	rucham
μαρμαρόθετος	marmarothetos	mermere benzer şekilde	رخامي	ruchamie
θαλασσινή άμμος *f*	thalassini ammos	deniz kumu	رمل البحر	raml elbahr
επισήμανση *f*	episimansi	etiketleme, işaretleme	علامة	alama
βάλτος *m*	valtos	bataklik	مسيرة	masira
μάσκα *f*, προσωπίδα *f*	maska, prosopida	mask, maske	قناع	kinaa
συνδετική ζώνη τοιχοοποιΐας *f*	sindetiki zoni toichoopoiias	taş örgüsü	ربط الجدار	rabt elgidar
ομαδική ταφή *f*	omadiki tafi	toplu mezar	مقبرة جماعية	makbara gamaeija
μαζικός, ομαδικός	mazikos, omadikos	kaba, kütle halinde	مصمت	musmat
φασματομετρία μαζών/μάζας *f*	fasmatometria mazon/mazas	kütle spektrometrisi	قياس الطيف الكتلي	kijas eltief elkotalie
υλικό *n*	iloko	malzeme, materyal	مادة	mada
χαλάκι *n*, ψάθα *f*	chalaki, psatha	hasır	حصيرة	hasira
μητριαρχία *f*	mitriarchia	anaerkilik	النظام الأمومي	elnisam elumumi
ματ, θαμπός	mat, thabos	uçuk, soluk	مطفي	matfie
αποτύπωμα ψάθας *n*	apotipoma psathas	hasır baskısı, hasır izi	الطبع علي الحصائر	eltaba ala elhasaer
μαυσωλείο *n*	mafsoleio	maussoleion	ضريح	darih
λιβάδι *n*	livadi	çayır	مرج	marg
μαίανδρος *m*	maiandros	meander	منعطف النهر	munataf elnahr
μέτρηση *f*	metrisi	ölçme, ölçümleme	قياس	kijaas
σημείο μέτρησης *n*	simeio metrisis	ölçme noktası	نقطة القياس	nuktet elkijas
μετροταινία *f*	metrotainia	mezura, şerit metre	شريط قياس	scherit kijas
μετάλλιο *n*	metallio	madalyon	ميدالية	medalja
Μεσαίωνας *m*	Mesaionas	Ortaçağ	العصور الوسطى	elusur elwosta
μεσογειακός	mesogeiakos	akdeniz	خاص بالبحر الأبيض المتوسط	chaas belbahr elabjad elmotawaset
μεγάλιθος *m*	megalithos	megalit	حجر ضخم	hagar dachm
μεγαλιθικός τάφος *m*	megalithikos tafos	megalit mezar	مقبرة من الحجارة الضخمة	makbara men elhigara eldachma
μέγαρο *m*	megaro	megaron	غرفة رئيسية بشرفة	gurfa raiseja bischorfa

English	German	French	Italian	Spanish
melting pot	Schmelztiegel *m*	creuset *m*	crogiolo *m* (di fusione)	crisol *m*
menhir	Menhier *m*	menhir *m*	menhir *m*	menhir *m*
merchant	Händler *m*	marchand *m*	commerciante *m/f*	comerciante *m/f*
merlon	Zinne *f*	créneau *m*	merlo *m*	almena *f*
mesoamericanistics	Mesoamerikanistik *f*	archéologie *f* méso-américaine	archeologia *f* della Mesoamerica	estudio *m* de mesoamerica
mesolithic	Mesolithikum *n*	Mésolithique *m*	mesolitico *m*	mesolítico *m*
mesopotamian	mesopotamisch	mésopotamien/-ienne	mesopotamico/-a	mesopotámico/-a
metal	Metall *n*	métal *m*	metallo *m*	metal *m*
Metal Age	Metallikum *n*, Metallzeit *f*	âge *m* des Métaux	età *f* del metallo	era *f* metálica
metal detector	Metalldetektor *m*	détecteur *m* de métaux	metal detector *m*	detector *m* de metales
metallurgical process, smelting	Verhüttung *f*	fonte *f*, extraction *f* par fusion	trattamento *m* dei minerali	tratamiento *m* metalúrgico
metallurgy	Metallurgie *f*	métallurgie *f*	metallurgia *f*	metalurgia *f*
metal sheet	Blech *n*	tôle *m*	lamiera *f*, lamina *f*	chapa *f*, metal *m*
metamorphic	metamorph	métamorphique	metamorfo/-a	metamórfico/-a
metamorphism	Metamorphismus *m*	métamorphisme *m*	metamorfismo *m*	meatmorfismo *m*
methode	Methode *f*	méthode *f*	metodo *m*	método *m*
methodical	methodisch	méthodique	metodico/-a	metódico/-a
methodology	Methodologie *f*	méthodologie *f*	metodologia *f*	metodología *f*
method, procedure, process	Verfahren *n*	méthode *f*, procédé *m*	metodo *m*, procedimento *m*	método *m*, procedimiento *m*
metope	Metope *f*	métope	metopa *f*	métopa *f*
metre	Meter *m*	mètre *m*	metro *m*	metro *m*
microlith	Mikrolith *m*	microlithe *m*	microlite *f*	microlito *m*
microorganism	Mikroorganismus *m*	microorganisme *m*	microorganismo *m*	micoorganismo *m*
microscope	Mikroskop *n*	microscope *m*	microscopio *m*	microscopio *m*
migration period	Völkerwanderung *f*	Grandes Invasions *f pl*	migrazione *f* di popoli	migración *f* de pueblos
mildew	Schimmel *m*	moisissure *f*	muffa *f*	moho *m*
milestone	Meilenstein *m*	milliaire *m*, borne *f* milliaire	miglio *m*	miliario *m*, columna *f* miliar
millimetre	Millimeter *m*	millimètre *m*	millimetro *m*	millímetro *m*
millstone	Mühlstein *m*	meule *f*	mola *f*	muela *f*
minaret	Minarett *n*	minaret *m*	minareto *m*	alminar *m*
mineral	Mineral *n*	minéral *m*	minerale *m*	mineral *m*
miniature	Miniatur *f*	miniature *f*	miniatura *f*	miniatura *f*
mining	Bergbau *m*	exploitation *f* minière	industria *f* mineraria	explotación *f* minera, minería *f*
Minoan	minoisch	minoen/-enne	minoico/-a	minoico/-a
misfired pottery	Fehlbrand *m*	raté *m* de cuisson	ceramica *f* di scarto	producto *m* de mala cocción
mixture	Mischung *f*	mélange *m*	mescolamento *m*	mezcla *f*, mixtura *f*

Greek		Turkish	Arabic	
χωνευτήρι *n*	choneftiri	döküm potası	بوتقة الانصهار	bawtaket elensihar
μενχίρ *n*	menchir	menhir	حجر قائم للطقوس	Hagar kaem letukus
έμπορος *m*	eboros	esnaf, satıcı, tüccar	تاجر	tager
πολεμίστρα *f*	polemistra	kale mazgalı	سور مدبب	suur modabab
Μεσοαμερικανικές Σπουδές *f pl*	Mesoamerikanikes Spoudes	Orta Amerika Bilimi	علم الأمريكانيات السيط	elm elamrikanijat elwasiet
Μεσολιθική Περίοδος *f*	Mesolithiki Periodos	Mezolitik Çağ	العصر الحجري الأوسط	elasr elhagarie elawst
μεσοποταμιακός	mesopotamiakos	mezopotamyalı	خاص ببلاد الرافدين	chaas bebilad elrafidein
μέταλλο *m*	metallo	metal	معدن	maadan
Εποχή των Μετάλλων *f*	Epochi ton Metallon	metal çağı	العصر المعدني	elasr elmadenie
ανιχνευτής μετάλλων *m*	anichneftis metallon	metal detektörü	كاشف المعدن	kaschef elmaadan
καμίνευση μεταλλεύματος *f*	kaminefsi metallevmatos	işleme	صهر المعادن	sahr elmaaden
Μεταλλουργία *f*	Metallourgia	Metalurji	علم المعادن	elm elmaaden
μεταλλικό έλασμα *n*	metalliko elasma	sac	صفيح	safieh
μεταμορφωσιγενής, μεταμορφωμένος	metamorfosigenis, metamorfomenos	metamorf	متحول	motahawel
μεταμόρφωση *f*	metamorfosi	başkalaşma	التحول	eltahawul
μέθοδος *f*	methodos	metot, yöntem	أسلوب	uslub
μεθοδικός	methodos	metodik, yöntemli	منهجي	manhagie
μεθοδολογία *f*	methodologia	Yöntem Bilimi	علم المنهجية	elm elmanhagija
διαδικασία *f*	diadikasia	yöntem	طريقة	tarika
μετόπη *f*	metopi	metop	زخرف بين تاج العمود والسقف	zachrafa bein tag elamud wi elsakf
μέτρο *n*	metro	metre	متر	metr
μικρόλιθος *m*	mikrolithos	mikrolit	حجر صوان صغير	hagar sawan sagier
μικροοργανισμός *m*	mikroorganismos	mikroorganizma	الكائنات الحية الدقيقة	elkaenat elheia eldakika
μικροσκόπιο *n*	mikroskopio	mikroskop	ميكروسكوب	mikruskub
περίοδος μεταναστεύσεων *f*	periodos metanastefseon	kavimler göçü	هجرة الشعوب	hegrat elschuub
μούχλα *f*	mouchla	küf	عفن	afan
μιλιάριο *n*	miliario	miltaşı	حجر المسافات	hagar elmasafat
χιλιοστόμετρο *n*	chiliostometro	milimetre	مللیمتر	melimetr
μυλόπετρα *f*	milopetra	değirmen taşı	حجر الرحى	hagar elraha
μιναρές *m*	minares	minare	منذنة	mezana
ορυκτό *n*	orikto	mineral	معدن	madan
μικρογραφία *f*	mikrografia	minyatür	حاجة مصغرة	haga musagar
εξόρυξη *f*	exorixi	madencilik	تعدين	tadien
μινωϊκός	minoikos	Minos ile ilgili	مينوسي	minusie
κακοψημένη κεραμική *f*	kakopsimeni keramiki	hatalı üretim	حرق خاطئ	hark chatea
ανάμιξη *f*	anamixi	karışım	خليط	chalit

English	German	French	Italian	Spanish
model	Modell *n*	modèle *m*	modello *m*	maqueta *f*, modelo *m*
model, role model	Vorbild *n*	modèle *m*	espempio *m*, modello *m*	ejemplo *m*, modelo *m*
moderate	gemässigt	modéré	moderato/-a	moderado/-a
modification	Abänderung *f*, Modifikation *f*	modification *f*	modificazione *f*	modificación *f*
moisture content	Wassergehalt *m*	teneur *m* en eau	contenuto *m* dell'acqua	contenido *m* de agua
molar tooth	Backenzahn *m*	dent *f* molaire	dente *m* molare	molar *m*
mollusc	Molluske *f*	mollusque *m*	mollusco *m*	molusco *m*
monochrome	einfarbig, monochrom	monochrome	monocromo	monocolor, unicolor
monogramme	Monogramm *n*	monogramme *m*	monogramma *m*	monograma *m*
monolith	Monolith *m*	monolithe *f*	monolito *m*	monolito *m*
monolithic	monolithisch	monolithique	monolitico/-a	monolítico/-a
monotheism	Monotheismus *m*	monothéisme *m*	monoteismo *m*	monoteísmo *m*
monument	Denkmal *n*	monument *m*	monumento *m*	monumento *m*
monument protection	Denkmalschutz *m*	protection *f* des monuments	protezione *f* dei monumenti	protección *f* del patrimonio nacional
moor, swamp	Moor *n*	marais *m*	palude *f*	pantano *m*
moraine	Moräne *f*	moraine *f*	morena *f*	morena *f*
mortar	Mörser *m*, Reibschale *f*	mortier *m*	mortaio *m*	mortero *m*
mortar, plaster	Mörtel *m*	gâchis *m*, mortier *m*	malta *f*	argamasa *f*, mortero *m*
mosaic	Mosaik *n*	mosaïque *f*	mosaico *m*	mosaico *m*
mosaic floor	Mosaikfußboden *m*	pavement *m* en mosaïque	pavimento *m* mosaicato	pavimento *m* de mosaico
mosque	Moschee *f*	mosquée *f*	moschea *f*	mezquita *f*
moss	Moos *n*	mousse *m*	musco *m*	musgo *m*
mother of pearl	Perlmutt *n*	nacre *f*	madreperla *f*	madreperla *f*, nácar *m*
motif	Motiv *n*	motif *m*	motivo *m*	motivo *m*
mounting	Beschlag *m*	garniture *f*	borchia *f*	herraje *m*
mouth	Mündung *f*	embouchure *f* (Fluss!), ouverture *f*	foce *f*, sbocco *m*	boca *f*, desembocadura *f*
mudbrick building	Lehmbau *m*	construction *f* / architecture *f* en terre crue	costruzione *f* in argilla	construcción *f* de adobe
mummy	Mumie *f*	momie *f*	mummia *f*	momia *f*
museum	Museum *n*	musée *m*	museo *m*	museo *m*
mushroom	Pilz *m*	champignon *m*	fungo *m*	hongo *m*, seta *f*
mutation	Mutation *f*	mutation *m*	mutazione *f*	mutación *f*
Mycenaean	mykenisch	mycénien/-ienne	miceneo/-a	micénico/-a
mythology	Mythologie *f*	mythologie *f*	mitologia *f*	mitología *f*
nail	Nagel *m*	ongle *m*	chiodo *m*	clavo *m*

Greek		Turkish	Arabic	
πρότυπο *n* , μοντέλο *n*	protipo, montelo	model, örnek	نموذج	namuzag
πρότυπο *n* , μοντέλο *n*	protipo, montelo	numune, örnek	نموذج	namuzag
μέτριος, μετρημένος	metrios, metrimenos	ılıman, orta dereceli	معتدل	moatadel
τροποποίηση *f*	tropopoiisi	morfolojik değişim	تعديل	tadil
βαθμός υγρασίας *m*	vathmos igrasias	su içeriği	محتوى الماء	mohtawa elmaa
τραπεζίτης *m*	trapezitis	azı dişi	ضرس	ders
μαλάκιο *n*	malakio	yumuşakçalar	حيوان رخوي	hajawan rachawi
μονόχρωμος	monochromos	tek renkli	أحادي اللون	ohadi ellon
μονόγραμμα *n*	monogramma	monogram	نيابة الحرف الاول عن المصطلح	nijabet elharf elawal an elmostalah
μονόλιθος *m*	monolithos	monolit	كتلة حجرية منحوتة من صخرة واحدة	kotla hagarija manhuta men sachra waheda
μονολιθικός	monolithikos	tektaşlı	أحادي	uhadi
μονοθεϊσμός *m*	monotheismos	tektanrıcılık	الوحدانية	elwahdanija
μνημείο *n*	mnimeio	anıt	نصب تذكاري	nasb teskari
Προστασία *f* Μνημείων	Prostasia Mnimeion	anıtları koruma, tarihi eserleri koruma	حماية التراث	himayt elturas
έλος *n*	elos	bataklık	مستنقع	mostanka
παγετώνιες αποθέσεις *f pl*	pagetonies apothesies	buzultaş, moren	ركام	rukam
γουδί *n* , ιγδίο *n*	goudi, igdio	dibek, havan	هون	hon
κονίαμα *n*	koniama	harç	مونة	muna
ψηφιδωτό *n*	psifidoto	mozaik	فسيفساء	fusaifisaa
ψηφιδωτό δάπεδο *n*	psfidoto dapedo	mozaik döşeme, mozaik döşeli taban	أرضية فسيفساء	ardija fusaifisaa
τζαμί *n*	tzami	cami	مسجد	masged
βρύα *n pl*	vria	yosun	طحلب	tahlab
φίλντισι *n*	fildisi	sedef	صدف	sadaf
μοτίβο *n*	motivo	motif	دافع / موضوع	dafea/ mawgua
επίθεμα *n*	epithema	kaplama	حلية واقية	helja wakeja
στόμιο *n*	stomio	ağız, akarsuyun döküldüğü yer, delik	مصب	masab
πηλοδομή *f*	pilodomi	kerpiç yapı	البناء بالطين	elbinaa beltien
μούμια *f*	moumia	mumya	مومياء	mumjaa
μουσείο *n*	mouseio	müze	متحف	mathaf
μανιτάρι *n*	manitari	mantar	عيش الغراب	aisch elgurab
παράλλαξη *f*	parallaxi	mutasyon	تحول	tahawol
μυκηναϊκός	mikinaikos	Myken ile ilgili	ميسيني	maisinie
μυθολογία *f*	mithologia	mitoloji	علم الأساطير	elm elasatier
νύχι *m*	vichi	sivri uç, tırnak	مسمار	mosmar

English	German	French	Italian	Spanish
narrow	eng	étroit/-te	stretto/-a	estrecho/-a
natural	natürlich	naturel/-elle	naturale	natural
natural science	naturwissenschaftlich	qui appartient aux sciences naturelles, scientifique	delle scienze naturali	científico/-a
natural sciences	Naturwissenschaft *f*	sciences *f pl* naturelles	scienze *f pl* naturali	ciencias *f pl* naturales
nave	Kirchenschiff *n*	nef *f*	navata *f*	nave *f*
Neanderthal	Neandertaler *m*	Néandertalien/-ienne	uomo *m* di Neandertal	hombre *m* de neandertal
necklace	Halsband *n*, -kette *f*	collier *m*	collana *f*	collar *m*
necropolis	Nekropole *f*	nécropole *m*	necropoli *f*	necrópolis *f*
needle	Nadel *f*	aiguille *f*	ago *m*, spillo *m*	alfiler *m*
negative	negativ	négatif/-ve	negativo/-a	negativo/-a
Neolithic	Neolithikum *n*	Néolithique *m*	neolitico *m*	neolítico m
neolithic	neolithisch	néolithique	neolitico/-a	neolítico/-a
net	Netz *n*	filet *m*	rete *f*	red
netting	Geflecht *n*	clayonnage *m*, entrelacs *m pl*, treillis *m*	reticolato *m*	enrejado *m*
network	Netzwerk *n*	réseau *m*	traliccio *m*	malla *f*, red social *m*
neutral	neutral	neutre	neutrale	neutro/-a
niello (work)	Niello *n*	nielle *m*, niellure *f*	niello *m*	nielado *m*
nomadic	nomadisch	nomade	nomade	nómado/-a
north	Norden *m*	nord *m*	nord *m*	norte *m*
northern	nördlich	nordique	del nord, settentrionale	septentrional
north point	Nordpfeil *m*	flèche *f* nord	freccia del nord *f*	flecha norte *f*
notebook	Notizblock *m*	bloc-notes *m*	bloc-notes *m*	bloc de notas *m*
noticeable	auffällig	frappant	vistoso	llamativo
numismatics	Numismatik *f*	numismatique *f*	numismatica *f*	numismática *f*
nut	Nuss *f*	noix *f*	noce *f*	nuez *f*
nymphaeum	Nymphaion *n*	nymphée *m*	ninfeo *m*	ninfeo *m*
oak tree	Eiche *f*	chêne *m*	quercia *f*	roble *m*
oat	Hafer *m*	avoine *f*	avena *f*	avena *f*
obelisk	Obelisk *m*	obélisque *m*	obelisco *m*	obelisco *m*
object of art	Kunstobjekt *n*	objet *m* d'art	oggetto artistico *m*	objeto *m* de arte
obsidian, volcanic glass	Obsidian *n*	obsidienne *f*	ossidiana *f*	obsidiana *f*
odeion	Odeion *n*	odéon *m*	odeion *m*	odeón *m*
opening	Öffnung *f*	orifice *m*, ouverture *f*	apertura *f*	abertura *f*
open-worked	durchbrochen	à jour, ajouré/-ée	a giorno *m*, traforato	calado/-a, perforado/-a
order	Ordnung *f*	ordre *m*	ordine *m*	orden *m*
order, sequence	Reihenfolge *f*	ordre *m*, suite *f*	successione *f*	sucesión *f*

Greek		Turkish	Arabic	
στενός	stenos	dar	ضيق	deiyek
φυσικός	fisikos	doğal	طبيعى	tabiie
των φυσικών επιστημών	ton fisikon epistimon	doğa bilimi ile ilgili	من علوم طبيعية	men elulum eltabiija
φυσική επιστήμη f	fisiki epistimi	Doğa bilimleri	علم طبيعي	elm tabiie
κλίτος n	klitos	nave	صحن الكنيسة	sahn elkanisa
Άνθρωπος του Νεάντερταλ m	Anthrops Neadertal	Neandertal insanı	الإنسان البدائي	elensan elbidaie
περιλαίμιο n	perilaimio	gerdanlık, kolye	عقد	ekd
νεκρόπολη f	nekropoli	nekropol	جبانة	gabana
βελόνα f	velona	iğne, ibre	إبرة	ibra
αρνητικός	arnitikos	negatif, olumsuz	سلبي	salbie
Νεολιθική Εποχή f	Neolithiki Epochi	Neolitik Çağ/ Cilalı Taş Devri	العصر الحجري الحديث	elasr elhagarie elhadies
νεολιθικός	neolithikos	neolitik	العصر الحجري الحديث	elasr elhagari elhadies
δίχτυ n	dichti	ağ	شبكة	schabaka
πλέγμα n	plegma	çelenk, örgü	أسياخ مُضفرة	asjach mudafara
δίκτυο n	diktio	ağ	شبكة اتصال	schabakat etesal
ουδέτερος	oudeteros	nöt(ü)r, tarafsız	محايد	muhajed
νιέλλο n	viello	savatlama	زخرفة بالمينا السوداء	zachrafa belmina elsawdaa
νομαδικός	nomadikos	göçebe gibi	بدوي	badawie
βορράς m	vorras	kuzey, kuzey bölgesi	شمال	schamal
βόρειος	voreios	kuzey, kuzeyde bulunan	شمالي	schamalie
βορράς m	vorras	kuzey oku	سهم الشمال	sahm elschmal
σημειωματάριο n	simeiomatario	not defteri	مفكرة	mufakera
επιδεικτικός	epideiktikos	dikkat çekici	ملفت للنظر	molfet lelnazar
νομισματική f	nomismatiki	nümizmatik	علم العملات	elm elumlat
ξηρός καρπός m	xiros karpos	ceviz fındık	بندق	bunduk
νυμφαίο n	nimafaio	nymphaion	معبد الآلهة نومفا (عزراء)	maabd elaleha numfe (elazraa)
βελανιδιά f, δρυς f	velanidia, dris	meşe	شجرة البلوط	schagart elbalut
βρώμη f	vromi	yulaf	شوفان	schufan
οβελίσκος m	oveliskos	obelisk	مسلة	misala
αντικείμενο τέχνης n	antikeimeno technis	sanatsal nesne	عمل فني	amal fani
οψιδιανός m, οψιανός m	opsidianos, opsianos	obsidien	زجاج بركاني أسود	zugag burkanie aswad
ωδείο n	odeio	odeion	قاعة للموسيقى و الحفلات	kaah lelmusika we elhafalat
άνοιγμα n	anoigma	aralık, boşluk, yarık	افتتاح / فتحة	iftetah/ fatha
διάτρητος	diatritos	delik, yarık, yarılmış	محطّم	muhatam
τάξη f	taxi	düzen, kanun, kural	نظام	nizam biie
ακολουθία f, σειρά f	akolouthia, seira	ardışıklık, sıra(lama)	ترتيب	tartieb

English	German	French	Italian	Spanish
ore	Erz *n*	minerai *m*	minerale *m*	mineral *m*
organic	organisch	organique	organico/-a	orgánico/-a
orientation	Orientierung *f*	orientation *f*	orientamento *m*	orientación *f*
origin	Ursprung *m*	origine *f*	origine *f*	origin *m* , procedencia *f*
original	Original *n*	original *m*	originale *m*	original *m*
origin, provenance	Herkunft *f* , Provenienz *f*	origine *f* , provenance *f*	origine *m*	procedencia *f*
ornament	Ornament *n*	ornement *m*	ornamento *m*	adorno *m*, ornamento *m*
osteology	Osteologie *f*	ostéologie *f*	osteologia *f*	osteología *f*
oval	oval	ovale	ovale	oval
oven	Ofen *m*	four *m* , fourneau *m*	fornace *f* , forno *m*	horno *m*
oven layer	Ofenschicht *f*	couche *f* d'un fourneau	strato *m* di fornace	estrato *m* de horno
overburden	Abraum *m*	déblai *m*	terra *f* di scarico	escombro *m*
overburden, surface soil	Oberboden *m*	horizon A *m*	solaio *m*	capa superficial *f*
oxidation	Oxidation *f* , Oxidierung *f*	oxydation *f*	ossidazione *f*	oxidación *f*
oxide	Oxid *n*	oxyde *m*	ossido *m*	óxido *m*
oxidized	oxidiert	oxydé/-ée	ossidato/-a	oxidado/-a
pad	Unterlage *f*	sous-main *m*	sostegno *m*	carpeta *f*
padding material	Polstermaterial (zum Lagern) *n*	matériel *m* de rembourrage	imbottitura *f*	material *m* de relleno
paintbrush	Pinsel *m*	brosse *f*	pennello *m*	pincel *m*
paint coating	Farbüberzug *m*	film *m* de couleur	verniciatura *f*	capa *f* de color
painting	Bemalung *f*	peinture *f*	pintura *f*	pintura *f*
palace	Palast *m*	palais *m*	palazzo *m*	palacio *m*
palaeoanatomy	Paläoanatomie *f*	paléoanatomie *f*	paleoanatomia *f*	paleoanatomía *f*
palaeoanthropology	Paläoanthropologie *f*	paléoanthropologie *f*	paleoantropologia *f*	paleoantropología *f*
palaeobotanic	Paläobotanik *f*	paléobotanique *f*	paleobotanica *f*	paleobotánica *f*
palaeogenetic	Paläogenetik *f*	paléogénétique *f*	paleogenetica *f*	paleogenética *f*
palaeolithic	Paläolithikum *n*	paléolithique *m*	paleolitico *m*	paleolítico *m*
palaeontology	Paläontologie *f*	paléontologie *f*	paleontologia *f*	paleontología *f*
palaestra	Palästra *f*	palestre *f*	palestra *f*	palestra *f*
pale	blass	pâle	pallido/-a, smorto/-a	livido/-a, pálido/-a
palisade	Palisade *f*	palissade *f*	palizzata *f*	empalizada *f*
palmette, palm leaf	Palmette *f*	palmette *f*	palmetta *f*	palmeta *f*
paper	Papier *n*	papier *m*	carta *f*	papel *m*
papyrus	Papyrus *m*	papyrus *m*	papiro *m*	papiro *m*

Greek		Turkish	Arabic	
μετάλλευμα *n*	metallevma	maden cevheri	خام	cham elhadid
οργανικός	organikos	organik	عضوي	udwie
προσανατολισμός *m*	prosanatolismos	yön tayin etme	توجيه	tawgieh
προέλευση *f*	proelefsi	asıl, kök, köken	أصل	asl
αρχικός, αυθεντικός	archikos, afthentikos	asıl, özgün gerçek	أصل	asl
προέλευση *f*	proelefsi	köken, menşe, soy	أصل / منشأ	asl/ manschaa
κόσμημα *n*	kosmima	bezek, süs, süsleme	زخرفة	zachrafa
οστεολογία *f*	osteologia	Osteoloji	علم العظام	elm elizam
ωοειδής	ooidis	oval	بيضوي	baidawie
φούρνος *m*	fournos	fırın, ocak	فرن	forn
στρώμα κλιβάνου *n*	stoma klivanou	fırın katmanı	طبقة فرن	tabaket forn
κατάλοιπα *n pl*	kataloipa	kazılmış toprak	رديم	rediem
επιφανειακό χώμα *n*	epifaneiako choma	humuslu toprak	تربة سطحية	torba sathija
οξείδωση *f*	oxeidosi	oksitleme, oksidasyon	أكسدة	aksada
οξείδιο *n*	oxeidio	oksit	أوكسيد	oksied
οξειδωμένος	oxeidomenos	okside edilmiş	مؤكسد	moaksada
βάση *f*	vasi	altlık	قاعدة / مستند	kaeda/ mustanad
(παρα)γέμισμα *n*	(para)gemisma	salmastra malzemesi	متطلبات التنجيد	motatalebat eltangied
πινέλο *n*	pinelo	fırça	فرشة	furscha
έγχρωμο επίχρισμα *n* , επικάλυψη *f* χρώματος	egchromo epichrisma, epikalipsi chromatos	renkli kaplama	طلاء بالألوان	tilaa belalwan
βαφή *f*	vafi	boyama	رسم	rasm natigat elbahs
παλάτιον *n*	palation	saray	قصر	kasr
παλαιοανατομία *f*	palaioanatomia	Paleoanatomi	علم التشريح القديم	elm eltaschrieh elkadiem
παλαιοανθρωπολογία *f*	palaioanthropologia	Paleoantropoloji	علم الإنسان القديم	elm elensan elkadiem
παλαιοβοτανική *f*	palaiovotaniki	Paleobotanik	علم النبات القديم	elm elnabat elkadiem
παλαιογενετική *f*	palaiogenetiki	Paleogenetik	علم الوراثة القديمة	elm elwirasa elkadima
Παλαιολιθική Εποχή *f*	Palaiolithiki Epochi	Paleotik Çağ	العصر الحجري القديم	elasr elhagarie elkadim
Παλαιοντολογία *f*	Palaiontologia	Fosil Bilimi, Paleontoloji	علم المتحجرات	elm elmotahagirat
παλαίστρα *f*	palaistra	palaestra	معهد المصارعة	maahad elmosarah
ανοιχτόχρωμος, χλωμός	anichtochromos, chlomos	solgun	شاحب	schaheb
πασσαλόπυκτος περίβολος *m*	passalopiktos perivolos	kazıklarla yapılmış set	سياج	siejag
ανθέμιο *n*	anthemio	palmet	سعف النخل	saaf elnachl
χαρτί *n*	charti	kağıt	ورق	warak rasm
πάπυρος *m*	papiros	papirüs	ورقة بردي	waraket bardie

English	German	French	Italian	Spanish
parallel	parallel	parallèle	parallelo/-a	paralelo
parapet walk	Wehrgang *m*	chemin *f* de ronde	cammino *m* di ronda	adarve *m*
parchment	Pergament *n*	parchemin *m*	pergamena *f*	pergamino *m*
paries	Gefäßwandung *f*	paroi *f* (du/des vases)	parete *f* del vaso	pared *f*
part	Teil *m*	part *f*, partie *f*	parte *f*	parte *f*
partition wall	Trennwand *f*	mur *m* de séparation	parete *f* divisoria	tabique *m*
partly	teilweise	partiel	parziale	parcial
passage	Übergang *m*	passage *m*	passaggio *m*	paso *m*, transición *f*
pathology	Pathologie *f*	Pathologie *f*	patologia *f*	patología *f*
patina	Patina *f*	patine *f*	patina *f*	pátina *f*
patriarchy	Patriarchat *n*	patriarcat *m*	partriarcato *m*	patriarcado *m*
pattern	Muster *n*	modèle *m*, motif *m*	esempio *m*, modello *m*	modelo *m*, patrón *m*
peak, summit	Gipfel *m*	cime *f*, sommet *m*	vertice *m*	cima *f*
pearl	Perle *f*	perle *f*	perla *f*	perla *f*
pebble	Bachkiesel *m*	galets *m* roulés, gravier *m* fluvial	ciottolo *m*	guijas del río *f*
peculiarity	Auffälligkeit *f*	caractère *m* frappant, particularité *f*	vistosità *f*	espectacularidad *f*, peculiaridad *f*
pedestal	Standfuß *m*	pied *m*	supporto *m*	pie *m* (alto)
pediment	Giebel *m*	pignon *m*	frontone *m*	frontón *m*
pedology	Pedologie *f*	pédologie *f*	pedologia *f*	pedología *f*
pen	Stift *m*	crayon *m*	matita *f*	clavija *f*
pencil	Bleistift *m*	crayon *m*	matita *f*	lápiz *m*
pendant	Anhänger *m*	pendentif *m*	pendaglio *m*	colgante *m*
penguin	Pinguin *m*	manchot *m*	pinguino *m*	pájaro *m*
period	Periode *f*	période *f*	periodo *m*	período *m*
period of prosperity	Blütezeit *f*	épanouissement m	periodo *m* aureo	apogeo *m*
peristyle, portico	Portikus *f*, Säulenhalle *f*	galerie *f*, portique *m*	portico *m*	pórtico *m*
permafrost	Dauer-/ Permafrost *m*	gel *m* persistant	permafrost *m*	helada permanente
persian	persisch	perse/ persique	persiano/-a	pérsico/-a
perspective	Perspektive *f*	perspective *f*	prospettiva *f*	perspectiva *f*
perturbation layer	Störungshorizont *m*	horizon *m* perturbé	fase *f* di distruzione	nivel *m* de derrumbe
pestle	Stößel *m*	pilon *m*	pestello *m*	mano *m* de almirez
phase	Phase *f*	phase *m*	fase *f*	fase *f*
Phoenician	phönizisch	phénicien/-ienne	fenicio/-a	fenicio/-a
photo dokumentation	Fotodokumentation *f*	documentation *f* photographique	documentazione *f* fotografica	documentación *f* fotográfica
photogrammetry	Photogrammetrie *f*	photogrammétrie *f*	fotogrammetria *f*	fotogrametría *f*
photo, picture	Foto *n*	photo *f*	fotografia *f*	foto *f*

Greek		Turkish	Arabic	
παράλληλος	parallilos	paralel	موازي	muwazie
έπαλξη f	epalxi	savunma geçidi	ممرللدفاع	mamar leldefaa
περγαμηνή f	pergamini	parşömen	مخطوط علي جلد حيوان	machtut ala geld heiwan
τοίχωμα αγγείουn	tichoma angioui	cidar	جدار الإناء	gedar elenaa
τμήμα n	tmima	bölüm, kısım, pay	جزء	guzaa
διαχωριστικός τοίχος m	diachoristikos toichos	ara duvar	جدار عازل	gedar azel
εν μέρει, μερικώς	en meri, merikos	kısmen	جزئي	guzie
μετάβαση f	metavasi	aşama, geçiş	انتقال	entikal
παθολογία f	pathologia	patoloji	علم الأمراض	elm elamrad
πατίνα f	patina	patina	صدأ النحاس	sadaa elnahas
πατριαρχία f	patriarchia	ataerkilik	النظام البطريكي	elnizam elbatriekie
μοτίβο n , σχήμα n	motivo, schima	desen, örnek	نموذج	namuzag
κορ(υ)φή f	kor(i)fi	zirve	قمة	kema
μαργαριτάρι n	margaritari	inci	لؤلؤة	loaloah
βότσαλο n	votsalo	çakıl taş, dere çakılı, yassı çakıl	حصى	hasa
ιδιαιτερότητα f	idiaterotita	alışılmamışlık, dikkati çeken, göze çarpan	إلفات النظر	ilfat elnazar
βάθρο n	vathro	sabit ayağı	حامل	haamel
αέτωμα n	aetoma	alınlık, çatı tepesi, fronton	جملون	gamalon
εδαφολογία f	edafologia	Pedoloji	علم التربة	elm eltorba
στυλό n	stilo	çivi, kalem	قلم	kalam
μολύβι n	molivi	kurşunkalem	قلم رصاص	kalam resas
περίαπτο n	periapto	pandantif	قلادة	keladah
πιγκουίνος f	pigkouinos	penguen	بطريق	batriek
περίοδος f	periodos	devre, dönem, periyot	فترة	fatra
ακμή f	akmi	en parlak dönem	عصر الإزدهار	asr elizdehaar
στοά f, υπόστυλη αίθουσα f	stoa, ipostili aithousa	Porticus, sütunlu avlu, sütunlu salon	بهو معمد	baho moamad
μόνιμα παγωμένο έδαφος n	monima pagomeno edafos	sürekli don	صقيع طويل الأمد	sakiea tawil elamad
περσικός	persikos	Fars, İran	فارسي	faresie
προοπτική f	prooptiki	derinlik çizimi, persfektif	منظور	manzur
στρώμα διατάραξης m	stroma diataraxis	tahrib edilmiş tabaka	أفق الاضطراب	ufok eletiraab
κοπανιστήρι n	kopanistiri	tokmak	مدقة	medaka
φάση f	fasi	devre dönem, evre, safha	مرحلة	marhala
φοινικός	fonikos	Fenikeli	فينيقي	finikie
φωτογραφική καταγραφή f	fotografiki katagrafi	fotoğrafla belgeleme	توثيق بالصور	tawsiek belsowar
φωτογραμμετρία f	fotogrammetria	fotogrammetri	المسح التصويري	elmash eltaswirie
φωτογραφία f	fotografia	fotoğraf	صورة	sura

English	German	French	Italian	Spanish
photo tablet	Fototafel *f*	plaque *f* photo, tableau *m*	tavola *f* fotografica	pizarra *f* tablón para la documentación fotográfica
pH-value	PH-Wert *m*	pH *m*	pH *m*	valor pH *m*
pigment	Pigment *n*	pigment *m*	pigmento *m*	pigmento *m*
pile, post	Pfahl *m*	pieu *m*	palo *m*	estaca *f*, poste *m*
pillar	Pfeiler *m*	pilier *m*	pilone *m*	pilar *m*
pine	Kiefer *f*	pin *m*	pino *m*	pino *m*
pipe, tube	Rohr *n*	tube *m* , tuyau *m*	canna *f*, tubo *m*	tubo *m*
pitch	Pech *n*	poix *f*	pece *f*	betún *m*
pitched/ gable roof	Satteldach *n*	toit *m* à double pente	tetto a spioventi *m*	techo de dos vertientes *n*
pitcher	Gießgefäß *n*	vase *m* verseur	annaffiatoio *m*	vaso *m* para servir liquido
pithos burial	Pithosbestattung *f*	sépulture *f* en pithos	sepoltura *f* in pithos	tumba *f* en pithos
pithos, storage vessel	Pithos *m*, Vorratsgefäß *n*	jarre *f*, pithos *m*, vase *m* de stockage	dolio *m* , pithos *m*	pithos *m* , recipiente *m*
pithos, storage vessel	Vorratsgefäß *n*, Pithos *m*	pithos *m* , jarre *f*, vase *m* de stockage	dolio *m* , pithos *m*	pithos *m* , recipiente *m*
place of ritual activity	Kultplatz *m*	site *m* cultuel	luogo *m* consacrato al culto	lugar *m* de culto
place of sacrifice	Opferplatz *m*	lieu *m* de sacrifice	luogo *m* del sacrificio	lugar *m* del sacrificio
plain	tongrundig	brut/-e	a fondo argilloso	arcilloso/-a
plant	Pflanze *f*	plante *f*	pianta *f*	planta *f*
plant	pflanzlich	végétal/-e	vegetale	vegetal
plant remains	Pflanzenreste *pl*	restes *m pl* végétaux	resti *m pl* vegetale	restos *m pl* vegetales
plaster	Putz *m*	crépi *m*, enduit *m*	intonaco *m*	atavio *m* , revoque *m*
plaster bandage	Gipsbinde *f* (zum Abformen)	bande *f* plâtrée	benda *f* con gesso	gasa *f* enyesada
plaster, road pavement	Pflaster (Straße)	dallage *m* , pavé *m*	pavimentazione *f*, selciato *m*	empedrado *m*, pavimento *m*
plaster, stucco	Stuck *m*	stuc *m*	stucco *m*	estuco *m*
plastic	Kunststoff *m*	matière *m* plastique	materia *f* sintetica, plastica *f*	plástico *m*
plastic	Plastik *n*	plastique *m*	plastica *f*	plástico *m*
plastic bag	Plastikbeutel *m*	sachet *m* plastique	sacchetto *m* di plastica	bolsa *f* de plástico
plastic container	Kunststoffbehälter *m*	réservoir *m* plastique	contenitore *m* plastico	container *m* de plástico
plastic foil	Plastikfolie *f*	feuille *f* de plastique	pellicola *f* trasparente	malla *f* de plástico
Plasticine	Plastilin *n*	pâte *f* à modeler	plastilina *f*	plastilina *f*
plate	Teller *m*	assiette *f*	piatto *m*	plato *m*
plateau	Hochebene *f*, Plateau *n*	(haut) plateau *m*	altopiano *m*	altiplano *m*, meseta *f*
platform	Plattform *f*	estrade *f*, plate-forme *f*	piattaforma *f*	plataforma *f*
Pleistocene	Pleistozän *n*	Pléistocène *m*	pleistocene *m*	pleistoceno *m*

Greek		Turkish	Arabic	
φωτογραφικός πίνακας *m*	fotografikos pinakas	fotoğraf levhası	لوحة صور	lohat sowar
τιμή του pH *f*	timi tou pH	PH-değeri	قيمة درجة الحموضة	kimat daraget elhomuda
βαφή *f*, χρωστική *f*	vafi, chrostiki	boya ham maddesi	صبغة	sabga
πάσσαλος *m*, παλούκι *n*	passalos, palouki	direk, kazık	عمود خشبي	amud chaschabie
πεσσός *m*	pessos	dayanak, destek	عمود مربع	amud murabaa
πεύκο *n*	pefko	çene	خشب الصنوبر	chaschab elsanubar
σωλήνας *m*	solinas	boru, kamış, saz	ماسورة	masura
πίσσα, ξυλόπισσα *f*	pissa, xilopissa	çam katranı, zift	زفت / سوء الحظ	zeft/ sua elhaz
δικλινής στέγη *f*	diklinis stegi	beşik çatı	سقف جملوني	sakf gamalonie
κανάτα *f*, οινοχόη *f*	kanata inochoi	döküm kabı	إبريق	ibriek
εγχυτρισμός *m*	egchitrismos	pithos gömü	الدفن في الزير	eldafn fi elzier
πίθος *m*, αποθηκευτικό, αγγείο *n*	pithos, apothikeftikos, angio	depolama kabı, küp	وعاء للتخزين	wiaa leltachzien
πίθος *m*, πιθάρι *n*, αποθηκευτικό αγγείο *n*	pithos, pithari, apothikeftiko angio	pithos, vakum kabı	زير	zier
χώρος *m* λατρείας	choros latreias	kült alanı, kült yeri	مكان للعبادة	makan lelabada
χώρος θυσιών *m*	choros thision	adak yeri	مكان التضحية	makan eltadhija
στο χρώμα του πηλού	sto chroma tou pilou	kil zeminli	ذو أساس طيني	zo asas tienie
φυτό *n*	fito	bitki	نبات	nabat
φυτικός	fitikos	bitkisel	نباتي	nabatie
φυτικά κατάλοιπα *n pl*	fitika kataloipa	bitki artıkları	بقايا نباتات	bakaja nabat
γύψος *m*	gipsos	sıva	طلاء	tilaa
γυψόγαζα *f*, γυψοεπ ίδεσμος *m*	gipsogaza, gipsoepidesmos	alçı band, alçılı sargı bezi	رباط جبسي	rubat gebsie
κατάστρωμα οδού *n*, λιθόστρωτο *n*	katastoma odou, lithostroto	kaldırım	رصيف (الطريق)	rasief (eltariek)
γύψος *m*, stucco *n*	gipsos, stukko	mermer sıva, stuko	زخارف مُلصقة	zacharef molsaka
πλαστικό *n*	plastiko	plastik, suni madde	بلاستيك	blastik
πλαστικό *n*	plastiko	plastik	بلاستيك	blastik
πλαστική σακούλα *f*	plastiki sakoula	plastik torba, poşet	كيس بلاستيك	kies blastik
πλαστικό δοχείο *n*	plastikio dochio	plastik kap	حاوية بلاستيك	hawija blastik
νάιλον *n*	nailon	plastik folyo	مشمع بلاستيك	mischama blastik
πλαστελίνη *f*	plastelini	plastilin	صلصال ملون	selsal melawen
πιάτο *n*, πιν άκιο *n*	piato, pinakio	tabak	طبق	tabak
υψίπεδο *n*	ipsipedo	yüksek ova, yayla, plato	هضبة	hadaba
εξέδρα *f*	exedra	platform	أساس	asas
Πλειστόκαινο *n*	Pleistokaino	Buzul Çağı	العصر الجليدي	elasr elgalidie

English	German	French	Italian	Spanish
Pliocene	Pliozän n	Pliocène m	pliocene m	plioceno m
plug	Dübel m	cheville f	tassello m	clavija m
plumb	Lot n	fil m à plomb	filo m a piombo	plomada f
plumb	Senkblei n	fil f à plomb	piombino m	plomada f
pluvial period	Pluvialzeit f	période f pluviale	periodo m pluviale	período m pluvial
pluvial, rainy	pluvial, regnerisch	pluvieux/-euse	piovoso/-a	lluvioso/-a
podium, stage	Podium n	podium m	podio m	estrado m , podium m
pointed	spitz	pointu/-e	aguzzo/-a	agudo/-a
point of fracture	Bruchstelle f	cassure f	punto m di rottura	punto m de rotura
point of orientation	Orientierungspunkt m	repère m	punto m d'orientamento	punto m de referencia
point, tip	Spitze f	pointe f	punta f	punta f
poisoned	giftig	toxique	velenoso/-a	tóxico/-a, venenoso/-a
pole, post	Pfosten m	poteau m	palo m	poste m
polis	Polis f	polis f	polis f	polis f
polished ware	polierte Ware f	céramique f polie	ceramica f lucida	cerámica f lustrada/ pulida
polishing stone	Polierstein m	polissoir m	pietra f da politura	piedra f para pulir
pollen	Blütenstaub m, Pollen	pollen m	polline m	polen m
pollutant, toxin	Schadstoff m	polluant m	tossico m	sustancia f nociva
polychrome	mehrfarbig, polychrom	polychrome	policromo/-a	multicolor
polygonal	polygonal	polygonal	poligonale	poligonal
polytheism	Polytheismus m	polythéisme	politeismo m	politeísmo m
polyurethane foam	Polyurethanschaum (PU-Schaum) m	mousse f de polyuréthane	schiuma f poliuretanica	espuma f poliuretano
porosity	Porosität f	porosité f	porosità f	porosidad f
porous	porig, porös	poreux/-euse	poroso/-a	poroso/-a
portal	Portal n	portail m	portale m	portal m
portrait	Portrait n	portrait m	ritratto m	retrato m
position	Position f	position f	posizione f	posición f
positive	positiv	positif/-ve	positivo/-a	positivo/-a
post-Christian	nachchristlich	de l'ère chrétienne	dopo Cristo	después de Cristo
posthole	Pfostenloch n	trou m de poteau	buca f di palo	hoyo m de poste
postmortem	postmortal	postmortel/-elle	dopo la morte	pos(t)mortal
postprocessing	Nachbearbeitung f	aménagement m postérieur	rifinitura f, rilavorazione f	trabajo m de repaso
pot digger/ hunter	Raubgräber m	fouilleur m clandestin	scavatore m clandestino, tombarolo m	ladrón m
potsherd	Scherbe f	tesson m	coccio m	casco m , pedazos m

Greek		Turkish	Arabic	
Πλειόκαινο *n*	Pleiokaino	Pliosen	الفترة الأقرب للعصر الحديث	elfatra elakrab lelasr elhadies
βύσμα *n*	visma	dübel	خابور	chabur
μολυβδοκόλληση *f*	molivdokollisi	çekül, şakül	ميزان لتحديد الوضع العمودي	mizan letahdied elwada elamudie
νήμα της στάθμης *n*	nima tis stathmis	çekül, şakul	مطمار	metmar
περίοδος βροχών	periodos vrochon	yağmur çağı	العصر المطير	elasr elmatier
όμβριος, βρόχινος	omvrios, vrochinos	yağmurlu	مُمطر	momter
βήμα *n* , προσκήνιο *n*	vima, proskinio	platform, podyum	منصة	minasa
οξυκόρυφος	oxikorifos	keskin, sivri uçlu	حاد	haad
σημείο *n* θραύσης	simio thrafsis	kırık yeri	نقطة الانهيار	noktat elenhiear
σημείο προσανατολισμού *n*	simio prosanatolismou	nirengi noktası	نقطة التوجه	nuktet eltawgieh
κορυφή *f* , μύτη *f*	korifi, miti	üst kısım, uç	سن	sen
δηλητηριώδης	dilitiriodis	zehirli	سام	saam
πάσσαλος *m* , παλούκι *n*	passalos, palouki	destek direği, kazık	قائمة خشبية	kaima chaschabija
πόλις *f* , πόλη *f*	polis, poli	polis	مدينة مستقلة إداريا	madina mostakela idarijan
στιλβωμένη κεραμική *f*	stilvomeni keramiki	cilalı mal	سلعة ملمعة	sela molamaa
λειαντικός/ στιλβωτικός λίθος *m*	leiantikos/stilvotikos lithos	parlatma taşı	حجر للتنعيم	hagar leltaniem
γύρη *f*	giri	çiçek tozu, polen	اللقاح	ellekah
τοξική ουσία *f*	toxiki ousia	zararlı madde	مادة ضارّة	mada darah
πολύχρωμος	polichromos	çok renkli	متعدد الألوان	mutaaded elalwan
πολυγωνικός	poligonikos	çok köşeli	مضلع	modalaa
πολυθεϊσμός *m*	politheismos	çoktanrıcılık	تعدد الآلهة	taadod elaleha
αφρός πολυουρεθάνης *m*	afros poliourethanis	poliüretan köpüğü	رغاوي اليوريتان المتعدد	ragawie elyuretjan elmotaaded
πορώδες *n*	porodes	gözeneklilik	مسامية	masamija
πορώδης	porodis	gözenekli	مسامى	masamie
πυλώνας *m* , πύλη *f*	pilonas, pili	ana kapı, porta	بوابة	bawaba
προσωπογραφία *f* , πορτραίτο *n*	prosopografia, portraito	portre	صورة شخص	suret schachs
θέση *f*	thesi	durum, yer	وضع	wadaa
θετικός	thetikos	kati, olumlu, veri	إيجابي	igabie
μεταχριστιανικός	metachristianikos	İsa'dan, Milattan Sonra	بعد الميلاد	baad elmilad
πασσαλότρυπα *f*	passalotripa	direk çukuru	ثقب فى القائمة الخشبية	sokb fi elkaima elchaschbija
μεταθανάτιος	metathanatios	ölümden sonra olan	بعد الموت	bada elmawat
μετεπεξαργασία *f*	metepexargasia	tekrar işleme	معالجة لاحقة	mualaga laheka
λαθρανασκαφέας *m*	lathranaskafeas	kaçak kazıcılar, yağmacılar	مقابر مسروقة	makaber masruka
όστρακο *n*	ostrako	kırık çömlek parçası	كسرة فخارية	kesra fuchareja

English	German	French	Italian	Spanish
potter's mark	Töpfermarke *f*	marque *f* de potier	stampiglia *f* del vasaio	sellos *m* del alfarero
potter's wheel	Töpferscheibe *f*	tour *m* de potier	tornio *m* da vasaio	torno *m* de alfarero
pounder	Schlagstein *m*	percuteur *m*	percussore *m* di pietra	piedra *f* de percusión
praefurnium	Praefurnium *n*	praefurnium *m*	prefurnio *m*	prefurnio *m*
precautions/ safety measures	Schutzmaßnahmen *pl*	mesures *f pl* de protection	misure *f pl* di protezione	medida *f* preventiva
pre-Christian	vorchristlich	d'avant l'ère *f* chrétienne	avanti Cristo	antes de Cristo
precious metal	Edelmetall *n*	métal *m* précieux	metallo *m* nobile	metal *m* noble / precioso
prehistoric	frühzeitlich	archaïque	preistorico/-a	temprano/-a
prehistory	Vorgeschichte *f*	préhistoire *f*	preistoria *f*	prehistoria *f*
preparation	Präparation *f*	préparation *f*	preparazione *f*	preparación *f*
preparation	Vorbereitung *f*	préparation *f*	preparazione *f*	preparación *f*
preparation surface	Präparationsfläche *f*	face *f* de préparation	superficie da preparazione *f*	superficie preparatoria *f*
pressed	gepresst	pressé	pressato/-a, spremuto/-a	comprimido/-a
prestige goods	Prestigegüter *pl*	biens *m pl* de prestige	merce *f* di prestigio	cosas *f pl* del prestigio
prevention	Prävention *f*	prévention *f*	prevenzione *f*	prevención *f*
preventive	präventiv	préventif/-ve	preventivo/-a	preventivo/-a
priest	Priester *m*	prêtre *m*	sacerdote *m*	cura *m*, sacerdote *m*
primary	primär	primaire	primario/-a	primario/-a
primitive	primitiv	primitif/-ve	primitiv/-a	primitivo/-a
prismatic square	Winkelprisma *n*	prisme *m* angulaire	prisma *m* squadrato	escuadra *f* de agrimensor
process	Prozess *m*	processus *m*	processo *m*	proceso *m*
production	Herstellung *f*	production *f*	produzione *f*	producción *f*
production	Produktion *f*	production *f*	fabbricazione *f*, produzione *f*	fabricación *f*, producción *f*
production facility	Produktionsstätte *f*	centre *m* / site *m* de production	luogo *m* di produzione	lugar *f* de producción
production method/ process	Produktionsverfahren *n*	méthode *f*/ technique *f* de production	metodo *m* di produzione	método *m* de producción
professional	fachgerecht	approprié/-ée	a regola d'arte	profesional
profile	Profil *n*	profil *m*	profilo *m*	perfil *m*
(profile) section	Profilschnitt *m*	coupe *f*	profilo *m*	sección del profil
project	Projekt *n*	projet *m*	progetto *m*	proyecto *m*
projection	Projektion *f*	projection *f*	proiezione *f*	proyección *f*
proof	Beweis *m*	preuve *f*	prova *f*	muestra *f*, prueba *f*
proof	Nachweis *m*	preuve *f*	prova *f*	prueba *f*
proportion, relation	Verhältnis *n*	proportion *f*, relation *f*	proporzione *f*, relazione *f*	escala *f*, relación *f*
propylon	Propylon *n*	propylée *m*	propileo *pl*	propíleo *m*

Greek		Turkish	Arabic	
σήμα κεραμέως *n*	sima kerameos	çömlekçi işareti	علامة صانع الفخار	alamet sanea elfuchar
κεραμικός τροχός *m*	keramikos trochos	çömlekçi çarkı	عجلة صناع الفخار	agalet sanea elfuchar
γουδοχέρι *n*	goudocheri	yontma taş	مدقة حجرية	medaka hagarija
προπνιγείο *n*	propnigeio	praefurnium	حمام	hammam
προστατευτικά μέτρα *n pl*	prostateftika metra	koruyucu önlemler, koruma tedbirleri	إجراءات وقائية	igraat wikaija
προχριστιανικός	prochristianikos	İsa'dan önce, Milattan Önce	قبل الميلاد	kabl elmilad
πολύτιμο μέταλλο *f*	politimo metallo	değerli maden	معدن ثمين	madan samin
προϊστορικός	proistorikos	arkaik, erken dönem	مُبكر	mobaker
προϊστορία *f*	proistoria	tarihöncesi	عصور ما قبل التاريخ	usur ma kabl eltariech
προετοιμασία *f*	proetoimasia	hazırlanma	إعداد	iadad
προετοιμασία *f*	proetoimasia	hazırlanma	تحضير	tahdier
επιφάνεια προετοιμασίας *f*	epifania proetoimasias	hazırlanma alanı	منطقة الإعداد	manteket eliadad
πεπιεσμένος	pepiesmenos	basılmış, preslenmiş	مكبوس	makbus
αντικείμενα κύρους *n pl*	antikeimena kirous	prestijli ürünler	سلع للتباهى	sela leltabahie
πρόληψη *f*	prolipsi	önleme, önüne geçme	وقاية	wikaja
προληπτικός	proliptikos	koruyucu, önleyici	وقائي	wikaie
ιερέας *m*	iereas	rahip	كاهن	kahen
πρωτεύων	protevon	asıl, birincil, ilk	أساسي	asasie
πρωτόγονος	protogonos	basit, ham, ilkel	بدائي	bidaie
τοπογραφικό πρίσμα *n*	topografiko prisma	dikdörtgen prizma	موشور زاوية	moschur zawija
διαδικασία *f*	diadikasia	süreç	عملية	amaleja
κατασκευή *f*	kataskefi	imalat, üretim, yapım	إنتاج	intag
παραγωγή *f*	paragogi	imalat, mamul, ürün	إنتاج	entag
παραγωγική εγκατάσταση *f*	paragogiki egkatastasi	üretim yeri	مصنع	masna
μέθοδος παραγωγής *f*	methodos paragogis	üretim yöntemi	عملية الانتاج	amalejet elentag
επαγγελματικός	epangelmatikos	kuralınca, ustaca	متخصص	motachases
πλάγια όψη *f*, προφίλ *n*	plagia opsi, profil	profil, yatay kesit	مقطع عرضي / صورة جانبية	makta ardie/ sura ganibija
τμήμα κατατομής *n*	tmima katatomis	yanal kesit	مقطع جانبي	maktaa ganibie
πρόγραμμα *n* , σχέδιο *n*	programma, schedio	proje	مشروع	maschrua
προβολή *f*	provoli	projeksiyon, yansıtma	إسقاط	iskaat
απόδειξη *f*	apodexi	kanıt, ispat	دليل	dalil
απόδειξη *f*	apodexi	delil, ispat, kanıt	إثبات	isbat
σχέση *f*	schesi	ilişki	علاقة	ilaka
πρόπυλο(ν) *n*	propilo(n)	propylon	صرح أمامى	sarh amamie

English	German	French	Italian	Spanish
prospection	Prospektion *f*	prospection *f*	prospezione *f*	prospección *f*
protection	Schutz *m*	protection *f*	protezione *f*	protección *f*
protective coating	Schutzlack *m*	laque *f* de protection	lacca protettiva	barniz protector *m*
prove	beweisen	prouver	provare	demostrar, evidenciar
provincial Roman	provinzialrömisch	provincial romain/-e (gallo-romain/-e)	romano/-a provinciale	romano/-a provincial
provision, supply	Versorgung *f*	approvisionnement *m*	mantenimento *m*	provisión *f*
proximity, vicinity	Nähe *f*	proximité *f*, voisinage *m*	prossimità *f*, vicinanza *f*	proximidad *f*
publication	Publikation *f*	publication *f*	pubblicazione *f*	publicación *f*
pumice stone	Bimsstein *m*	pierre *f* ponce	pietra *f* pomice	piedra *f* pómez
pyramid	Pyramide *f*	pyramide *f*	piramide *f*	pirámide *f*
pyroclastic cloud	pyroklastische Wolke *f*	nuage *m* pyroclastique	nube *f* piroclastica	nube piroclástica *f*
quadrant	Quadrant *m*	quadrant *m*	quadrante *m*	cuadrante *m*
quarry	Steinbruch *m*	carrière *f*	cava *f* di pietra	cantera *f*
quartz crystal	Quarz *n*	quartz *m*	quarzo *m*	cuarzo *m*
quartz sand	Quarzsand *m*	sable *m* de quartz	sabbia *f* quarzifera	arena *m* de cuarzo
queen	Königin *f*	reine *f*	regina *f*	reina *f*
question	Frage *f*	question *f*	domanda *f*	cuestión *f*
question	Fragestellung *f*	problème *m*, question *f*	formulazione *f* della domanda	cuestión *f*
race	Rasse *f*	race *f*	razza *f*	raza *f*
raddle	Rötel *m*	ocre rouge *f*	sanguigna *f*	almagre *m*
radioactivity	Radioaktivität *f*	radioactivité *f*	radioattività *f*	radiactividad *f*
radiocarbon dating	Radiocarbon-Datierung *f*	datation *f* par le radiocarbone	datazione *f* con il radiocarbonio	datación *f* por radiocarbono
radius	Radius *m*	rayon *m*	raggio *m*	radio *m*
raft	Floß *n*	radeau *m*	zattera *f*	almadía *f*
rain	Regen *m*	pluie *f*	pioggia *f*	lluvia *f*
rampart	Festungswall *m*, Wallanlage *f*	enceinte *f*	bastione *m*	fortificación *f*, valla *f*
rampart, wall	Wall *m*	rempart *m*	vallo *m*	terraplén *m*
ranging pole/ rod	Fluchtstange *f*	jalon *m*	palina *f*	báston *m*, jalon
rank, status	Status *m*, Stellung *f*	position *f*, situation *f*	posizione *f*	posición *f*
raster	Raster *n*	quadrillage *m*	retino *m*	retículo *m*
raw	roh	brut	crudo/-a, grezzo/-a	bruto/-a, crudo/-a
raw material	Rohmaterial *n*	matière *f* brute/ première	materiale *m* grezzo	material *m* en bruto
raw material	Rohstoff *m*	matière *f* première	materia *f* prima	materias *f* primas
recess, residue	Rückstand *m*	résidu *m*	residuo *m*, resto *m*	residuo *m*
reconstruction	Rekonstruktion *f*	reconstruction *f*	ricostruzione *f*	reconstrucción *f*

Greek		Turkish	Arabic	
αναζήτηση *f*	anazitisi	prospeksiyon	تنقيب	tankib
προστασία *f*	prostasia	koruma, savunma	حماية	himaja
προστατευτικό βερνίκι *n*	prostateftiko verniki	koruma cilası, verniği	طلاء واقي	tilaa wakie
αποδεικνύω	apodeiknio	ispatlamak, kanıtlamak	يثبت	yusbit
επαρχιακός ρωμαϊκός	eparchiakos romaikos	Roma vilayetleri ile ilgili	مقاطعات رومانية	mukataat rumaneia
εφοδιασμός *m*	efodiasmos	bakım, temin etme	إمداد	imdad
εγγύτητα *f*	engitita	çevre, civar, yakınlık	قرب	korb
δημοσίευση *f*	dimosiefsi	basılan eser, yayın	نشر	naschr
ελαφρόπετρα *f*	elafropetra	sünger/ pomza taşı	حجر خفيف	hagar chafif
πυραμίδα *f*	piramida	piramit	هرم	haram
πυροκλαστικό νέφος *n*	piroklastiko nefos	piroklastik bulut	سحابة من الحُمم البركانية	sahaba men elhomam el borkanija
τεταρτοκύκλιο *n*	tetartokiklio	plankare	ربع دائرة	ruba daera
λατομείο *n*	latomeio	taş ocağı	محجر	mahgar
χαλαζίας *m*	chalazias	akik taşı, kuvars	بلور	balur
χαλαζιακή άμμος *f*	chalaziaki ammos	kuvars kumu	رمل بلوري	raml balurie
βασίλισσα *f*	vasilissa	kraliçe	ملكة	maleka
ερώτηση *f*	erotisi	soru	سؤال	suaal
ερώτημα *n*	erotima	soru sorma, soruş	سؤال	suaal
φυλή *f*	fili	ırk, soy	عنصر	unsur
ώχρα *f*	ochra	kırmızı tebeşir	حجر أحمر	hagar ahmar
ραδιενέργεια *f*	radienergia	radyoaktivite	نشاط إشعاعي	naschat eschaie
ραδιοχρονολόγηση *f*	radiochronologisi	Radyokarbon Tarihleme Yöntemi	تأريخ الكربون المشع	taarich elkarbon elmuschea
ακτίνα *f*	aktina	ön kol kemiği, yarıçap	نصف القطر	nesf elkutr
σχεδία *f*	schedia	sal	طوافة	tawafa
βροχή *f*	vrochi	yağmur	مطر	matar
οχυρωματικό ανάχωμα/ τείχος *n*	ochiromatiko anachoma/teichos	kale duvarı	جسر	gesr
ανάχωμα *n* , τείχος *n*	anachoma, teichos	sur	سد	sad
σταδία *f*	stadia	jalon	عصى للقياس	asa lelkijas
κύρος *n* , θέση *f*	kiros, thesi	iş, statü	وضع	wadaa
κάνναβος *m*	kannavos	kafes, örtücü, yatay ve dikey hatlar sistemi	شبكة خطية	schabaka chatija
ωμός, ακατέργαστος	omos, akatergastos	ham, işlenmemiş	خام	cham
ακατέργαστο υλικό *n*	akatergasto iliko	ham madde	مادة خام	mada cham
πρώτη ύλη *f*	proti ili	ham madde	مادة خام	mada cham
υπόλειμμα *n*	ipolimma	artık, kalıntı, tortu	رواسب	rawaseb
αποκατάσταση *f* , αναπαράστα ση *f*	apokatastasi, anaparastasi	eski durumuna getirme, rekonstrüksiyon	إعادة بناء	iadet benaa

English	German	French	Italian	Spanish
reconstruction drawing	Rekonstruktionszeichnung *f*	dessin *m* de restitution	disegno *m* ricostruttivo/ ricostruzione *f*	dibujo de reconstrucción *m*
recovery	Bergung *f*	sauvetage *m*	salvataggio *m*	salvamento *m*
rectangle	Rechteck *n*	rectangle *m*	rettangolo *m*	rectángulo *m*
rectangular	rechtwinklig	rectangulaire	rettangolo/-a	rectangular
reduced	reduziert	réduit/-e	ridotto/-a	reducido/-a
reduction	Reduktion *f*	réduction *f*	riduzione *f*	reducción *f*
reed, thatch	Reed *n*	roseau *m*	canneto *m*	caña *f*
reed, thatch	Schilf *n*	roseau *m*	canne *f pl*	cañaveral *m*
refridgerator	Kühlschrank *m*	réfrigérateur *m*	frigorifero *m*	nevera *f*
region	Region *f*	région *f*	regione *f*	región *f*
regional	regional	régional	regionale	regional
regular	regelmäßig	régulier/-ière	regolare	regular
related	verwandt	apparenté/-e	imparentato/-a	emparentado/-a, pariente
relative	relativ	relatif/-ve	relativo/-a	relativo/-a
relief	Relief *n*	relief *m*	rilievo *m*	relieve *m*
religious	religiös	religieux/-euse	religioso/-a	religioso/-a
reparation	Reparatur *f*	réparation *f*	riparazione *f*	reparación *f*
replica	Replik *f*	réplique *f*	replica *f*	réplica *f*
report	Bericht *m*	rapport *m*	rapporto *m*	informe *m* , memoria *f*
reproduction	Reproduktion *f*	reproduction *f*	riproduzione *f*	reproducción *f*
rescue excavation	Notgrabung *f*	fouille de sauvetage *f*	scavi di salvataggio *pl*	excavación de urgencia *f*
rescue excavation	Rettungsgrabung *f*	fouille *f* de sauvetage	scavo *m* di emergenza	excavación *f* de urgencia
research	Forschung *f*	recherche *f*	ricerche *f*	investigación *f*
research excavation	Forschungsgrabung *f*	fouille *f* de recherche	scavo *m* di ricerca	excavación *f* de investigación
resin	Harz *n*	résine *f*	resina *f*	resina *f*
result	Ergebnis *n*	résultat *m*	risultato *m*	resultado *m*
rhomboid	rautenförmig	en losange, rhombique	romboidale	romboidal
rhomboid pattern	Rautenmuster *n*	motif *m* en losange	decorazione *f* romboidale	muestra *f* de rombo
rhombus	Raute *f*	losange *m*	rombo *m*	rombo *m*
rhyton	Rhyton *m*	rhyton *m*	rhyton *m*	rhyton *m,* ritón
rib	Rippe *f*	côte *f*	costola *f*	costilla *f*
ribbon, tape	Band *n*	cordon *m,* ficelle *f*	filetto *m*	banda *f,* cinta *f*
ridge, spine	Grat *m*	arête *f,* crête *f*	cresta *f*	cresta *f*
rim	Rand *m*	bord *m*	orlo *m*	borde *m* , orilla *f*
ring	Ring *m*	anneau *m*	anello *m*	anillo *m*
ripped	gerissen	déchiré/-ée	strappato/-a	rompido/-a
risk	Risiko *n*	risque *m*	rischio *m*	riesgo *m*
rite	Ritus *m*	rite *m*	rito *m*	rito *m*

Greek		Turkish	Arabic	
σχέδιο αναπαράστασης	schedio anaparastasis	rekonstrüksiyon çizimi	رسم إعادة البناء	ras iadet elbenaa
ανάκτηση *f*	anaktisi	çıkarma, kurtarma	إنقاذ	enkaaz
ορθογώνιο *n*	orthogonio	dikdörtgen	مستطيل	mostatiel
ορθογώνιος	orthogonios	dikey açı, dikgen	قائم الزوايا	kaem elzawija
μειωμένος	meiomenos	indirgenmiş	مخفض	muchafad
μείωση *f*	meiosi	azaltma, eksiltme	تخفيض	tachfied
καλάμι *n*	kalami	hasırotu, kamış, saz	قصبة	kasaba
άχυρο *n*	achiro	hasırotu, kamış	بوص	buus
ψυγείο *n*	psigeio	buzdolabı	ثلاجة	salaga
περιοχή *f*	periochi	alan, bölge, yer	إقليم	ekliem
τοπικός	topikos	bölgesel, yerel	إقليمي	ekliemie
τακτικός	taktikos	düzenli, kurallı	منتظم	montazem
συγγενής	singenis	akraba, benzer	متعلق	motaalek
σχετικός	schetikos	ait, bağıntılı, ilintili, nispeten	نسبي	nesbie
ανάγλυφο *n*	anaglifo	kabartma, rölyef	نقش	naksch
θρησκευτικός	thriskeftikos	dindar, dini	دينى	dienie
επισκευή *f*	episkevi	onarma, tamir etme	إصلاح	islah
αντίγραφο *n*	antigrafo	kopya sanat eseri	نسخة طبق الأصل	noscha tebk elasl
αναφορά *f*	anafora	rapor	تقرير	takrier
αναπαραγωγή *f*	anaparagogi	çoğaltma	استنساخ	istensach
σωστική ανασκαφή *f*	sostiki anaskafi	kurtarma kazısı	حفريات طارئة	hafrijat tareaa
σωστική ανασκαφή *f*	sostiki anaskafi	kurtarma kazısı	حفريات للانقاذ	hafrijat lelenkaz
έρευνα *f*	erevna	araştırma, inceleme	بحث	bahs
ερευνητική ανασκαφή *f*	erevnitiki anaskafi	araştırma kazısı	حفر إستكشافى	hafr estekschafi
ρητίνη *f*	ritini	reçine	صمغ	samg
αποτέλεσμα *n*	apotelesma	netice, sonuç	نتيجة	natiga
ρομβοειδής	romvoeidis	ağ şeklinde, baklava şeklinde	شكل معين	schakl muajan
ρομβοειδές μοτίβο *n*	romvoeides motivo	baklava motifi	نموذج على شكل مُعيّن	namuzg ala schakl muajan
ρόμβος *m*	romvos	eşkenar dörtgen	معين	muajan
ρυτό *n*	rito	rhyton	إناء على شكل رأس حيوان	inaa ala schakl raas hajawan
πλευρό *n* , νεύρωση *f*	plevro, nevrosi	kaburga, yan kemer	ضلع	delaa
ταινία *f*	tainia	kordon, kuşak, şerit	رباط	rubat
κορυφογραμμή *f*	korifogrammi	bayır, sırt	حافة	hafa bareza
χείλος *n*	cheilos	kenar, kıyı, sınır	حافة	hafa
δαχτυλίδι *n*	dachtilidi	halka, yüzük	خاتم	chatem
σπασμένος	spasmenos	yarılmış, yırtılmış	مُمزق	momazak
κίνδυνος *m*	kindinos	risk	مخاطرة	muchatara
τελετή *f*	teleti	dini adet, dinsel tören	طقس	taks dinie

English	German	French	Italian	Spanish
ritual	Ritual *n*	rituel *m*	rituale *m*	ritual *m*
river	Fluss *m*	fleuve *m*, rivière *f*	fiume *m*	río *m*
riverbank	Flussrand *m*, Ufer *n*	berge *f*, bord *m*, rive *f*	riva *f*	orilla *f*
riverbed	Flussbett *n*	lit *m* de rivière/de fleuve	letto *m* del fiume	cauce *m*
rivet	Niete *f*	rivet *m*	rivetto *m*	roblón *m*
rock	Fels *m*	rocher *m*	roccia *f*	roca *f*
rock	Gesteinsart *f*	type *m* de roches	tipo *m* di roccia	tipos *f* de rocas
rock grave	Felsgrab *n*	tombe *f* rupestre	tomba *f* di roccia	sepultura *f* excavada en la roca
rock, stone	Gestein *n*	roche *f*	roccia *f*	roca *f*
Roman, etc.	römisch	romain/-e	romano/-a	romano/-a
roof	Dach *n*	toit *m*	tetto *m*	techo *m*
roof tile	Dachziegel *m*	tuile *f*	tegola *f*	ímbrix *m*, *teja m*
root	Wurzel *f*	racine *f*	radice *f*	raíz *f*
rope	Seil *n*	corde *f*	corda *f*	cuerda *f*, soga *f*
rope	Tau *n*	câble *m*, cordage *m*	cavo *m*	cuerda *f*
rosette	Rosette *f*	rosace *f*, roson *f*	rosetta *f*	rosetón *m*
rough	rau	bourru/-e	ruvido/-a, scabroso/-a	áspero/-a
round	rund	ronde	rotondo/-a	circular
rubber	Radiergummi *n*	gomme *f*	gomma *f*	goma *f* de borrar
rubbish pit	Abfallgrube *f*	fosse à détritus *m pl*	buca *f* per i rifiuti	vertedero *m* de basuras
ruin	Ruine *f*	ruine *f*	rovina *f*	ruina *f*
ruinous	ruinös	ruineux/-euse	rovinoso/-a	ruinoso/-a
ruler	Lineal *n*	règle *f*	righello *f*	regla *f*
rural	ländlich	rural/-e	rurale, rustico/-a	rural
rust	Rost *m*	rouille *f*	ruggine *f*	orín *m*, óxido *m*
rust-free, stainless	rostfrei	inoxydable, sans rouille	non arrugginito/-a	inoxidable
sacrifice	Opfer *n*	offrande *f*, sacrifice *m*	sacrificio *m*	sacrificio *m*
salinity level	Salzgehalt *m*	salinité *f*	salinità *f*	salinidad *f*
sallow, wan	fahl	blafard, terne	sbiadito/-a	descolorido/-a, lívido/-a
salt	Salz *n*	sel *m*	sale *m*	sal *f*
sample taking, sampling	Beprobung *f*	prélèvement *m* d'échantillons	campionamento *m*	muestreo *m*, tomar muestra
sample, test	Probe *f*	échantillon	prova *f*	prueba *f*
sanctuary	Heiligtum *n*	sanctuaire *m*	santuario *m*	santuario *m*
sand	Sand *m*	sable *m*	sabbia *f*	arena *f*
sanded, smoothed	geschliffen	poli/-e, taillé/-ée	affilato/-a, levigato/-a	afilado/-a, filoso/-a
sandstone	Sandstein *m*	grès *m*	pietra *f* arenaria	arenisca *f*, gres *m*
sandy	sandig	sableux/-euse	sabbioso/-a	arenoso/-a

Greek		Turkish	Arabic	
τελετουργικό *n*	teletourgiko	ibadetle ilgili tören, ritüel	طقوس	tukus dineja
ποτάμι *n*	potami	ırmak, nehir	نهر	nahr
όχθη *f*	ochthi	nehir kıyısı/ kenarı ☐	ضفة النهر	dafet elnahr
κοίτη ποταμού *f*, πυθμένας *m*	koiti potamou, pithmenas	ırmak yatağı, nehir yatağı	مجرى النهر	magra elnahr
πριτσίνι *n*	pritsini	perçin, perçin çivisi	مسمار قلاووظ معدني	mosmar kalawoz madenie
βράχος *m*	vrachos	kaya	صخرة	sachra
είδος πετρώματος *n*	eidos petromatos	kaya türü, taş türü	نوع الصخر	noaa elsachr
λαξευτός τάφος *m*	laxeftos tafos	kaya mezarı	مقبرة منقورة فى الصخر	makbara makura fi elsachr
λίθος *m* , πέτρωμα *f*	lithos, petroma	kaya, taş	صخرة	sachra
ρωμαϊκός	romaikos	Roma ile ilgili, Romalı	روماني	romanie
στέγη *f* , σκεπή *f*	stegi, skepi	çatı	سقف	sakf
κεραμίδα στέγης *f*	keramida stegis	çatı kiremidi	قرميد	karmid
ρίζα *f*	riza	kök	جذر	gezr
σκοινί/ σχοινί *n*	skoini/schini	halat, urgan	حبل	habl
σκοινί/ σχοινί *n*	skoini/schini	çiy, halat	حبل	habl
ρόδακας *m* , ροζέτα *f*	rodakas, rozeta	gül yaprağı şeklinde dairesel süsleme	رشيد	raschied
αδρός	adros	kaba, küflü, paslı	خشن	cheschen
κυκλικός, στρόγγυλος	kiklikos, strongilos	dairesel	دائري	daerie
γομολάστιχα *f*	gomolasticha	silgi	ممحاة	mumhah
αποθέτης *m*	apothetis	çöp çukuru	حفرة القمامة	hufrat elkemamah
ερείπιο *n*	ereipio	harabe, yıkıntı	أنقاض	ankad
ερειπιώδης	ereipiodis	garip, yıkıcı	مدمر	modamar
χάρακας *m*	charakas	cetvel	مسطرة	mastara
αγροτικός	agrotikos	kırsal	ريفي	rifi
οξείδωση *f*, σκωρία *f*	oxeidosi, skoria	pas	صدأ	sadaa
ανοξείδωτος	anoxeidotos	paslanmaz, passız	مقاوم للصدأ	mukawem lelsadaa
θυσία *f*	thisia	kurban	ضحية	dahija
αλμυρότητα *f*	almirotita	tuz içeriği, tuz miktarı	ملوحة	moloha
ωχρός	ochros	donuk, mat	شاحب	schaheb
αλάτι *n*	alati	tuz	ملح	malh
δειγματοληψία *f*	deigmatolipsia	numune alma	أخذ العينات	achz elajenat
δείγμα *n*	deigma	deney, örnek	عينة	aijena
ιερό *n*	iero	kutsal yer, tapınak	مكان مقدس / حرم	makan mukadas/ haram
άμμος *f*	ammos	kum	رمل	raml balurie
λειασμένος	leiasmenos	bilenmiş, zımparalı	حاد	haad
ψαμμίτης *m*	psammitis	kum taşı	حجر رملي	hagar ramlie
αμμώδης	ammodis	kumlu	رملي	ramlie

English	German	French	Italian	Spanish
sarkophagus	Sarkophag *m*	sarcophage *m*	sarcofago *m*	sarcófago *m*
savety	Sicherheit *f*	protection *f*	sicurezza *f*	seguridad *f*
saw	Säge *f*	scie *f*	sega *f*	sierra *f*
sawn	gesägt	scié/-e	segato/-a	serrado/-a
scabbard	Schwertscheide *f*	fourreau *m*	fodero *m*	vaina *f* de la espada
scale	Maßstab *m*	échelle *f*	scala *f*	escala *f*, proporción *f*
scale drawing	maßstäbliche Zeichnung *f*	dessin *m* à l'échelle	disegno *m* in scala	dibujo *m* a escala
scale paper	Millimeterpapier *n*	papier *m* millimétré	carta *f* millimetrata	papel *m* milimetrado
scales	Waage *f*	balance *f*	bilancia *f*	balanza *f*, báscula *f*
scale, scute	Schuppe *f*	écaille *f*	scaglia *f*	escama *f*
scalpel	Skalpell *n*	scalpel *m*	scalpello *m*	escalpelo *m*
science	Wissenschaft *f*	science *f*	scienza *f*	ciencia *f*
(science of) history	Geschichtswissenschaft *f*	histoire *f*	scienza *f* storica	historiografía *f*
scientific	wissenschaftlich	scientifique	scientifico/-a	científico/-a
scientific field	Wissenschaftsbereich *m*	domaine *m* scientifique	ambito *m* scientifico	ramo *m* de ciencia
scissors	Schere *f*	ciseaux *m*	forbici *f pl*	tijeras *f pl*
scratch decoration	Ritzverzierung *f*	décor *m* gravé	decorazione *f* scalfitta	ornamento *m* con incisuras
scratching	Ritzung *f*	incision *m*	incisione *f*, scalfittura *f*	incisura *f*
sculptor	Bildhauer *m*	sculpteur *m*	scultore *m*/-trice *f*	escultor *m*
sculpture	Plastik (Statue) *f*	sculpture *f*	scultura	escultura *f*
Scythian	skythisch	scythe	scitico/-a	escitico/-a
sea	Meer *n*	mer *f*	mare *m*	mar *m/f*
sea gate	Meeresenge *f*	détroit *m*	stretto *m*	estrecho *m*
seal	Siegel *n*	sceau *m*	sigillo *m*	sello *m*
season	Jahreszeit *f*	saison *f*	stagione *f*	estaciónes *f* del año
seasonal	jahreszeitlich	saisonnier	stagionale	estacional, temporal
seasonal rhythm	Jahresrhythmus *m*	rythme *m* annuel	ritmo *m* annuale	ritmo *m* anual
secondary	sekundär	secondaire	secondario/-a	secundario/-a
secondary burial	Nachbestattung *f*	sépulture *f* secondaire	sepoltura *f* secondaria	sepultura *f* secundaria
secondary layer	sekundäre Lage *f*	contexte *m* secondaire	giacitura *f* secondaria	posición *f* secundaria
secondhand bookshop	Antiquariat *n*	librairie *f* d'occasion	antiquariato *m*	librería *f* de ocasión/ de lance
security	Sicherung *f*	sécurisation *f*	garanzia *f*, tutela *f*	protección *f*
sediment	Sediment *n*	sédiment *m*	sedimento *m*	sedimento *m*
sediment analysis	Sedimentanalyse *f*	analyse *f* de sédiments	analisi *f* dei sedimenti	análisis *f* de sedimentos
sedimentary rock	Sedimentgestein *n*	roche *f* sédimentaire	roccia *f* sedimentaria	roca *f* sedimentaria
seed(s)	Samen *m*	semence *f*	seme *m*	semilla *f*
segment	Segment *n*	segment *m*	segmento *m*	segmento *m*
semicircular	halbkreisförmig	semi-circulaire	semicircolare	semicircular
semicolumn	Halbsäule *f*	demi-colonne *f*	semi-colonna *f*	semi-columna *f*

Greek		Turkish	Arabic	
σαρκοφάγος *f*	sarkofagos	lahit, sanduka	تابوت حجري	tabut hagarie
ασφάλεια *f*	asfaleia	kesinlik	أمن	amn
πριόνι *n*	prioni	bıçkı, testere	منشار	menschar
πριστός	pristos	testere ile kesilmiş	منشور	manschur
θηκάρι *n* , θήκη ξίφους *f*	thikari, thiki xifous	kılıç kılıfı	غمد السيف	gemd elseif
κλίμακα *f*	klimaka	ölçek	معيار	mejar
σχέδιο υπό κλίμακα *n*	schedio ipo klimaka	ölçekli çizim	رسم معياري	rasm mejari
χαρτί μιλιμετρέ *n*	charti milimetre	milimetrik kâğıt	ورق رسم بيانى	warak rasm bajani
ζυγαριά *f* , ζυγός *m*	zigaria, zigos	terazi	ميزان	mizan
φολίδα *f*	folida	pul	قشر	keschr
νυστέρι *n*	nisteri	neşter	مشرط	maschrat
επιστήμη *f*	epistimi	bilim	علم	elm
ιστορική επιστήμη *f*	istoriki epistimi	Tarih Bilimi	علم التاريخ	elm eltariech
επιστημονικός	epistimonikos	bilimsel	علمي	elmie
επιστημονικό πεδίο *n*	epistimoniki pedio	bilim alanı	مجال العلم	magal elelm
ψαλίδι *n*	psalidi	makas	مقص	mekas
εγχάρακτη διακόσμηση *f*	egcharakti diakosmisi	çentik bezeme	زخرفة خدوش	zachrafet chodusch
χάραξη *f*	charxi	çentik	خدش	chadsch
γλύπτης *m*	gliptis	heykeltraş	نحات	nahat
πλαστική *f*	plastiki	heykel	تمثال	temsal
σκύθικός	skithikos	iskit	سكيثي	sikiesie
θάλασσα *f*	thalassa	deniz, okyanus	بحر	bahr
πορθμός *m* , στενό *n*	porthmos, steno	deniz darlığı	مضيق	madik
σιγίλλιον *n*	sigillion	mühür	ختم	chetm
εποχή *f*	epochi	mevsim	فصل السنة	fasl elsana
εποχιακός	epochiakos	mevsimlik	موسمي	mawsimie
ετήσιος ρυθμός *m*	etisios rithmos	yıllık döngü	إيقاع سنوي	ikaa sanawie
δευτερεύων	defterevon	ikincil	ثانوي	sanawie
επανενταφιασμός *m*	epanentafiasmos	ikincil gömüt	دفن ملحق	dafn molhak
δεύτερη χρήση *f*	defteri chrisi	ikincil konum	وضع ثانوي	wadaa sanawie
παλαιοβιβλιοπωλείο *n*	palaiovivliopoleio	antikacı, sahaf	مكتبة لبيع الكتب القديمة	maktaba libea elkutob elkadima
ασφάλιση *f*	asfalisi	emniyet, güvence	تأمين	tamien
ίζημα *n*	izima	tortu	راسب	raseb
ανάλυση ιζήματος *f*	analisi izimatos	tortu analizi	تحليل الرواسب	tahliel elrawaseb
ιζηματογενές πέτρωμα *n*	izimatogenes petroma	tortul kaya/ kayaç	صخور رسوبية	sochor rosobija
σπόρος/-οι *m s/pl*	sporos/oi/s	tohum	بذور	bozur
τομέας *m* , τμήμα *n*	tomeas, tmima	katman, parça, tabaka	قطعة	ketaa
ημικυκλικός	imikiklikos	yarım daire şeklinde	نصف دائرى	nesf dairi
ημικίονας *m*	imikionas	yalancı sütun, yarım sütun	نصف عامود	nesf amud

English	German	French	Italian	Spanish
separation layer	Trennschicht *f*	couche *f* de séparation	strato *m* di separazione	nivel *m* de separación
sequence dating	Staffeldatierung *f*	séquence *f* de datation	datazione *f* per sequenze	datación *f* de secuencia
serial production	Serienproduktion *f*	fabrication *f* en série	produzione *f* in serie	fabricación *f* en serie
set square	Geodreieck *n*	équerre *f*	squadra *f*	escuadra *f*
settlement history	Siedlungsgeschichte *f*	histoire *f* du peuplement	storia *f* dell'insediamento	historia *f* de asentamiento
shading	Schattierung *f*	dégradé *m*	ombreggiatura *f*	sombreado *m*
shaft	Schaft *m*	bois *m*, hampe *f*	fusto *m*	mango *m*
shaft grave	Schachtgrab	tombe *f* à fosse	tomba *f* a fossa	sepultura *f* de pozo
sharp	scharf (Messer)	aigu/-ë, tranchant/-e	affilato/-a, pungente	cortante
sharpener	Anspitzer *m*	taille-crayon *m*	temperino *m*	sacapuntas *m*
shellac	Schellak *n*	gomme-laque *f*	gommalacca *f*	goma laca *f*
shellac varnish	Lackschicht *f*	couche *f* de laque	strato di lacca	capa de barniz *f*
shifting sand dune/ wandering	Wanderdüne *f*	dune *f* mouvante	duna *f* mobile	duna *f* movediza
shipwreck	Schiffswrack *n*	épave *f*	relitto *m*	buque *m* naufragado
short	kurz	court	corto/-a, breve	breve, corto/-a
shovel	Schaufel *f*	pelle *f*	pala *f*, paletta *f*	pala *f*
shrine	Schrein *m*	châsse *f*, reliquaire *m*	scrigno *m*	relicario *m*
shroud	Leichen-, Grabtuch *n*	linceul *m*, drap *m* mortuaire	sudario *m*	sudario *m*
side	Seite *f*	côté *m*	lato *m*	lado *m*
sieve, sifter, strainer	Sieb *n*	crible *m*, tamis *m*	colino *m*, setaccio *m*	criba *f*, tamiz *f*
signature	Signatur *f*	signature *f*	segnatura *f*	firma *f*
silicone	Silikon *n*	silicone *f*	silicone *m*	silicona *f*
siltstone	Schluff-/ Siltstein *m*	phtanite *m*	siltite *f*	limolita *f*
silver	Silber *n*	argent *m*	argento *m*	plata *f*
similar	ähnlich	similaire	simile	similar
similarity	Ähnlichkeit *f*	ressemblance *f*, similarité *f*	somiglianza *f*	similtud *f*
sink	sinken	baisser	calare	hundirse
sinter	Sinter *m*	concrétion *f*	concrezione *f*, scoria *f*	escoria *f*
sintering, vitrification	Sinterung *f*	fusion *f*, grésage *m*	sinterizzazione *f*	sinterización *f*
site	Stätte *f*	site *m*	luogo *m*	lugar *m*, sitio *m*
site map	Lageplan *m*	plan *m* topographique	piantina *f*	plano *m*
site model	Geländemodell *n*	modèle *m* de terrain, modèle *m* d'élévation	modello *m* di terreno	modelo *m* topográfico
situation of discovery	Fundumstände *m pl*	circonstances *f pl* de la découverte	circostanza *f* del rinvenimento	circunstancias *f* del hallazgo
skeleton	Skelett *n*	squelette *m*	scheletro *m*	esqueleto *m*
sketch	Skizze *f*	croquis *m*	schizzo *m*	croquis *m*, esbozo *m*
skin	Haut *f*	peau *m*	pelle *f*	piel *f*

Greek		Turkish	Arabic	
διαχωριστικό στρώμα *n*	diachoristiko stroma	ara, ayırıcı tabaka	طبقة عازلة	tabaka azela
ακολουθιακή χρονολόγηση *f*	akolouthiaki chronologisi	stratigrafik tarihleme	تأريخ مُوازى	taarich muwazie
μαζική παραγωγή *f*	maziki paragogi	seri üretim	إنتاج	entag motatebea
γεωμετρικό τρίγωνο *n*	geometriko trigono	gönye	منقلة	mankala
ιστορικό κατοίκησης *n*	istoriko katoikisis	yerleşim tarihi	تاريخ المستوطنة	tariech elmostawtana
σκίαση *f*	skiasi	gölgelenme, nüans	تظليل	tazliel
ράβδος *f*, στέλεχος *n*	ravdos, stelechos	direk, ağaç gövdesi, sütunun asıl bölümü	ساق العمود	saak elamud
κιβωτιόσχημος τάφος *m*	kivotioschimos tafos	yer altı kaya mezar	مقبرة بها بئر للدفن	makbara biha beer leldafn
οξύς	oxis	keskin, net, sert	حاد	haad
ακονιστήρι *n*	akonistiri	kalemtraş	مبراة	mibrah
γομμαλάκα *f*	gommalaka	vernik	صمغ اللك	samg ellak
στρώμα χρώματος *n*	stroma chromatos	cila/ vernik tabakası	طبقة ورنيش	tabaket warniesch
αμμόλοφος *m*	ammolofos	göçmen kumul	كثبان رملية متحركة	kosbaan ramlija motahareka
ναυάγιο *n*	nafagio	gemi enkazı/ batığı	حطام سفينة	hutam safina
κοντός, βραχύς	kontos, vrachis	kısa	قصير	kasir
φτυάρι *n*	ftiari	büyük kepçe, kürek	مجرفه	megrafa
ιερό *n*	iero	mabet, türbe	ناووس	nawoos
σάβανο *n*	savano	kefen	كفن	kafan
πλευρά *f*	plevra	kenar, taraf, yan	جانب	ganeb
κόσκινο *n*	koskino	süzgeç, elek	غربال	gorbaal
υπογραφή *f*	ipografi	damga	إمضاء	imdaa
σιλικόνη *f*	silikoni	silikon	سيليكون	sieliekon
ιλυόλιθος *m*	iliolithos	silt taşı	حجر الغرين	hagar elgarien
άργυρος *m*, ασήμι *n*	argiros, asimi	gümüş	فضة	fada
παρόμοιος	paromoios	benzer	مشابه	muschabeh
ομοιότητα *f*	omoiotita	benzerlik	تشابه	taschabuh
βυθίζομαι	vithizomai	alçalmak, batmak, eksilmek	يهبط / يغرق	yahbet/ yagrak
συσσωμάτωση *f*	sissomatosi	kireçli tortu, kül	صخور متكلسة	sochur motakalesa
συσσωμάτωση *f*, υαλοποίηση η *f*	sissomatosi, ialopoiisi	yumuşama	تكلس	takalos
χώρος *m*	choros	alan, mevki	مكان	makan
τοπογραφικό *n*	topografiko	durum planı	خريطة للموقع	charita lelmawkea
μοντέλο *n* εδάφους	montelo edafous	arazi rölyefi	نموذج الموقع	namuzak elmawkea
συνθήκες *f pl* εύρεσης	sinthikes evresis	buluntu durumu	سياق الإكتشاف	sijak elektischaf
σκελετός *m*	skeletos	iskelet	هيكل عظمي	heikal azmie
σκαρίφημα *n*	skarifima	eskiz, kroki, taslak	رسم تخطيطي	rasm tachtitie
δέρμα *n*	derma	cilt, deri, ten	بشرة	baschra

English	German	French	Italian	Spanish
skull	Schädel *m*	crâne *m*	cranio *m*	cráneo *m*
slag	Schlacke *f*	scorie *f*	scoria *f*	cagafierro *m*, escoria *f*
slaked lime	Löschkalk *m*	chaux *f* éteinte	calce *f* spenta	cal *f* apagada
slate	Schiefer *m*	schiste *m*	scisto *m*	pizarra *f*
slide	Dia (positiv) *n*	diapositive *f*	diapositiva *f*	diapositiva *f*
slope	Hang *m*	pente *f*	pendio *m*	pendiente *f*
small area	kleinflächig	de (sur une) petite surface *f*	a superficie ridotta	de extensión *f* reducida
small find	Kleinfund *m*	petit objet *m*, trouvaille mineure	reperto *m* di piccole dimensioni	hallazgo *m* de pequeño tamaño
soapstone, steatite	Steatit *m*, Speckstein *m*	stéatite *f*	steatite *f*	esteatita *f*, talco *m*
social	sozial	social/-e	sociale	social
society	Gesellschaft *f*	société *m*	società *f*	sociedad *f*
soft	weich	doux/ douce	molle, morbido/-a	blando/-a, elástico/-a
soil	Boden *m*	sol *m*	suolo *m*	suelo *m*
soil	Erde *f*	terre *f*	terra *f*	tierra *f*
sonar mapping	Sonarkartierung *f*	relevé *m* au sonar	mappatura *f* sonar	cartografía *f* de sonar
sondage	Sondage *f*, Sondierung *f*	sondage *m*	sondaggio *m*	sondeo *m*
sorting	Sortierung *f*	triage *m*	classificazione *f*	clasificación *f*
source	Quelle (Forschung) *f*	source *f*	fonte *f*	fuente *f*
south	Süden *m*	sud *f*	sud *m*	sur *m*
southern	südlich	méridional/-e	del sud, meridionale	meridional
spade	Spaten *m*	bêche *f*	vanga *f*	azada *f*, laya *f*
spatial	räumlich	relatif/-ve à l'espace, spatial/-e	spaziale	espacial
spattle	Spachtel *m*	spatule *f*	spatola *f*	espátula *f*
spatula	Spatel *m*	spatule *f*	spatola *f*	espátula *f*
spear	Speer *m*	lance *f*	lancia *f*	jabalina *f*
spearhead	Speerspitze *f*	pointe *f* de lance	punta *m* di lancia	punto *m* de lanza
special form	Sonderform *f*	forme *f* particulière	forma *f* particolare	forma especial *f*
spectroscopy	Spektroskopie *f*	spectroscopie *f*	spettroscopia *f*	espectroscopia *f*
spectrum	Spektrum *n*	spectre *m*	spettro *m*	espectro *m*
sphere	Wirkungskreis *m*	rayon *m* d'action	sfera di attività *f*	ámbito de acción *m*
spherical	kugelig	globulaire	sferico/-a	esférico/-a
spiral	spiralförmig	en spirale	spiraliforme	espiral
spit of land	Landzunge *f*	langue *f* de terre	lingua *f* di terra	lengua *f* de tierra
splitting wedge	Spaltkeil *m*	hachereau *m*	cuneo *m*	división de cuña
sponge	Schwamm *m*	éponge *f*	spugna *f*	esponja *f*
spot, stain	Fleck *m*	tache *f*	macchia *f*	mácula *f*, mancha *f*
spotted, stained	fleckig	tacheté/-ée moucheté/-ée	macchiato/-a	manchado/-a
spout	Ausguss *m*	bec (verseur) *m*	beccuccio *m*	boquilla *f*, pitorro *m*
spout	Tülle *f*	douille *f*	becco *m*	pico *m*

Greek		Turkish	Arabic	
κρανίο *n*	kranio	kafatası	جمجمة	gomgoma
σκωρία *f*	skoria	cüruf	خبث / شوائب	chabas/ schwaeb
σβησμένος ασβέστης *m*	svismenos asvestis	söndürülmüş kireç	جير مطفي	gir matfi
σχιστόλιθος *m*	schistolithos	kara taş, kayrak	شظية	schazja
διαφάνεια *f*	diafaneia	diyapozitif	شفافية	schfafeia
πλαγιά *f*	plagia	yamaç	انحدار	inhedar
περιορισμένος, μικρής έκτασης	periorismenos, mikris ektasis	küçük alan	ضيق	keijek
μικροεύρημα *n*	mikroevrima	küçük buluntu	اكتشاف صغير	ekteschaf sagier
στεατίτης *m*	steatitis	sabuntaşı	حجر أملس	hagar amlas
κοινωνικός	koinonikos	sosyal, toplumsal	اجتماعي	igtemaie
κοινωνία *f*	koinonia	toplum	مجتمع	mogtamaa
μαλακός	malakos	yumuşak	لين	lein
έδαφος *n*	edafos	yer, zemin	أرض	ard
χώμα *n*	choma	dünya, toprak	أرض	aard
χαρτογράφηση sonar *f*	chartografisi sonar	sonar haritalama	رسم خرائط بالموجات الصوتية	rasm charaet belmawgat elsawtija
δοκιμαστική/ διερευνητική τομή *f*	dokimastiki/dierevnitiki tomi	sondaj	حفر تمهيدى لإختبار طبقات الأرض	hafr tamhidie leechtibar tabakat el ard
ταξινόμηση *f*	taxinomisi	ayırma, seçme	فرز	farz
πηγή *f*	pigi	bilgi kaynağı, kaynak	مرجع	margiea
νότος *m*	notos	güney	جنوب	ganub
νότιος	notios	güneyinde	جنوبي	ganubie
φτυάρι *n*	ftiari	bel	كُريك	koreek
χωρικός	chorikos	alan bakımından, hacimsel	مكاني	makanie
σπάτουλα *f*	spatoula	mala, spatula	سكينة معجون	sekinet magoon
σπάτουλα *f*	spatoula	harç malası	ملعقة	malaet tabieb
δόρυ *n*	dori	kargı, mızrak	حربة	harba
αιχμή δόρατος *f*	aichmi doratos	kargı ucu, mızrak ucu	رأس الحربة	raas elharba
ειδικό έντυπο *n*	eidiko entipo	özel şekil	شكل خاص	schakl chaas
φασματοσκοπία *f*	fasmatoskopia	spektroskopi	تحليل طيفي	tahliel teefie
φάσμα *n*	fasma	çeşitlilik	طيف	teef
σφαίρα επιρροής *f*	sfaira epirrois	etki alanı	نطاق التأثير	netaak eltasier
σφαιρικός	sfairikos	yuvarlak	كُروى	kurawi
σπειροειδής	speiroeidis	helezon biçiminde	حلزوني	halzonie
χερσόνησος *f*	chersonisos	burun	لسان الأرض	lisan elard
καλέμι *n*	kalemi	kama	شق طويلي	schaak tulie
σφουγγάρι *n*	sfoungari	sünger	إسفنجة	esfenga
λεκές *m* , σπίλος *m*	lekes, spilos	leke	بقعة	bokaa
κατάστικτος	katastikos	lekeli	ملطخ	mulatach
στόμιο απορροής *n*	stomio aporrois	ağız, boşaltma deliği	صنبور	sonbur
προχοή *f*	prochoi	başlık	فوهة / وصلة	fowaha/ wasla

English	German	French	Italian	Spanish
spouted jug	Tüllenkanne *f*	cruche *f* à bec tubulaire	brocca *f* a beccuccio	jarra *f* de pico
spring, well	Quelle *f*	source *f*	sorgente *f*	fuente *f*
spruce	Fichte *f*	épicéa *m*	abete *m* rosso	pícea *f*
square	Platz *m*	lieu *m* , place *f*	piazza *f*	plaza *f*
square	quadratisch	carré/-e	quadrato/-a	cuadrado/-a
squat lekythos	Bauchlekytos *f*	lécythe *m* aryballisque	lekythos *m* a piede largo	lécito *m* aribalístico
stabilisation	Festigung *f*	affermissement *m* , consolidation *f*	stabilizzazione *f*	consolidación *f*
stability	Stabilität *f*	stabilité *f*	stabilità *f*	estabilidad *f*
stable	Stall *m*	étable *f*	scuderia *f*, stalla *f*	establo *m*
stable, sturdy	stabil	stable	stabile	estable
stadium	Stadium *n*	stade *m*	stadio *m*	estadio *m*
stairs	Treppe *f*	escalier *m*	scala *f*	escalera *f*
stalactite	Stalaktit *m*	stalactite *f*	stalattite *m*	estalactita *f*
stalagmite	Stalagmit *m*	stalagmite *f*	stalagmite *m*	estalagmita *f*
stamp	Stempel *m*	étampe *m*	impronta *f*, timbro *m*	sello *m* , timbre *m*
stamp seal	Stempelsiegel *n*	cachet *m* , sceau *m*	sigillo *m* a stampo	sello *m*
stand	Ständer *m*	support *m*	sostegno *m*	soporte *m*
stand, tripod	Stativ *n*	trépied *m*	stativo *m*	trípode *m*
statue	Statue *f*	sculpture *f*, statue *f*	statua *f*	estatua *f*
status	Status *m*	état *m*, statut *m*	status *m*	estado *m*
steel	Stahl *m*	acier *m*	acciaio *m*	acero *m*
steel brush	Drahtbürste *f*	brosse *f* métallique	spazzola *f* metallica	cepillo *m* metálico
steep	steil	raide	ripido/-a	escarpado/-a
step	Stufe *f*	degré *m*, marche *f*	gradino *m*	escalón *m*, g rada *f*
steppe	Steppe *f*	steppe *f*	steppa *f*	estepa *f*, pampa *f*
stirrup jar	Bügelkanne *f*	vase *m* / jarre *m* à étrier	olla *f*	jarra *f* con asa
stoa	Stoa *f*	stoa *f*	stoa *f*	estoa, stoa *f*
stolen goods	Diebesgut *n*	butin *m*	bottino *m*	botín *m*
stone	Stein *m*	pierre *f*	pietra *f*	piedra *f*
stone age	Steinzeit *f*	âge *m* de la Pierre	età *f* della pietra	edad *f* de piedra
stone block	Steinblock *m*	bloc *m* de pierre	blocco *m* di pietra	bloque *m* de piedra
stone fundament	Steinfundament *n*	soubassement *m* en pierre	fondamento *m* di pietra	cimiento *m*, fundamento *m*
stone tools	Steingerät *n*	outil *m* de/ en pierre	utensile *m* di pietra	instrumento *m* de piedra
stone tools	Steinwerkzeug *n*	outil *m* lithique/ de pierre	arnesi *f* di pietra	herramienta *f* de piedra
storage room	Lager *n*, Magazin *n*	dépôt *m* , magasin *m*	magazzino *m*	almacén *m*, depósito *m*
straight	gerade	direct/-e, droit/-e	dritto/-a	recto/-a
strata, stratigraphic sequence	Schichtenfolge *f*	séquence *f* stratigraphique	stratigrafia *f*, successione *f* degli strati	sucesión *f* estratigráfica

Greek		Turkish	Arabic	
οινοχόη με προχοή *f*	oinochoi me prochoi	emzikli kap	دورَق بفوهة	dawrak befowaha
πηγή *f*	pigi	ılıca, kaynak, pınar	عين ماء	aein maa
έλατο *n*	elato	çam ağacı	شجرة التنوب	schagrat eltanub
πλατεία *f*	plateia	alan, bölge, mekân	مكان	makan
τετραγωνικός	tetragonikos	kare	مربع	murabaa
αρυβαλλοειδής λήκυθος *f*	arivalloeidis likithos	karınlı lekythos	إناء لحفظ زيت الزيتون	inaa lehefz zeit elzeitun
στερέωση *f*	stereosi	konsolidasyon, sağlamlaştırma	تثبيت	tasbiet
σταθερότητα *f*	statherotita	sabitlik, sağlamlık	ثبات	sabaat
στάβλος *m*	stavlos	ağıl, ahır, dam	إسطبل	establ
σταθερός	statheros	sabit, sağlam	ثابت	saabet
στάδιο *n*	stadio	stadion	مرحلة / مسرح	marhala/ masrah
σκάλα *f*	skala	basamak, merdiven	سلالم	salalem
σταλακτίτης *m*	stalaktitis	sarkıt	مقرنصات	mukarnasat
σταλαγμίτης *m*	stalagmitis	dikit	صخر عمودى (طبيعى)	sachr amudie (tabiie)
σφραγίδα *f*	sfragida	damga, mühür	ختم	chetm
σφραγίδα *f*	sfragida	baskı mühür	ختم	chetm
στήριγμα *n*	stirigma	ayaklık	حامل	haamel
τρίποδο *n*	tripodo	üçayak	حامل بثلاث أرجل	haamel besalas argol
άγαλμα *n*	agalma	heykel, yontu	تمثال	temsal
κατάσταση *f*	katastasi	durum	حالة	hala
ατσάλι *n* , χάλυβας *m*	atsali, chalivas	çelik	صلب	solb
συρματόβουρτσα *f*	sirmatovourtsa	tel fırça	فرشة سلك	furscha selk
απόκρημνος, απότομος	apokrimnos, apotomos	dik, sarp	شديد الانحدار	schadied elenhedar
σκαλί *n* , σκα λοπάτι *n*	skali, skalopati	basamak, derece	مرحلة	marhala
στέπα *f*	stepa	bozkır, step	البادية	elbadija
ψευδόστομος αμφορέας *m*	psefdostomos amforeas	Bügel Kanne	إبريق مقوَّس	ebrik mokawas
στοά *f*	stoa	stoa	مدرسة للفلسفة اليونانية	madrasa lelfalsafa elyunanija
λεία *f*, κλ οπιμαία *n pl*	leia, klopimaia	çalıntı mal	بضائع مسروقة	badaia masruka
λίθος *m* , πέτρα *f*	lithos, petra	taş	حجر	hagar
Εποχή του Λίθου *f*	Epochi tou Lithou	Taş Çağı	العصر الحجري	elasr elhagari
ογκόλιθος *m*	ogkolithos	taş blok	كُتلة صخرية	kotla sachreija
λίθινο θεμέλιο *n*	lithino themelio	taş temel	أساس حجري	asas hagarie
λίθινα εργαλεία *n pl*	lithina ergaleia	taş alet	أدوات حجرية	adawat hagarija
λίθινο εργαλείο *n*	lithino ergaleia	taş alet	أدوات حجرية	adawat hagareija
αποθήκη *f*	apothiki	ambar, depo	مخزن	machzan
ευθύς	efthis	direkt, düz	مستقيم	mostakiem
διαδοχή στρωμάτων *f*	dadochi stromaton	tabaka dizisi, tabaka sıralanması	تسلسل الطبقات	tasalsol eltabakat

English	German	French	Italian	Spanish
stratification	Stratifikation f	stratification f	stratificazione f	estratificación f
stratigraphic	stratigraphisch	stratigraphique	stratigrafico/-a	estratificado/-a
stratigraphy	Stratigraphie f	stratigraphie f	stratigrafia f	estratigrafía f
stratum	Stratum n	strate f	strato m	capa f, estrato m
stray find	Einzelfund m	trouvaille f isolée	reperto m singolo	hallazgo m aislado
stray find	Streufund m	trouvaille f isolée	rinvenimento m sporadico	hallazgo m en dispersión
strength	Stärke f	force f	forza f	fuerza f, solidez f
structurally engineered	bautechnisch	relatif à la technique de construction	architettonico/-a	arquitectónico/-a
structure	Struktur f	structure m	struttura f	estructura f
structure, texture	Gefüge n, Tektur f	structure f, texture f	struttura f, tessuto m	textura f
stump	Stumpf m	moignon m	troncone m	tronco m
style	Stil m	style m	stile m	estilo m
stylised	stilisiert	stylisé	stilizzato/-a	estilizado/-a
stylus	Stichel m	burin m, poinçon m	bulino m	buril m, punzón m
suborder	Unterordnung f	sous-ordre m	subordine m	subordinacíon f
subspecies	Unterart f	sous-espèce m, variété f	sottospecie f	subclase f, subspecie f
subterranean, underground	unterirdisch	souterrain/-e	sotteraneo/-a	subterranéo/-a
Sumerian	sumerisch	sumérien/-ienne	sumero/-a	sumerico/-a
Sumeriology	Sumerologie f	sumérologie f	sumerologia	sumerología f
sun	Sonne f	soleil m	sole m	sol m
supporting wall	Stützmauer f	mur m de soutènement	muro m di sostegno	muro m de contención
support structure	Abstützung f	étaiement m	sostegno m, supporto m	soporte m
supraregional	überegional	suprarégional/-e	sovraregionale	supraregional
surface	Oberfläche f	surface m	superficie f	superficie f
surface find	Oberflächenfund m	trouvaille f de surface	scoperta f di superficie	hallazgo m de superficie
surface structure	Oberflächenstruktur f	structure f de surface	struttura f superficiale	estructura f de la superficie
survey	Begehung f, Survey m	prospection f	ispezione f	prospección (arqueológica) f, survey m
survey	Oberflächenbegehung f	prospection f de surface	ricognizione di superficie f	prospección f (de superfiecie)
(surveyor's) level	Nivelliergerät n	niveau m	livello (strumento) m	nivel m óptico
surveyor's pole/ rod	Nivellierlatte f	mire (parlante) f	stadia f	mira f de nivelación
swamp	Sumpf m	marécage m	palude f	pantano m
symbol	Symbol n	symbole m	simbolo m	emblema m, símbolo m

Greek		Turkish	Arabic	
διαστρωμάτωση *f*	diastromatosi	katmanlaşma	تكون الطبقات	takawon eltabakat
στρωματογραφικός	stromatografikos	stratigrafik	خاص بطبقات الأرض	chaas betabakaat elard
στρωματογραφία *f*	stromatografia	katman, stratigrafi	علم طبقات الأرض	elm tabakat elard
στρώμα *n*	stroma	biyotop yaşam alanı	طبقة	tabaka
μεμονωμένο/ τυχαίο εύρημα *n*	memonomeno/tichaio evrima	tek buluntu	إكتشاف فريد	ektischaf farid
τυχαίο εύρημα *n*	tichaio evrima	yüzey buluntusu	اكتشاف منعزل	ekteschaf monazel
δύναμη *f*, ισχύς *f*	dinami, ischis	güç, kudret	قوة	kowa
δομικά σχεδιασμένος	domika schediasmenos	yapı tekniği ile ilgili	فنى بناء	fani binaa
δομή *f*	domi	yapı	تركيب	tarkieb
δομή *f*	domi	tadilat	تشابك	taschabuk
κορμός *m*, κούτσουρο *n*	kormos, koutsouro	kütük	قرمة	kirma
στυλ *n*	stil	stil, teknik	أسلوب	uslub
σχηματοποιημένος	schimatopoimenos	stilize	منمق	monamak
γραφίδα *f*	grafida	keski	إزميل	ezmil
υποκατηγορία *f*	ipokatigoria	ast olma, tabii olma	تبعية	tabaija
υποείδος *n*	ipoeidos	alt tip, alt tür	سلالة	sulala
υπόγειος	ipogeios	yer altında bulunan	تحت الارض	taht elard
σουμερικός	soumerikos	Sümer, Sümer ile ilgili (Sümerce, Sümerli vb.)	سومري	somerie
Σουμεριολογία *f*	Soumeriologia	Sümeroloji	علم السومريات	elm elsomerijat
ήλιος *m*	ilios	güneş	شمس	schams
αναλημματικός τοίχος *m*	analimmatikos toichos	istinat/ destek duvarı	جدار ساند	gidar saned
υποστήρηξη *f*	ipostirixi	destekleme	دعم	daam
υπερτοπικός	ipertopikos	bölgeler üstü	مُتجاوز حدود الإقليم	motagawez hudud elekliem
επιφάνεια *f*	epifaneia	yüzey	سطح الأرض	sath elard
επιφανειακό εύρημα *n*	epifaneiako evrima	yüzey buluntusu	اكتشاف في سطح الأرض	ikteschaf fi sath elard
επιφανειακή κατασκευή *f*	epifaneiaki kataskevi	satıh yapısı, yüzeysel yapı	بنية سطح الأرض	binjet sath elard
επιφανειακή έρευνα *f*, survey *n*	epifaneiaski erevna, survey	göz atma, yerinde denetim	تفتيش	taftiesch
επιφανειακή έρευνα *f*	epifaneiaki erevna	yüzey araştırması	معاينة سطح الأرض	muajanat sath elard
γεωδαιτικός σταθμός *m*	geodaitikos stathmos	nivo ölçme aleti	جهاز تسوية	gihaz taswija
σταδία *f*	stadia	mira	عارضة خشب للتسوية	aredat chaschab leltaswija
βάλτος *m*	valtos	bataklık	مستنقع	mostankaa
σύμβολο *n*	simvolo	sembol, simge	رمز	ramz

English	German	French	Italian	Spanish
symbol	Zeichen *n*	marque *m* , signe *f*	marchio *m* , segno *m*	signo *m*
symmetrical	symmetrisch	symétrique	simmetrico/-a	simétrico/-a
symmetry	Symmetrie *f*	symétrie *f*	simmetria *f*	simetría *f*
synagogue	Synagoge *f*	synagogue *f*	sinagoga *f*	sinagoga *f*
synchronical	synchron	synchrone	sincrono/-a	sincrónico/-a
synchronism	Synchronismus *m*	synchronisme *m*	sincronismo *m*	sincronismo *m*
system	System *n*	système *f*	sistema *f*	sistema *m*
systematic	systematisch	stystématique	sistematico/-a	sistemático/-a
table	Tafel *f*	plaque *f* photo, tableau *m*	lastra *f*, tavola *f*	lámina *f*, tabla *f*
tablet, tray	Tablett *n*	plateau *m*, tablette *f*	vassoio *m*	bandeja *f*
tachymeter	Tachymeter *m*	tachéomètre *m*	tacheometro *m*	taquímetro *m*
teaching excavation	Lehrgrabung *f*	fouille *f* école	scavo didattico *m*	excavación prácticas *f*
technical	technisch	technique	tecnico/-a	técnico/-a
technician	Grabungstechniker *m*	technicien *m* de fouilles (archéologiques)	tecnico/-a di *m/f* scavo	técnico *m* de excavación
technique	Technik *f*	technique *f*	tecnica *f*	técnica *f*
technology	Technologie *f*	technologie *f*	tecnologia *f*	tecnología *f*
tectonic	tektonisch	tectonique	tettonico/-a	tectónico/-a
tectonic trench	tektonischer Graben *m*	fossé *m* tectonique	fossa *f* tettonica	fosa *f* tectónica
tell formation	Tellbildung *f*	formation *f* d'un tell	formazione *f* dei tell	formación *f* de un tell
temperature	Temperatur *f*	temperature *f*	temperatura *f*	temperatura *f*
temper, tempering	Magerung *f*	dégraissant *m*	sgrassaggio *m* dell'impasto ceramico	degrasante *m*
temple	Tempel *m*	temple *m*	tempio *m*	templo *m*
temple offering	Weihgabe *f*	objet *m* consacré	offerta votiva *f*	exvoto *m*, ofrenda *f*
tent	Zelt *n*	tente *f*	tenda *f*	entoldado *m*
tepidarium	Tepidarium *n*	tepidarium *m*	tepidario *m*	tepidario *m*
terrace	Terrasse *f*	terrasse *f*	terrazzo *m*	terraza *f*
terracotta	Terrakotte *f*	(figurine en) terre cuite *f*	terracotta *f*	figurillas de terracota *f*
terrazzo floor(ing)	Terrazzoboden *m*	sol *m* en terrazzo	pavimento *m* alla veneziana, terrazzo	terrazo *m*
territory	Territorium *n*	territoire *f*	territorio *m*	territorio *m*
tesselated	mosaikartig	en mosaïque	mosaicato/-a	mosaico/-a
textile	Textilie *f*	textile *m*	tessuto *m*	tejidos *m pl*
texture	Textur *f*	texture *f*	tessuto *m*	textura *f*
thatched roof	Schilfdach *n*	toit *m* de chaume	tetto *m* di canne	tejado *m* de caña
theatre	Theater *n*	théâtre *m*	teatro *m*	teatro *m*
theodolite	Theodolit *m*	théodolite *m*	teodolite *m*	teodolito *m*
theory	Theorie *f*	théorie *f*	teoria *f*	teoría *f*
thermoluminescence	Thermoluminiszenz *f*	thermoluminescence *f*	termoluminescenza *f*	termoluminiscencia *f*
thickness	Dicke *f*	épaisseur *f*	grossezza *f*	espesor *m* , grosor *m*

Greek		Turkish	Arabic	
σημείο *n*, σήμα *n*	simeio, sima	belirti, işaret	علامة	alama
συμμετρικός	simmetrikos	simetrik	متناسق	motanasek
συμμετρία *f*	simmetria	simetri	تناسق	tanasok
συναγωγή *f*	sinagogi	havra, sinagog	معبد يهودي	maabad yahudie
σύγχρονος	sigchronos	eş zamanlı	متزامن	mutazamen
συγχρονισμός *m*	sigchronismos	eş zamanlılık	تزامن	tazamun
σύστημα *n*	sistima	düzen, sistem	نظام	nizam
συστηματικός	sistimatikos	sistemli, sistematik	منظم	munazam
πίνακας *m*	pinakas	cetvel, levha, tahta	لوحة	loha
πινακίδα *f*	pinakida	tablet	صينية	sinija
ταχύμετρο *n*	tachimetro	takometre	مقياس السرعة	mikjas elsoraa
εκπαιδευτική ανασκαφή *f*	ekpaideftiki anaskafi	öğretim amaçlı kazı	حفريات للتعليم	hafrijat leltaliem
τεχνικός	technikos	tekniksel	تقني	tekanie
τεχνίτης *m*	technitis	kazı teknikeri	خبير فني الحفريات	chbier fani elhafrijat
τεχνική *f*, τεχνολογία *f*	techniki, technologia	metod, teknik	تقنية	teknija
τεχνολογία *f*	technologia	teknoloji	تكنولوجيا	teknologija
τεκτονικός	tektonikos	tektonik	فى القشرة الأرضية	fi elkischra elardija
τεκτονική τάφρος *f*	tektoniki tafros	tektonik vadi	حفر في القشرة الأرضية	hafr fi elkischra elardija
σχηματισμός τούμπας *m*	schimatismos toubas	höyükleşme	تكوين تل	takwien tall
θερμοκρασία *f*	thermokrasia	ısı, sıcaklık	درجة الحرارة	daraget elharara
μετριασμός *m*	metriasmos	katkı	تنحيف	tanhief
ναός *m*	naos	tapınak	معبد	mabad
ανάθημα *n*	anathima	adak	نذر	nazr
σκηνή *f*	skini	çadır, tente	خيمة	chema
χλιαρός χώρος *m*	chliaros choros	ılıklık odası	حمام ماء ساخن	hamam maa sachen
ανάλημμα *n*, άνδηρο *n*	analimma, anthiro	seki, taraça, teras	شرفة	schurfa
τερακότα *f*	terakota	terrakotta	أشكال صغيرة من الطين المحروق	aschkal sagiera men eltin elmahruk
αδρό ψηφιδωτό δάπεδο *n*	edro psifidoto dapedo	terarazzo döşeme	أرضية موزاييك	ardeija muzaiek
χώρα *f*, περιοχή *f*	chora, periochi	teritoryum	إقليم	ekliem
ψηφιδωτός	psifidotos	mozaiğe benzer	فسيفسائى	fusaifisaie
ύφασμα *n*	ifasma	dokuma, tekstil	نسيج	nasieg
υφή *f*	ifi	yapı	بنية	benja
αχυροσκεπή *f*	achiroskepi	kamıştan yapılma çatı	سقف من البوص	sakf men elbuus
θέατρο *n*	theatro	tiyatro	مسرح	masrah
θεοδόλιχος *m*	theodolichos	teodolit	جهاز قياس الزوايا	gihaz kijas elzawaja
θεωρία *f*	theoria	kuram, teori	نظرية	nazareja
θερμοφωταύγεια *f*	thermofotafgeia	termolüminesans	لمعان بالحرارة	lamaan belharara
πάχος *n*	pachos	kalınlık	سُمك	sumk

English	German	French	Italian	Spanish
thick-walled	dickwandig	à paroi épaisse	a parete spessa	de paredes gruesas
thin	dünn	fin/-e, mince	fino/-a, sottile	delgado/-a, fino/-a
thin-walled	dünnwandig	à paroi mince	a parete sottile	de paredes finas
tholos tomb	Tholos *m* , Kuppelgrab *n*	tholos *m*	tolos *m*	tholos *m*
thread	Faden *m*	fil *m*	filo *m*	hilo *m*
three-dimensional	dreidimensional	à trois dimensions	tridimensionale	tridimensional
three-dimensional	plastisch	plastique	scultoreo/-a	plástico/-a
threshold	Schwelle *f*	seuil *m*	soglia *f*	umbral *m*
throwing marks	Drehspuren *f pl*	traces *f pl* de tour	tracce *f pl* di tornitura	marcas *f pl* de torno
tide	Tide *f*, Gezeiten *pl*	marée *f*	maree *f*	marea *f*
tile	Fliese *f*	carreau *m* , dalle *f*	piastrella *f*	azulejo *m*, plaqueta *f*
tillage	Feldbau *m*	agriculture *f*	agricoltura *f*	agricultura *f*
timber, wood	Holz *n*	bois *m*	legno *m*	madera *f*
tin	Zinn *n*	étain *m*	stagno *m*	estaño *m*
to accord, to agree	übereinstimmen	concorder	concordare	coincidir, corresponder con
to add, to amend	ergänzen	compléter	completare	completar
to analyse, to evaluate	auswerten	exploiter	analizzare	evaluar
to appeal	einwirken	agir, influencer sur	agire	actuar
to apply	auftragen	appliquer	applicare	aplicar
to assign	zuordnen	classer	assegnare	añadir
to attach sth., to fix	befestigen	attacher, fixer	attaccare, fissare	fijar, fortificar
to attach, to bind, to bond	binden	attacher, lier	attaccare, legare	espesar
to blur, cloud	trüben	opacifier	intorbidire	enturbiar
to brake	zerbrechen	briser, casser	rompere, spezzare	romper
to brush	aufpinseln	appliquer au pinceau, peindre sur	spennellare	aplicar
to build	bauen	édifier, élever	costruire, edificare	construir, edificar
to build up, to construct	aufbauen	construire, édifier, ériger	costruire	construir
to calibrate	kalibrieren	calibrer	calibrare	calibrar
to calibrate, to measure	vermessen	arpenter, mesurer	misurare, rilevare	apear, medir
to camp, to store	lagern	camper stocker	accampare, immagazinare	acampar, almacenar
to carve	schnitzen	sculpter (sur bois)	intagliare	tallar en madera
to carve, scratch	einritzen	graver	incidere, scalfire	grabar
to cast, to pour	gießen	fondre, mouler	colare, fondere	fundir, vaciar
to chip, flake (off)	abplatzen	s'écailler, sauter	staccarsi	desprenderse, saltar
to chisel	meißeln	tailler	scalpellare	cincelar
to chisel, to engrave	ziselieren	ciseler, graver	cesellare	cincelar
to clean	putzen	nettoyer	pulire	limpiar

Greek		Turkish	Arabic	
με παχείς τοίχους	me pacheis toichous	kalın cidarlı, kalın duvarlı	سميك الجدران	samik elgudran
αραιός, λεπτός	araios, leptos	ince, zarif, zayıf	رفيع	rafia
λεπτότοιχος	leptotoichos	ince cidarlı	ذو جدران رقيقة	zu gudran rakikah
θολωτός τάφος *m*	tholotos tafos	tholos	مقبرة بقبة	makbara bikoba
νήμα *n*	nima	iplik	خيط	cheet
τρισδιάστατος	trisdiastatos	üç boyutlu	ثلاثي الأبعاد	sulasi elabaad
πλαστικός, γλυπτός, ολόγλυφος	plastikos, gliptos, ologlifos	maddesel, yumuşak	مُجسم	mogasam
κατώφλι *n*	katofli	eşik, temel hatılı	عتبة	ataba
δαχτυλιές *f pl* , ίχνη *n pl* διάπλασης	dachtilies, ichni diaplasis	dönme izleri, torna izleri	مسارات اللف	masarat ellaf
παλίρροια *f*	palirroia	gelgit, med cezir	المد والجزر	elmad wi elgazr
πλακίδιο *n*	plakidio	fayans, çini	بلاط	balat
καλλιέργεια *f*	kalliergeia	ziraat	زراعة	zeraa
ξύλο *n*	xilo	ağaç, odun	خشب	chaschab salb
κασσίτερος *m*	kassiteros	kalay	قصدير	kasdier
συμφωνώ	simfono	uymak, uyuşmak	يطابق	yutabek
συμπληρώνω	siblirono	tamamlamak	يكمل	yukammel
αξιολογώ	axiologo	değerlendirmek	يقيم	yukajem
επιδρώ	epidro	etki etmek	يؤثر	yoaser
επιθέτω	epitheto	üzerine sürmek	يكلف	yukalef
κατατάσσω	katatasso	gruplandırmak	يُلحق	yolhek
στερεώνω	stereono	sağlamlaştırmak	يثبت	yusabet
δένω, συνδέω, προσδένω	deno, sindeo, prosdeno	bağlamak	يربط	yarbet
θολώνω	tholono	bulan(dır)mak	يُعتّم	yuatem
σπάζω, θρμματίζω	spazo, thrimmatizo	kırmak, parçalamak	يكسر	yakser
βουρτσίζω	vourtsizo	üstüne boya sürmek, üzerini boyamak	يدهن بالفرشاة	yadhen belforscha
χτίζω	chtizo	inşa etmek, yapmak	يبنى	yabni
δομώ	domo	inşa etmek, kurmak, yapılandırmak	يشيّد	yoschajed
βαθμονομώ, διακριβώνω	vathmonomo, diakrivono	ayarlamak	يعاير	yuajer
μετρώ	metro	ölçmek, ölçümlemek	يقيس	yakies
αποθηκεύω	apothikevo	depolamak, kamp yapmak	يُخزن	yuchazen
σκαλίζω	skalizo	oymak	ينحت	yanhet
εγχαράσσω, χαράζω	egcharasso, charazo	çizmek, oymak	ينقش	yankisch
χύνω, χυτεύω	chino, chitevo	döküm yapmak, kalıba dökmek	يصب	yasob
απολεπίζομαι, ξεφλουδίζομαι	apolepizomai, xefloudizomai	kopmak, yerinden oynamak	يسقط	yaskut
αποξύνω	apoxino	yontmak	ينحت	yanhet
εγχαράζω	egcharazo	oymak, yiv açmak	ينقش	yankesch
καθαρίζω	katharizo	temizlemek	ينظف	yunazef

English	German	French	Italian	Spanish
to clean	reinigen	nettoyer	pulire	limpiar
to climb, to increase	steigen	augmenter, monter	aumentare, salire	aumentar, subir
to clump	klumpen	s'agglomérer	raggrumarsi	agrumarse, formar grumos
to collapse	einstürzen	s'écrouler	crollare	derrumbarse
to collect	sammeln	collecter, ramasser	raccogliere	coleccionar
to colour	färben	colorer, teindre	colorare	entintar, tiñir
to compose	zusammensetzen	composer, remonter	comporre	componer, reunir
to comprehend, to gather	erfassen	comprendre, saisir	afferere, comprendere	alistar, comprender
to conduct	ausführen	accomplir, réaliser	realizzare	efectuar, realizar
to conserve	erhalten	conserver	conservare	conservar
to conserve, preserve	konservieren	conserver	conservare	conservar
to construct	konstruieren	construire	costruire	construir
to copy	kopieren	copier	copiare	copiar
to corrode	ätzen	corroder	corrodere	corroer
to (cross-)link	vernetzen	interconnecter, relier	reticolare	encadenar
to crush, to mash	zerdrücken	écraser	schiacciare	aplastar
to cut	schneiden	couper	tagliare	cortar
to damage	beschädigen	endommager	danneggiare	dañar, deteriorar
to date	datieren	dater	datare	datar, fechar
to decay, to decompose	zersetzen	décomposer, détruire	decomporre	descomponer
to demarcate, to mark out	abstecken	délimiter, tracer	tracciare i confini di un saggio	estacar, jalonar, trazar
to demineralize, to desalt	entsalzen	dessaler	desalinizzare	desalar
to demolish	demolieren	démolir	demolire	demoler
to demolish, to shatter	zertrümmern	démolir	fracassare	destrozar, destruir
to dessicate, to dry	austrocknen	dessécher	seccare	desecar
to destroy, to devastate	verwüsten	dévaster, ravager	devastare	desvastar, vastar
to detect, to find out	ermitteln	rechercher	indagare	averiguar, determinar
to determine	bestimmen, definieren	déterminer	definire, determinare	definir
to determine, to observe	feststellen	constater, déterminer	constatare, stabilire	constatar
to dig	graben	fouiller	scavare	excavar
to disconnect	unterbrechen	interrompre	interrompere	interrumpir
to disinfect	desinfizieren	désinfecter	disinfettare	desinfectar
to dissolve	auflösen	décomposer, dissoudre	dissolvere	disolver
to document	dokumentieren	documenter	documentare	documentar
to draw	zeichnen	dessiner	disegnare, schizzare	dibujar
to drill	bohren	forer, percer	forare, trapanare	barrenar, horadar
to emboss	punzen	ciseler, poinçonner	punzonare	repujar
to emerge, to occur	auftreten	apparaître	comparire, trovarsi	aparecer

Greek		Turkish	Arabic	
καθαρίζω	katharizo	temizlemek	يُنظّف	yunazef
ανεβαίνω, αυξάνομαι	anevaino, afxanomai	artmak, yükselmek	يصعد	yasad
συσσωματώνω, αθροίζω	sissomatono, athroizo	topaklaşmak	كتلى	kotali
καταρρέω	katarreo	çökmek	ينهار	yanhar
συλλέγω	sillego	toplamak	يجمع	yagmaa
βάφω, χρωματίζω	vafo, chromatizo	boyama, renk verme	يلون	yulawn
συνθέτω	sintheto	bir araya getirmek	يجمع	yegamaa
κατανοώ, συμπεραίνω	katanoo, siberaino	idrak etmek, kavramak	يشمل	yaschmal
διεξάγω	diexago	gerçekleştirmek	ينفّذ	yunkiz
διατηρώ	diatiro	korumak, saklamak	يحصل على	yahsol ala
συντηρώ	sintiro	konservasyon yapmak	يحفظ	yahfaz
κατασκευάζω	kataskevazo	inşa etmek, kurmak	يصمم	yusamem
αντιγράφω	antigrafo	kopyalamak	يصوّر	yusawer
χαράζω	charazo	aşındırmak, asitlendirmek	يكوي	yakwie
δικτυώνω	diktiono	ağ kurmak	يربط بشبكة إتصال	yarbot beschabeket etesaal
συνθλίβω	sinthlivo	ezmek	يسحق	yashak
κόβω	kovo	kesmek	يقطع	yaktaa
βλάπτω, φθείρω	vlapto, ftheiro	hasar vermek	يتلف	yotlef
χρονολογώ	chronologo	tarihlemek	يؤرخ	yoarech
αποσυνθέτω	aposintheto	ayrıştırmak, eritmek	يتحلل	yatahalal
χαράζω, σημαδεύω	charazo, simadevo	sınırları ölçmek	يحدد	yuhaded
αφαλατώνω	afalatono	tuzdan arındırmak, tuzunu almak	يُحلى	yuhalie
κατεδαφίζω	katedafizo	bozmak, kırmak	يدمر	yudamer
διαλύω, κατεδαφίζω	dialio, katedafizo	parçalamak, yıkmak	يحطم	yohatem
(απο)ξηραίνω	(apo)xiraino	kurumak	يُجفّف	yugafef
ερημώνω, καταστρέφω	erimono, katastrefo	yerle bir etmek, yakıp yıkmak	يدمر	yudamer
διαγιγνώσκω	diagignosko	araştırmak	يكشف عن	yakschen an
καθορίζω	kathorizo	belirlemek	يحدد	yuhaded
διαπιστώνω	diapistono	saptamak, tespit etmek	يثبت	yosbet
σκάβω	skavo	kazmak	يحفر	yahfur
διακόπτω	diakopto	ara vermek, kesintiye uğra(t)mak	يقطع	yaktaa
απολυμαίνω	apolimaino	dezenfekte etmek	يُطهر	yutaher
λιώνω	liono	çözme, çözülme	يحل	yahel
καταγράφω	katagrafo	belgelemek	يوثق	yuwasek
σχεδιάζω	schediazo	çizmek	يرسم	yarsem
διατρυπώ	diatripo	delmek	يحفر	yahfur
εμπιέζω	ebiezo	kakma işi yapmak	يدمغ	yadmag
απαντώ, εμφανίζομαι	apanto, emfanizomai	ortaya çıkma	يدوس / يظهر	yadus, yazhar

English	German	French	Italian	Spanish
to evaluate, to judge	beurteilen	évaluer, juger	giudicare, valutare	censurar, valorar
to examine, to treat	behandeln	traîter	trattare	tratar
to excavate, to uncover	freilegen	dégager	mettere allo scoperto	descubrir
to exfoliate, peel off	abblättern	exfolier, s'écailler	sfaldarsi	desconcharse, exfoliar
to expand, to stretch	dehnen	étendre, étirer	tendere	distender, extender
to fake, to forge	fälschen	falsifier, fausser	falsificare	falsear, falsificar
to find	finden	trouver	trovare	descubrir, hallar
to fix	fixieren	fixer	fissare	fijar
to float	flotieren	flotter	sfangare	flotar
to float, to letigate	schlämmen	tamiser à l'eau	sfangare	fregar
to flow	fließen	couler	scorrere	fluir
to forge, hammer	schmieden	forger	forgiare	forjar
to fracture	aufbrechen	briser, casser	scassinare	fracturar, rompe
to frame	einrahmen	encadrer	incorniciare	encuadrar, enmarcar
to glue, to stick	kleben	coller	attaccare	adherir, pegar
to grade, to level	nivellieren	niveler, prendre les altitudes	livellare	nivelar
to grate, to rub, to scrape	schaben	racler, gratter	grattare, raschiare	raspar
to grate, to scatch	kratzen	gratter	grattare	arañar, rascar
to grind	schleifen	aiguiser	arrotare, levigare	afilar, pulir, tallar
to hammer	hämmern	marteler	martellare	martillar
to harden	aushärten	tremper	invecchiare	endurecerse
to impregnate	tränken	imprégner	impregnare	empapar, impregnar
to interprete	interpretieren	interpréter	interpretare	interpretar
to label	beschriften	étiqueter	etichettare	rotular
to lacquer, to varnish	lackieren	laquer	verniciare	barnizar
to lift	abheben (Schicht)	enlever	asportare	levantar
to lift, to elevate	heben	lever, soulever	alzare, levare	levantar
to lift up	anheben	soulever	sollevare	alzar, elevar
to limit	begrenzen	limiter	limitare	delimitar, limitar
tomb	Grabmal *n*	tombeau *m*	monumento *m* sepolcrale	tumba *f*
to measure	messen	mesurer	misurare	medir
to melt	schmelzen	fondre	fondere	fundir
to mummify	mumifizieren	momifier	mummificare	momificar
to observe, regard	betrachten	observer, regarder	considerare, ritenere	mirar, observar
tool marks	Werkzeugspuren *pl*	traces d'outil *f pl*	tracce di arnesi *pl*	marcas de fabricación *f*
tooth	Zahn *m*	dent *m*	dente *m*	diente *m*

Greek		Turkish	Arabic	
κρίνω	krino	değerlendirmek, yargılamak	يقيم	yukajem
διερευνώ, επεξεργάζομαι	dierevno, epexergazomai	ele almak, yapmak	يعالج	yoaleg
αποκαλύπτω	apokalipto	kazıp açmak	يكشف	yakschef
ξεφλουδίζομαι, απολεπίζομαι	xefloudizomai, apolepizomai	pul pul dökülmek	تقشر	takascher
εκτείνομαι	ekteinomai	genişletmek, germek	يمدد	yumaded
παραποιώ, παραχαράσσω	parapoio, paracharasso	sahtesini yapmak, taklit etmek	يزوّر	yuzawer
βρίσκω	vrisko	bulmak	يجد	yaged
στερεώνω, συγκολλώ	stereono, sigkollo	sabitleştirmek	يثبّت	yusabet
(επι)πλέω	(epi)pleo	yüzdürmek	يطفو	yatfu
επιπλέω	epipleo	yüzdürmek	يُزيل الطين / يشطف	yusiel eltien/ yaschtof
ρέω	reo	akmak	يسيل	yasiel
χυτεύω	chitevo	çekiçle dövmek	يُشگّل بالطرق	yuschakel beltark
σπάζω	spazo	kırarak açmak	يكسر	yakser
πλαισιώνω	plaisiono	çerçeve içine almak, çerçevelemek	يضع فى إطار	yadaa fi itar
κολλώ	kollo	yapıştırma	يلصق	yalsik
αποτυπώνω, ισοπεδώνω	apotipono, isopedono	düzlemek, eşitlemek, nivo ölçmek	يمهد / يسوى	yomahed/ yosawie
ξύνω	xino	kazımak	يكشط	yakschet
χαράζω	charazo	kazımak	يخدش	yachdesch
αλέθω	aletho	bilemek	يُصقل / يُنَعّم	yoskel/ yenaam
σφυρηλατώ	sfirilato	çekiçlemek, çekiçle dövmek	يطرق	yatrok
σκληραίνω	skliraino	sertleştirmek	يصلد	yuslad
εμποτίζω	ebotizo	emdirmek, ıslatmak	ينقع	yankaa
ερμηνεύω	erminevo	yorumlamak	يفسير	yufaser
βάζω ετικέτα, επιγράφω	vazo etiketa, epigrafo	üzerine yazmak, yazılandırmak	ينقش	yankisch
βερνικώνω, λουστράρω	vernikono, loustraro	cilalamak, verniklemek	يطلى	yatli
σηκώνω, ανυψώνω	sikono, anipsono	açmak, kaldırmak	يُزيل (طبقة)	yoziel (tabaka)
σηκώνω	sikono	kaldırmak	يرفع	yarfaa
ανυψώνω	anipsono	yukarı kaldırmak, yükseltmek	يرفع	yarfaa
περιορίζω	periorizo	sınırlamak	يحدد	yuhaded
μνήμα *n*	mnima	anıtmezar, türbe (Islam)	شاهد القبر	schahed elkabr
μετρώ	metro	ölçmek	يقيس	yakies
λιώνω	liono	eritmek	يصهر	yashar
ταριχεύω	tarichevo	mumyalamak	يحنيط	yuhanet
παρατηρώ	paratiro	incelemek	يعتبر	yaateber
ίχνη εργαλείου *n pl*	ichni ergaleiou	alet izleri	آثار عمل	asaar amal
δόντι *n*	dodi	diş	سن	sen

English	German	French	Italian	Spanish
toothbrush	Zahnbürste *f*	brosse *f* à dents	spazzolino *m* da denti	cepillo *m* de dientes
to penetrate, soak	durchdringen	imprégner, pénétrer	penetrare	atravesar
to photograph, to take a picture	fotografieren	photographier	fotografare	fotografiar, sacar fotos
to plan	planen	planifier	progettare	planear, proyectar
to plumb	loten	sonder	scandagliare	echar la plomada, sondar
topographic	topographisch	topographique	topografico/-a	topográfico/-a
topography	Topographie *f*	topographie *f*	topografia *f*	topografía *f*
to polish	polieren	polir	polire	pulir
to prepare	präparieren	préparer	preparare	preparar
to prevent	vorbeugen	prévenir	prevenire	prevenir
to probe	sondieren	sonder	fare un sondaggio, sondare	sondar
to process sth., to work sth.	bearbeiten	étudier, travailler	lavorare, trattare	labrar, trabajar
to prove	nachweisen	prouver	provare	probar
to publish	publizieren	publier	pubblicare	publicar
to recognise	erkennen	apercevoir	riconoscere	reconocer
to reconstruct	rekonstruieren	reconstruire	ricostruire	reconstruir
to reconstruct	wiedererrichten	reconstruire	restaurare	reconstruir, reedificar
to recover	bergen	recueillir, sauver	recuperare, salvare	recuperar, salvar
to remove	abnehmen	ôter	togliere	descolgar, quitar
to remove	entfernen	éloigner	allontanare, rimovere	eliminar, remover
to renew	erneuern	rénouver	rinnovare	renovar, restaurar
to repair	reparieren	réparer	riparare	reparar
to reproduce	reproduzieren	reproduire	riprodurre	reproducir
to research	forschen	rechercher	ricercare	investigar
to restore	restaurieren	conserver	restaurare	restaurar
torso	Torso *m*	torse *m*	torso *m*	torso *m*
to rust	rosten (ver-)	rouiller	arrugginire	oxidarse
to rust	verrosten	rouiller	arrugginire	oxidarse
to scrunch	zertreten	piétiner	calpestare	aplastar, pisotear
to secure	sichern (techn.)	consolider	salvaguardare	asegurar
to separate	trennen	séparer	separare	separar
to shape	drechseln	tourner	tornire	tornear
to sieve, to sift, to strain	sieben	tamiser	setacciare	cribar
to soak	einweichen	tremper	ammollare	abrevar
to sort	sortieren	classer, trier	classificare, ordinare	clasificar, seleccionar
to span	aufspannen	fixer, monter	tendere	abrir
to spray	einsprühen	imprégner	spruzzare	pulverizar, rociar
to spray	sprühen	asperger, cracher	spruzzare	pulverizar

Greek		Turkish	Arabic	
οδοντόβουρτσα *f*	ododovourtsa	diş fırçası	فرشاة أسنان	forschet asnan
εισχωρώ	eischoro	arasından geçmek	يخترق	yachtarek
φωτογραφίζω	fotografizo	fotoğraf çekmek	يصّور	yusawer
σχεδιάζω	schediazo	planlamak	يخطط	yuchatet
μολυβδοκολλώ	molivdokollo	şakullemek, sondaj yapmak	يحدد الوضع العمودي بالميزان	yuhaded elwada elamudie belmizan
τοπογραφικός	topografikos	topografik	تضاريسى	tadariesie
τοπογραφία *f*	topografia	topografya	وصف تضاريس	wasf eltadaries
γυαλίζω, στιλβώνω	gializo, stilvono	cilalamak, parlatmak	ينعم / يُلْمَع	yonaam/ yolamea
προετοιμάζω	proetoimazo	hazırlamak	يعد	yued
προλαμβάνω	prolamvano	bir şeyi önlemek	يقي	yakie
εξετάζω	exetazo	sondaj yapmak, sondalamak	يفحص	yafhas
επεξεργάζομαι	epexergazomai	işlemek, üzerinde çalışmak	ينحت	yanhat
αποδεικνύω	apodeiknio	ispatlamak, kanıtlamak	يُثبت	yosbet
δημοσιεύω	dimosievo	yayınlamak	ينشر	yanschor
αναγνωρίζω	anagnorizo	anlamak, tanımak	يعرف	yaaref
αποκαθιστώ, αναπαριστώ	apokathisto, anaparisto	eski haline geri getirmek	يُعيد بناء	yoied benaa
ανακατασκευάζω	anakatastevazo	yeniden kurmak	يعيد بناء	yuied binaa
ανακτώ	anakto	çıkarmak, kurtarmak	ينقذ	yonkez
απομακρύνω, αφαιρώ	apomakrino, afairo	azaltmak, eksiltmek, kaldırmak	يزيل	yoziel
απομακρύνω	apomakrino	çıkarmak, uzaklaştırmak	يُزيل	yuziel
ανανεώνω	ananeono	yenilemek	يجدد	yugaded
επισκευάζω	episkevazo	onarmak, tamir etmek	يُصلح	yosleh
αναπαράγω	anaparago	basarak çoğaltmak	يستنسخ	yastansech
ερευνώ	erevno	araştırmak, incelemek	يبحث	yabhas
αποκαθιστώ	apokathisto	restore etmek	يُرمَّم	yoramem
κορμός *m* , τόρσο *n*	kormos, torso	torso	جذع تمثال	geza temsaal
σκουριάζω	skouriazo	paslanmak	يصدأ	yasdaa
σκουριάζω, οξειδώνομαι	skouriazo, oxeidonomai	paslanmak	يصدأ	yasdaa
συντρίβω	sintrivos	ayakla ezmek, çiğnemek	يدوس	yadhas
ασφαλίζω	asfalizo	emniyete alma	يؤمّن	yuamen
διαχωρίζω	diachorizo	ayırmak	يعزل/ يفصل	yaazel/ yafsel
τορνεύω	tornevo	tornadan geçirmek	يخرط	yachret
κοσκινίζω	koskinizo	elemek, süzmek	يُغربل	yugarbel
εμποτίζω, μουσκεύω	ebotizo, mouskevo	yumuşatmak	ينقع	yankaa
ταξινομώ	taxinomo	ayırmak, seçmek	يفرز	yafrez
καλύπτω	kalipto	açma, germe	يشد	yasched
ψεκάζω	psekazo	spreylemek	يرش	yarosch
ψεκάζω	psekazo	püskürtmek	يرش	yarosch

English	German	French	Italian	Spanish
to support	stützen	supporter	sorreggere	sostener
total station	Totalstation *f*	station *f* totale	stazione *f* totale	estación *f* total
totem	Totem *n*	totem *m*	totem *m*	tótem *m*
to turn, spin	drehen	tourner	tornire	girar
to urbanise	urbanisieren	urbaniser	urbanizzare	urbanizar
to varnish	firnissen	vernir	verniciare	barnizar
to wash	waschen (aus-)	laver	lavare	lavar
to wear, to weather	verwittern	s'éroder, se désagréger	disgregarsi	descomponerse, desmoronarse
to weigh	wiegen	peser	pesare	pesar
tower	Turm *m*	tour *f*	torre *f*	torre *f*
to wrap	umwickeln	envelopper	avvolgere	envolver
to wrap	verpacken	emballer	imballare	embalar
to wrap (up)	einwickeln	envelopper	avvolgere	envolver
tracing paper	Transparentpapier *n*	papier *m* transparent	carta *f* velina	papel *m* vegetal
trade	Handel *m*	commerce *m*	commercio *m*	comercio *m*
trading goods	Handelsware *f*	article *m* de commerce	merce *f*	artículo *m* comercial
trading route	Handelsweg *m*	voie *f* commerciale	via *f* commerciale	ruta *f* comercial
tradition	Tradition *f*	tradition *f*	tradizione *f*	tradición *f*
traditional	traditionell	traditionnel/-elle	tradizionale	tradicional
transparent	durchsichtig	transparent	trasparente	diáfano/-a, transparente
transparent	transparent	transparent/-e	trasparente	transparente
transport	Transport *m*	transport *m*	trasporto *m*	transporte *m*
transversal	quer, transversal	transversal/-e	traverso/-a	al través, transversal
trapezoid	trapezförmig	trapézoïdal/-e	trapezoidale	trapezoidal
travertine	Travertin *n*	travertin *m*	travertino *m*	travertino *m*
treasure	Schatz *m*	trésor *m*	tesoro *m*	tesoro *m*
tree	Baum *m*	arbre *m*	albero *m*	árbol *m*
trefoil mouth	Kleeblattmündung *f*	embouchure *f* trilobée	bocca *f* di trifoglio	boca *f* trilobulada
trench	Grabungsschnitt *m*	tranchée *f*	taglio *m*	trinchera *f*, zanja *f*
triangle	Dreieck *n*	triangle *m*	triangolo *m*	triángulo *m*
triangular	dreieckig	triangulaire	triangolare	triangular
triglyph	Triglyphe *f*	triglyphe *m*	triglifo *m*	triglifo *m*
tripod	Dreifuß *m*	trépied *m*	tripode *m*	trípode *m*
triumphal arch	Triumphbogen *m*	arc *m* de triomphe	arco *m* di trionfo	arco *m* triunfal
trowel	Kelle *f*	louche *f*	cazzuola, trowel *f*	llana *f*, paleta *f*
trunk	Baumstamm *m*	tronc *m* d'arbre	tronco *m*	tronco *m*
tuff/ tufo	Tuff *m*	tuf *m*	tufo *m*	(piedra) toba *f*
turf	Torf *m*	tourbe *f*	torba *f*	turba *m*
turned, twisted	gedreht	tourué/-ée	tornito/-a	realizado a torno/ torneado/-a
turquoise	Türkis *m*	turquoise *f*	turchese	turquesa *f*

Greek		Turkish	Arabic	
στηρίζω	stirizo	desteklemek	يدعم	yudaem
γεωδαιτικός σταθμός *m*	geodaitikos stathmos	ölçüm aleti	جهاز قياس بخصائص مُتعددة	gehaz kijas bechasaes motadeda
τοτέμ *n*	totem	totem	رمز مُقدّس	ramz mokadas
στρέφω, περιστρέφω, διαπλάθω	strefo, peristrefo, diaplatho	çevirmek, torna etmek	يُدير	yudir
αστικοποιώ	astikopoio	yerleşime açmak	يتحضر	yatahadar
βερνικώνω	vernikono	cilalama, vernikleme	يورنش	yewarnisch
πλένω	pleno	yıkamak	يغسل	yagsel
φθείρω, αποσαθρώνω	ftheiro, aposathrono	aşınmak, bozulmak	يتآكل بفعل العوامل الجوية	yataakal befeal elawamel elgaweija
ζυγίζω	zigizo	tartmak	يزن	yazen
πύργος *m*	pirgos	kule	برج	borg
τυλίγω	tiligo	etrafını sarmak	يلف	yalef
συσκευάζω	siskevazo	paketlemek	يُغلّف	yogalef
τυλίγω	tiligo	çevrelemek, sarmak	يلفّ	yalef
αδιάσταλτο χαρτί *n*	adiastalto charti	yağlı ozalit kağıdı	ورق شفاف	warak schafaf
εμπόριο *n*	eborio	alışveriş, ticaret	تجارة	tigarah
εμπορικά προϊόντα *n pl*	eborika proionta	emtia, ticari mal	بضاعة تجارية	bidaah tugarija
εμπορική οδός *f*	eboriki odos	ticaret yolu	طريق تجاري	tarik tugari
παράδοση *f*	paradosi	gelenek	تقاليد	takalied
παραδοσιακός	paradosiakos	geleneksel	تقليدي	takliedie
διαφανής	diafanis	saydam	شفاف	schafaf
διαφανής	diafanis	duru, saydam	شفاف	schafaf
μεταφορά *f*	metafora	nakliye, sevk	نقل	nakl
εγκάρσιος	egkarsios	enine	أفقى	ufukie
τραπεζιόσχημος	trapezioschimos	trapez şeklinde	شبه منحرف	schebh monharef
τραβερτίνης *m*	travertinis	traverten	حجر جيري	hagar gierie
θησαυρός *m*	thisavros	gömü, hazine	كنز	kanz
δέντρο *n*	dentro	ağaç	شجرة	schagara
τριφυλλόσχημο ράμφος *n*	trifilloschimo ramfos	yonca ağızlı	فوهة بشكل ورقة البرسيم	fuwaha beschakl waraket elbarsim
ανασκαφική τομή *f*	anaskafiki tomi	açma	جُزء من منطقة الحفريات	guza mens manteket elhafrijat
τρίγωνο *n*	trigono	gönye, üçgen	مثلث	musalas
τριγωνικός	trigonikos	üç köşeli	مثلث الشكل	musalas elschakl
τρίγλυφος *f*, τρίγλυφο *n*	triglifos, triglifo	triglyph	حلية ثلاثية الأخدود	hilja sulasijat elochdud
τρίποδας *m*	tripodas	üç ayaklı	مقعد بثلاث أرجل	makad bisalas argol
θριαμβικό τόξο *n*	thriamviko toxo	zafer takı	قوس النصر	koos elnasr
μυστρί *n*	mistri	mala	مسطرين	mastarin
κορμός *m*	kormos	ağaç gövdesi/ kütüğü	جذع الشجرة	geza elschagara
μολυβδοσφραγίδα *f*, τόφφος *m*	molivdosfragida, toffos	tüf	حجر بركاني	hagar borkanie
τύρφη *f*	tirfi	bataklık kömürü	فحم المستنقعات	fahm elmostankaat
στρεπτός	streptos	döndürülmüş, tornalanmış	ملفوف	malfuf
τιρκουάζ *n*	tirkouaz	turkuaz	فيروز	fairuuz

English	German	French	Italian	Spanish
type of find	Fundgattung *f*	catégorie *f* d'objets	genere *m* di reperto *m*	cartegoría *f*
type of wood	Holzart *f*	espèce *f* de bois fessence	tipo *m* di legno	clase *f* de madera
typological	typologisch	typologique	tipologico/-a	tipologico/ -a
typology	Typologie *f*	typologie *f*	tipologia *f*	tipología *f*
underground	Untergrund *m*	sous-sol *m*	sottosuolo *m*	subsuelo *m*
underwater	unterwasser	subaquatique	acqua sotterranea *f*	submarino/-a
undisturbed	ungestört	intact/-e	non disturbato/-a	intacto/-a
uneven	uneben	inégal/-e	accidentato/-a	desigual, escabroso/-a
unguentarium	Unguentarium *n*	unguentarium *m*	unguentario *m*	ungüentario *m*
unity	Einheit *f*	unité *f*	unità *f*	unidad *f*
university	Universität *f*	université *f*	università *f*	universidad *f*
unornamented	unverziert	non décoré/ée	non decorato/-a	liso/-a, sin decoración
untidy	unsauber	malpropre	sudicio/-a	poco limpio/-a
untreated	unbehandelt	non traité/-e	non trattato/-a	sin tratar
upper edge of the terrain	Geländeoberkante *f*	niveau *m* de sol	livello *m* del terreno	nivel *m* superficial
urbanisation	Urbanisation *f*	urbanisation *f*	urbanizzazione *f*	urbanización *f*
urn	Urne *f*	urne *f*	urna *f*	urna *f*
urn grave, urn burial	Urnengrab *n*	tombe *f* à urne	tomba *f* ad urna	sepultura *f* en urna
use	Gebrauch *m*	emploi *m*, usage *m*	uso *m*	uso *m*
use trace	Gebrauchsspur *f*	trace *f* d'utilisation □	tracce *f pl* di utilizzo	huella(s) de uso *f*
utensil	Utensil *n*	outil *m*	utensili *pl*	utensilio *m*
utili	Öl *n*	huile *m*	olio *m*	aceite *m*
utilisation layer	Nutzungshorizont *m*	horizon *m* d'occupation	piano di calpestio *m*	nivel/ estrato *m* de uso
valley	Tal *n*	vallée *f*	valle *f*	valle *m*
value	Wert *m*	valeur *f*	valore *m*	valor *m*
varnish	Firnis *m*	vernis *m*	vernice *f*	barniz *m*
varnished ware	Firnisware *f*	céramique *f* vernie	ceramica *f* a vernice	cerámica *f* de barniz
vase, vessel	Vase *f*, Gefäß *n*	vase *m*	vaso *m*	jarrón *m*, vaso *m*
vegetation	Vegetation *f*	végétation *f*	vegetazione *f*	vegetación *f*
vertical	senkrecht, vertikal	vertical/-e	verticale	vertical
village	Dorf *n*	village *m*	villagio *m*	aldea *f*, pueblo *m*
visible	sichtbar	visible	visibile	visible
volcanic	vulkanisch	volcanique	vulcanico/-a	volcánico/-a
volcanic chronology	Vulkanchronologie *f*	téphrochronologie *f*	cronologia *f* vulcanica	cronología *f* vulcánica
volcanic rock	Vulkangestein *n*	roche *f* volcanique	roccia *f* vulcanica	roca *f* vulcánica
volcano	Vulkan *m*	volcan *m*	vulcano *m*	volcán *m*
volume	Volumen *n*	volume *m*	volume *m*	volumen *m*
volute	Volute *f*	volute *f*	voluta *f*	voluta *f*
votive	Votiv *n*	objet *m* votif, offrande *f* votive	votivo *m* / votiva *f*	exvoto *m*

Greek		Turkish	Arabic	
κατηγορία *f* ευρήματος	katigoria evrimatos	buluntu türü	نوع الإكتشاف	noa elektischaf
είδος ξύλου *n*	eidos xilou	ağaç, odun türü, türü	نوع الخشب	noaa elchaschab
τυπολογικός	tipologikos	tipolojik	تصنيفي	tasniefie
τυπολογία *f*	tipologia	tipoloji	تصنيف	tasnief
υπόγειο *n*	ipogeio	yer altı	العمق	elumk
ενάλιος, υποβρύχιος	enalios, ipovrichios	sualtı	تحت الماء	taht elmaa
αδιατάρακτος	adiatarktos	tahrip olmamış	غير مُضطرب	geer motareb
ανώμαλος	anomalos	engebeli	غير مُستوى	geer mostawie
μοιροδοχείο *n*	moirodocheio	unguentarium	قارورة	karura
ενότητα *f*	enotita	beraberlik, birlik	وحدة	wehda
πανεπιστήμιο *n*	panepistimio	üniversite	جامعة	gameaa
ακόσμητος	akosmitos	bezemesiz	غير مزخرف	geer mozachraf
ακάθαρτος	akathartos	kirli, pis, özensiz	غير نظيف	geer nazief
ανεπεξέργαστος	anepexergastos	ham, işlem görmemiş	غير معالج	geer mualeg
επιφάνεια *f* εδάφους	epifaneia edafous	arazi seviyesi, yer seviyesi	منسوب الموقع	mansub elmawkea
αστικοποίηση *f*	astikopoiisi	kentleşme, şehirleşme	تحضر	tahador
λάρνακα *f*, τεφροδόχος *f*	larnaka, tefro dochos	urne	وعاء	wiaa
ταφή σε λάρνακα *f*	tafi se larnaka	urne mezar	قبر الوعاء	kabr elwiaa
χρήση *f*, συν ήθεια *f*	chrisi, sinitheia	kullanılış, kullanma	إستخدام	istechdam
ίχνη *f pl* χρήσης	ichni chrisis	kullanım izi	أثر إستخدام	asar estechdam
εργαλείο *n*	ergaleio	araç-gereç	أداة	adah
λάδι *n*	ladi	akaryakıt, yağ	زيت، الخ ...	zeet elach
ορίζοντας χρήσης *m*	orizontas chrisis	kullanım seviyesi, kullanım tabakası	أفق الإستخدام	ufuk elestichdam
κοιλάδα *f*	koilada	vadi	وادي	wadie
αξία *f*	axia	değer	قيمة	kiema
βερνίκι *n*	verniki	cila, vernik	ورنيش	warniesch
γανωμένη κεραμική *f*	ganomeni kermiki	cilalı/ firnisli seramik	منتجات الورنيش	montagat elwarnisch
αγγείο *n*	angeio	vazo	زهرية	zohrija
βλάστηση *f*	vlastisi	bitki örtüsü	الحياة النباتية	elhaja elnabatija
κατακόρυφος, κάθετος	katakorifos, kathetos	dikey	عمودي رأسي	amudie, raasie
χωριό *n*	chorio	köy	قرية	karia
ορατός	oratos	görülebilir	مرئي	marie
ηφαιστειακός	ifaisteiakos	volkanik	بركاني	borkanie
ηφαιστειακή χρονολόγηση *f*	ifaisteiaki chronologisi	volkanik tabaka tarihlemesi	التسلسل الزمني للبركان	eltasalsol elzamanie lelborkan
ηφαιστειακό πέτρωμα *n*	ifaisteiako petroma	yanardağ kayası	صخور بركانية	sochur borkanija
ηφαίστειο *n*	ifaisteio	volkan	بركان	burkan
όγκος *m*	ogkos	hacim, volüm	حجم	hagm
έλικα *f*, σπείρα *f*	elika, speira	bezeme kıvrımı, volüt	حلية حلزونية	helja halazonija
αναθηματικός	anathimatikos	adak	نذر	nazr

English	German	French	Italian	Spanish
wall	Mauer *f*	mur *m*	muro *m*	muro *m*
wall	Wand *f*	paroi *f*	parete *f*	pared *f*
Wall painting	Wandmalerei *f*	peinture murale *f*	pintura *f* murale	pintura *f* mural/ al fresco
ware	Ware *f*	céramique *f*, poterie *f*	ceramica *f*, merce *f*	artículo *m*, mercancía *f*
waste	Abfall *m*	déchets *m pl*, détritus *m*	residuo *m*, rifiuto *m*	desecho *m*, residuos *m*
waste heap	Abfallhaufen *m*	déchet *m*, détritus *m pl*	mucchio *m* di rifiuti	montón *m* de vertidos
water	Wasser *n*	eau *f*	acqua *f*	agua *f*
water inflow	Wassereinfluss *m*	influence *f* de l'eau	influsso *m* dell'acqua	entrada *f* de agua
water level	Wasserspiegel *m*	niveau *m* d'eau	superficie *f* dell'acqua	nivel *m* del agua
waterproof	wasserdicht	imperméable à l'eau	impermeabile	impermeable al agua
wattle and daub	Flechtwerkwand *f*	paroi *m* en entrelacs/ clayonnage	parete *f* all'intreccio	muro *m* con trenzado interno
wattle work	Flechtwerk *n*	clayonnage *m*, entrelacs *m*	intreccio *m*	rejilla *f*, trenzado de ramas y barro *m*
wave	Welle *f*	onde *f*, vague *f*	onda *f*	ola *f*, onda *f*
wavy line	Wellenlinie *f*	ligne ondulée *f*	linea ondulata *f*	línea ondulada *f*
wax	Wachs *n*	cire *f*	cera *f*	cera *f*
wax tablet	Wachstafel *f*	tablette *f* de cire	lavagna *f* di cera	tabla/ tablillas de cera *f*
weapon	Waffe *f*	arme *f*	arma *f*	arma *f*
weapon component	Waffenbestandteil *m*	élément *m* d'arme	parte *f* dell'armamento	parte *f* de una arma
weaving loom	Webstuhl *m*	métier à tisser *m*	telaio *m*	telar *m*
weight	Gewicht *n*	poids *m*	peso *m*	peso *m*
well	Brunnen *m*	puits *m*	pozzo *m*	fuente *f*, pozo *m*
west	Westen *m*	ouest *m*	occidente *m*, ovest *m*	occidente *m*, oeste *m*
western	westlich	d'ouest, occidental/-e	dell'ovest, occidentale	del oeste, occidental
wet	nass	mouillé/-e	bagnato/-a	mojado/-a
wheat	Weizen *m*	blé *m*	frumento *m*	trigo *m*
wheel-thrown ware	scheibengedrehte Ware *f*	vaiselle *f*/ céramique *f* tournée	ceramica tornita *f*	cerámica *f* (realizado) a torno
whitewash	Tünche *f*	badigeon *m*	intonaco *m*	blanqueo *m*, revoque *m*
wide	breit	ample, large	ampio, largo	amplio, ancho
width	Breite *f*	largeur *f*	ampiezza *f*, larghezza *f*	anchura *f*, extensión *f*
willow	Weide *f*	saule *m*	salice *m*	mimbrera *f*, sauce *m*
window	Fenster *n*	fenêtre *f*	finestra *f*	ventana *f*
window jamb	Fensterlaibung *f*	embrasure *f* de fenêtre	intradosso *m*	alféizar *m*
wine	Wein *m*	vin *m*	vino *m*	vino *m*
wire	Draht *m*	fil *m*	filo *m* metallico	alambre *m*, hilo *m*
wooden	hölzern	en bois	di legno, ligneo/-a	de madera
woodworking lathe	Drechselbank *f*	tour *m*	tornio *m*	torno *m* para madera
work	arbeiten	travailler	lavorare	trabajar

Greek		Turkish	Arabic	
τοίχος *m* , τείχος *n*	toichos, teichos	duvar	جدار	gidar
τοίχος *m*	toichos	duvar	حائط	haet
τοιχογραφία *f*	toichografia	duvar resmi	رسم على الحائط	rasm ala elhaet
κεραμική *f*	keramiki	eşya, mal	سلعة	selaa
απορρίμματα *n pl*	aporrimmata	artık çöp	إنحدار / قمامة	inhedar, kemamah
σωρός *m* απορριμμάτων	soros aporrimmaton	çöplük, çöp yığını	كوم قمامة	kom kemamah
νερό *n*	nero	su	ماء	maa
εισροή νερού *f*	eisroi nerou	su sızıntısı	تأثير الماء	tasier elmaa
επιφάνεια νερού *f*	epifaneia nerou	su seviyesi, su yüzeyi	منسوب الماء	mansub elmaa
αδιάβροχος	adiavrochos	su geçirmez	لا يسرب الماء	la yusareb elmaa
χυτή πηλοδομή *f*	chiti pilodomi	dal örgü	جدار ذو زخرفة مضفرة	gidar zu zachrafa mudafara
καλαμωτή *f*, πλέγμα *f*	kalamoti, plegma	örgü, örgü süsleme, örme işi	زخرفة مضفرة	zachrafa mudafara
κύμαn	kima	dalga	موجة	moga
κυματιστή γραμμή *n*	kimatisti grammi	dalgalı çizgi	خط متموج	chat motamaweg
κερί *n*	keri	balmumu	شمع	schama
κηρωμένη πινακίδα *f*	kiromeni pinakida	balmumu tablet	قرص الشمع	kors elschama
όπλο *n*	oplo	silah	سلاح	silah
εξάρτημα όπλου *n*	exartima oplou	silah bileşeni	جزء من السلاح	gozaa men elsilah
αργαλειός *m*	argaleios	dokuma tezgahı	نول	nool
βάρος *n*	varos	ağırlık, kilo	وزن	wazn
πηγάδι n, κρήνη *f*	pigadi, krini	çeşme	بئر	biar
δύση *f*	disi	batı	غرب	garb
δυτικός, δυτικά	distikos, distika	batısında, batıda	غربي	garie
υγρός	igros	ıslak, nemli, yaş	مبلل	mobalal
σιτάρι *n*	sitari	buğday	قمح	kamh
τροχήλατη κεραμική *f*	trochilati keramiki	çarkta döndürülmüş eşya (seramik)	منتج على القرص الدوّار	montag ala elkors eldawar
ασβέστης *m*	asvestis	badana, boyama	محلول للتبييض	mahlul leltabjied
ευρύς, πλατύς	evris, platis	geniş	واسع	wasiea
εύρος *n*, πλάτος *n*	evros, platos	en	العرض	alard
ιτιάf	itiaf	söğüt ağacı	شجرة صفصاف	schagaret safsaf
παράθυρο *n*	parathiro	pencere	شباك	schebak
παραθυρόφυλλο *n*	parathirifillo	pencere takmak için duvarda açılan delik	إطار الشباك	itar elschebak
κρασί *n* , οίνος *m*	krasi, oinos	şarap	خمر	chamr
σύρμα *n*	sirma	tel	سلك	selk
ξύλινος	xilinos	ahşap, odundan	خشبي	chaschabie
τόρνος *m*	tornos	ağaç işleme tornası	مخرطة	mechrata
δουλεύω	doulevo	çalışmak	يعمل	yamal

English	German	French	Italian	Spanish
work gloves	Arbeitshandschuhe *m pl*	gants *m pl*	guanti *m pl* da lavoro	guantes *m pl* de trabajo
work safety	Arbeitsschutz *m*	sécurité *f* au travail	tutela *f* del lavoro	protección *f* laboral
workshop	Atelier *n*, Werkstatt *f*	atelier *m*	atelier *m* / bottega *f*	taller *m*
worm	Wurm *m*	ver *m*	verme *m*	gusano *m*
wrapping	Verpackung *f*	emballage *m*	imballaggio *m*	embalaje *m*
written	schriftlich	écrit/-e	scritto/-a	escrito/-a
X-ray spectroscopy	Röntgenspektroskopie *f*	spectroscopie *f* à rayons X	spettroscopia *f* a raggi X	espectroscopia *f* de rayos X
year	Jahr *n*	an *m* , année *f*	anno *m*	año m
ziggurat	Zikkurat *f*	ziggourat *f*	ziqqurat *f*	zigurat *m*
zigzag pattern	Zickzackmuster *n*	zigzag *m*	motivo *m* a zigzag	zigzag *m*
zinc	Zink *n*	zinc *m*	zinco *m*	cinc *m*
zoology	Zoologie *f*	zoologie *f*	zoologia *f*	zoología *f*
zoomorphic	tierförmig	zoomorphe	a forma di animale	zoomórfico/-a

Greek		Turkish	Arabic	
γάντια *n pl*	gantia	iş eldiveni	قفازات العمل	kofasat elamal
ασφάλεια *f* κατά την εργασία	asfaleia kata tnv ergasia	iş güvenliği	السلامة المهنية	alsalama almihaneiea
εργαστήριο *n*	ergastirio	atölye, imalathane	ورشة عمل فنان	warschet amal fanan
σκουλήκι *n*	skouliki	kurt, solucan	دودة	duda
συσκευασία *f*	siskevasia	paketleme	التعبئة والتغليف	eltabea weltaglief
γραπτός	graptos	yazılı	كتابي	ketabie
υπεριώδης φασματοσκοπία *f*	iperiodis fasmatoskopia	X-ışını spektroskopisi	التحليل الطيفي بالأشعة السينية	eltahliel eltefie belaschea elsineja
έτος *n* , χρονιά *f* , χρόνος *m*	etos, chronia, chronos	sene, yıl	سنة	sana
ζιγκουράτ *n*	zigkourat	zigurat	برج معبد متدرج	borg maabad motadareg
μοτίβο ζικ ζακ *n*	motivo zik zak	zikzak motifi	نموذج متعرج	namuzag motaareg
ψευδάργυρος *m*	psevdargiros	çinko	زنك	zenk
ζωολογία *f*	zoologia	Zooloji	علم الحيوان	elm elhajawaan
ζωόμορφος	zooomorfos	hayvan formlu	على شكل حيوان	ala schakl hajawan